T0185612

C++/CLI
The Visual C++ Language for .NET

Gordon Hogenson

Apress®

C++/CLI: The Visual C++ Language for .NET

Copyright © 2006 by Gordon Hogenson

ISBN-13: 978-1-4842-2027-6

ISBN-10: 1-59059-705-2

DOI 10.1007/978-1-4302-0282-0

Lead Editors: Ewan Buckingham, James Huddleston
Technical Reviewer: Damien Watkins
Editorial Board: Steve Anglin, Ewan Buckingham, Gary Cornell, Jason Gilmore, Jonathan Gennick, Jonathan Hassell, James Huddleston, Chris Mills, Matthew Moodie, Dominic Shakeshaft, Jim Sumser, Keir Thomas, Matt Wade
Project Manager: Julie M. Smith
Copy Edit Manager: Nicole Flores
Copy Editor: Ami Knox
Assistant Production Director: Kari Brooks-Copony
Production Editor: Laura Cheu
Compositor: Susan Glinert Stevens
Proofreader: Elizabeth Berry
Indexer: John Collin
Artist: Kinetic Publishing Services, LLC
Cover Designer: Kurt Krames
Manufacturing Director: Tom Debolski

Distributed to the book trade worldwide by Springer-Verlag New York, Inc., 233 Spring Street, 6th Floor, New York, NY 10013. Phone 1-800-SPRINGER, fax 201-348-4505, e-mail orders-ny@springer-sbm.com, or visit http://www.springeronline.com.

For information on translations, please contact Apress directly at 2560 Ninth Street, Suite 219, Berkeley, CA 94710. Phone 510-549-5930, fax 510-549-5939, e-mail info@apress.com, or visit http://www.apress.com.

The source code for this book is available to readers at http://www.apress.com in the Source Code/Download section.

To my parents, Arlin and Judy Hogenson, who built their character growing up on the farms of the Great Plains and passed on the time-honored virtues of personal responsibility, frugality, and integrity to their children.

Contents at a Glance

Contents

Foreword
By Stanley B. Lippman,
Former Architect, Visual C++

A person standing on the side of a river shouts to someone on the opposite bank: "How do you get to the other side?" The second person replies: "You are on the other side."

—Chris Gosden

C++/CLI is a binding of C++ to Microsoft's .NET programming environment. It integrates ISO C++ with the Unified Type System (UTS) of the Common Language Infrastructure (CLI). It supports both source-level and binary interoperability between native and managed C++. As the Gosden quote suggests, it is how one gets to the other side, regardless of where you happen to be standing. The actual details of how you do this are covered in Gordon's fine text.

In primitive societies and adolescent fantasy novels, such as *The Lord of the Rings* (which, along with *Remembrance of Things Past,* is one of *my* favorite books), names have a kind of magical aura to them—they need to be handled with extreme care and protected. The same holds true in computer science, apparently—or at least within Microsoft. Although you hold in your hand the first book devoted solely to C++/CLI, I couldn't for the life of me find any specific reference to C++/CLI in the Visual Studio 2005 release—at least not in the Visual C++ IDE, in order to open a C++/CLI project, or in the "What's New" section of the documentation. This whole notion of binding C++ to .NET has a sort of fantasy aspect to it that has clung to it since the original Managed Extensions to C++ in the Visual Studio .NET release of 2001. C++/CLI is the noncompatible and more elegant replacement for the Managed Extensions. It is how we program .NET using what the book's subtitle calls "the Visual C++ Language for .NET." That's what Gordon's book will teach you how to do.

As Gordon states in his introduction, C++/CLI represents an evolution of C++. This does not, of course, imply that C++/CLI is a better language than C++; rather, C++/CLI is better adapted to the current and future computing environment that we work in. If you are a Visual C++ programmer with legacy "native applications" and need to move or extend these applications to .NET, C++/CLI is an essential tool for your survival, and Gordon's text is an essential first step to mastering this tool.

An aspect of evolution is an increase in structural complexity, and this, too, is reflected in C++/CLI: knowing C++ may or may not be a help in understanding C++/CLI! For example, there is no such thing as a destructor in .NET, so although the syntax resembles that of the native C++ destructor, its behavior is oddly counterintuitive: you simply can't fully understand its operation by its analogous form. And this is where Gordon's text becomes invaluable both as a tutorial and a desktop reference. It is for this reason that I highly recommend it.

Foreword
By Herb Sutter, Architect

A Design Rationale for C++/CLI

—Excerpted from "A Design Rationale for C++/CLI" by Herb Sutter. (Full text available online at http://www.gotw.ca/publications/C++CLIRationale.pdf.)

1 Overview

A multiplicity of libraries, runtime environments, and development environments are essential to support the range of C++ applications. This view guided the design of C++ as early as 1987; in fact, it is older yet. Its roots are in the view of C++ as a general-purpose language.

—B. Stroustrup (*Design and Evolution of C++,* Addison-Wesley Professional, 1994, p. 168))

C++/CLI was created to enable C++ use on a major runtime environment, ISO CLI (the standardized subset of .NET).

A technology like C++/CLI is essential to C++'s continued success on Windows in particular. CLI libraries are the basis for many of the new technologies on the Windows platform, including the WinFX class library shipping with Windows Vista, which offers over 10,000 CLI classes for everything from web service programming (Communication Foundation, WCF) to the new 3D graphics subsystem (Presentation Foundation, WPF). Languages that do not support CLI programming have no direct access to such libraries, and programmers who want to use those features are forced to use one of the 20 or so other languages that do support CLI development. Languages that support CLI include COBOL, C#, Eiffel, Java, Mercury, Perl, Python, and others; at least two of these have standardized language-level bindings.

C++/CLI's mission is to provide direct access for C++ programmers to use existing CLI libraries and create new ones, with little or no performance overhead, with the minimum amount of extra notation, and with full ISO C++ compatibility.

1.1 Key Goals

- *Enable C++ to be a first-class language for CLI programming.*

  - Support important CLI features, at minimum those required for a CLS consumer and CLS extender: CLI defines a Common Language Specification (CLS) that specifies the subsets of CLI that a language is expected to support to be minimally functional for consuming and/or authoring CLI libraries.

  - Enable C++ to be a systems programming language on CLI: a key existing strength of C++ is as a systems programming language, so extend this to CLI by leaving no room for a CLI language lower than C++(besides ILASM).

- Use the fewest possible extensions.

  - Require zero use of extensions to compile ISO C++ code to run on CLI: C++/CLI requires compilers to make ISO C++ code "just work"—no source code changes or extensions are needed to compile C++ code to execute on CLI, or to make calls between code compiled "normally" and code compiled to CLI instructions.

  - Require few or no extensions to consume existing CLI types: to use existing CLI types, a C++ programmer can ignore nearly all C++/CLI features and typically writes a sprinkling of gcnew and ^. Most C++/CLI extensions are used only when authoring new CLI types.

  - Use pure conforming extensions that do not change the meaning of existing ISO C++ programs and do not conflict with ISO C++ or with C++0x evolution: this was achieved nearly perfectly, including for macros.

- Be as orthogonal as possible.

  - Observe the principle of least surprise: if feature X works on C++ types, it should also seamlessly work on CLI types, and vice versa. This was mostly achieved, notably in the case of templates, destructors, and other C++ features that do work seamlessly on CLI types; for example, a CLI type can be templated and/or be used to instantiate a template, and a CLI generic can match a template parameter.

Some unifications were left for the future; for example, a contemplated extension that the C++/CLI design deliberately leaves room for is to use new and * to (semantically) allocate CLI types on the C++ heap, making them directly usable with existing C++ template libraries, and to use gcnew and ^ to (semantically) allocate C++ types on the CLI heap. Note that this would be highly problematic if C++/CLI had not used a separate gcnew operator and ^ declarator to keep CLI features out of the way of ISO C++.

1.2 Basic Design Forces

Four main programming model design forces are mentioned repeatedly in this paper:

1. It is necessary to add language support for a key feature that semantically cannot be expressed using the rest of the language and/or must be known to the compiler.

Classes can represent almost all the concepts we need. . . . Only if the library route is genuinely infeasible should the language extension route be followed.

—B. Stroustrup (*Design and Evolution of C++*, p. 181)

In particular, a feature that unavoidably requires special code generation must be known to the compiler, and nearly all CLI features require special code generation. Many CLI features also require semantics that cannot be expressed in C++. Libraries are unquestionably preferable wherever possible, but either of these requirements rules out a library solution. Note that language support remains necessary even if the language designer smoothly tries to slide in a language feature dressed in library's clothing (i.e., by choosing a deceptively library-like syntax). For example, instead of

```
property int x; // A: C++/CLI syntax
```

the C++/CLI design could instead have used (among many other alternatives) a syntax like

```
property<int> x; // B: an alternative library-like syntax
```

and some people might have been mollified, either because they looked no further and thought that it really was a library, or because they knew it wasn't a library but were satisfied that it at least looked like one. But this difference is entirely superficial, and nothing has really changed—it's still a language feature and a language extension to C++, only now a deceitful one masquerading as a library (which is somewhere between a fib and a bald-faced lie, depending on your general sympathy for magical libraries and/or grammar extensions that look like libraries).

In general, even if a feature is given library-like syntax, it is still not a true library feature when

- the name is recognized by the compiler and given special meaning (e.g., it's in the language grammar, or it's a specially recognized type) and/or

- the implementation is "magical."

Either of these make it something no user-defined library type could be. Note that, in the case of surfacing CLI properties in the language, at least one of these must be true even if properties had been exposed using syntax like B.

Therefore, choosing a syntax like B would not change anything about the technical fact of language extension, but only the political perception. This approach amounts to dressing up a language feature with library-like syntax that pretends it's something that it can't be. C++'s tradition is to avoid magic libraries and has the goal that the C++ standard library should be implementable in C++ without compiler collusion, although it allows for some functions to be intrinsics known to the compiler or processor. C++/CLI prefers to follow C++'s tradition, and it uses magical types or functions only in four isolated cases: `cli::array`, `cli::interior_ptr`, `cli::pin_ptr`, and `cli::safe_cast`. These four can be viewed as intrinsics—their implementations are provided by the CLI runtime environment and the names are recognized by the compiler as tags for those CLI runtime facilities.

2. It is important not only to hide unnecessary differences, but also to expose essential differences.

I try to make significant operations highly visible.

—B. Stroustrup (*Design and Evolution of C++*, p. 119)

First, an unnecessary distinction is one where the language adds a feature or different syntax to make something look or be spelled differently, when the difference is not material and could have been "papered over" in the language while still preserving correct semantics and performance. For example, CLI reference types can never be physically allocated on the stack, but C++ stack semantics are very powerful, and there is no reason not to allow the lifetime semantics of allocating an instance of a reference type R on the stack and leveraging C++'s automatic destructor call semantics. C++/CLI can, and therefore should, safely paper over this difference and allow stack-based semantics for reference type objects, thus avoiding exposing an unnecessary distinction. Consider this code for a reference type R:

```
void f()
{
    R r;// OK, conceptually allocates the R on the stack
    r.SomeFunc(); // OK, use value semantics
    ...
} // destroy r here
```

In the programming model, r is on the stack and has normal C++ stack-based semantics. Physically, the compiler emits something like the following:

```
// f, as generated by the compiler
void f()
{
    R^ r = gcnew R; // actually allocated on the CLI heap
    r->SomeFunc();// actually uses indirection
    ...
    delete r;// destroy r here (memory is reclaimed later)
}
```

Second, it is equally important to avoid obscuring essential differences, specifically not try to "paper over" a difference that actually matters but where the language fails to add a feature or distinct syntax.

For example, although CLI object references are similar to pointers (e.g., they are an indirection to an object), they are nevertheless semantically not the same because they do not support all the operations that pointers support (e.g., they do not support pointer arithmetic, stable values, or reliable comparison). Pretending that they are the same abstraction, when they are not and cannot be, causes much grief. One of the main flaws in the Managed Extensions design is that it tried to reduce the number of extensions to C++ by reusing the * declarator, where T* would implicitly mean different things depending the type of T—but three different and semantically incompatible things, lurking together under a single syntax.

The road to unsound language design is paved with good intentions, among them the papering over of essential differences.

3. Some extensions actively help avoid getting in the way of ISO C++ and C++0x evolution.

Any compatibility requirements imply some ugliness.

—B. Stroustrup (*Design and Evolution of C++*, p. 198)

A real and important benefit of extensions is that using an extension that the ISO C++ standards committee (WG21) has stated it does not like and is not interested in can be the best way to stay out of the way of C++0x evolution, and in several cases this was done explicitly at WG21's direction.

For example, consider the extended for loop syntax: C++/CLI stayed with the syntax for each(T t in c) after consulting the WG21 evolution working group at the Sydney meeting in March 2004 and other meetings, where EWG gave the feedback that they were interested in such a feature but they disliked both the for each and in syntax and were highly likely never to use it, and so directed C++/CLI to use the undesirable syntax in order to stay out of C++0x's way. (The liaisons noted that if in the future WG21 ever adopts a similar feature, then C++/CLI would want to drop its syntax in favor of the WG21-adopted syntax; in general, C++/CLI aims to track C++0x.)

Using an extension that WG21 might be interested in, or not using an extension at all but adding to the semantics of an existing C++ construct, is liable to interfere with C++0x evolution by accidentally constraining it. For another example, consider C++/CLI's decision to add the gcnew operator and the ^ declarator. . . . Consider just the compatibility issue: by adding an operator and a declarator that are highly likely never to be used by ISO C++, C++/CLI avoids conflict with future C++ evolution (besides making it clear that these operations have nothing to do with the normal C++ heap). If C++/CLI had instead specified a new (gc)or new (cli) "placement new" as its syntax for allocation on the CLI heap, that choice could have conflicted with C++0x evolution that might want to provide additional forms of placement new. And, of course, using a placement syntax could and would also conflict with existing code that might already use these forms of placement new—in particular, new (gc) is already used with the popular Boehm collector.

4. Users rely heavily on keywords, but that doesn't mean the keywords have to be reserved words.

My experience is that people are addicted to keywords for introducing concepts to the point where a concept that doesn't have its own keyword is surprisingly hard to teach. This effect is more important and deep-rooted than people's vocally expressed dislike for new keywords. Given a choice and time to consider, people invariably choose the new keyword over a clever workaround.

—B. Stroustrup (*Design and Evolution of C++*, p. 119)

When a language feature is necessary, programmers strongly prefer keywords. Normally, all C++ keywords are also reserved words, and taking a new one would break code that is already using that word as an identifier (e.g., as a type or variable name).

C++/CLI avoids adding reserved words so as to preserve the goal of having pure extensions, but it also recognizes that programmers expect keywords. C++/CLI balances these requirements by adding keywords where most are not reserved words and so do not conflict with user identifiers.

For a related discussion, see also my blog article "C++/CLI Keywords: Under the hood" (November 23, 2003).

- *Spaced keywords*: These are reserved words, but cannot conflict with any identifiers or macros that a user may write because they include embedded whitespace (e.g., ref class).

- *Contextual keywords*: These are special identifiers instead of reserved words. Three techniques were used:

  1. Some do not conflict with identifiers at all because they are placed at a position in the grammar where no identifier can appear (e.g., sealed).

  2. Others can appear in the same grammar position as a user identifier, but conflict is avoided by using a different grammar production or a semantic disambiguation rule that favors the ISO C++ meaning (e.g., property, generic), which can be informally described as the rule "If it can be a normal identifier, it is."

  3. Four "library-like" identifiers are considered keywords when name lookup finds the special marker types in namespace cli (e.g., pin_ptr).

Note these make life harder for compiler writers, but that was strongly preferred in order to achieve the dual goals of retaining near-perfect ISO C++ compatibility by sticking to pure extensions and also being responsive to the widespread programmer complaints about underscores.

1.3 Previous Effort: Managed Extensions

C++/CLI is the second publicly available design to support CLI programming in C++. The first attempt was Microsoft's proprietary Managed Extensions to C++ (informally known as "Managed C++"), which was shipped in two releases of Visual C++ (2002 and 2003) and continues to be supported in deprecated mode in Visual C++ 2005.

Because the Managed Extensions design deliberately placed a high priority on C++ compatibility, it did two things that were well-intentioned but that programmers objected to:

- The Managed Extensions wanted to introduce as few language extensions as possible, and ended up reusing too much existing but inappropriate C++ notation (e.g., * for pointers CLI references). This caused serious problems where it obscured essential differences, and the design for overloaded syntaxes like * was both technically unsound and confusing to use.

- The Managed Extensions scrupulously used names that the C++ standard reserves for C++ implementations, notably keywords that begin with a double underscore (e.g., __gc). This caused unexpectedly strong complaints from programmers, who made it clear that they hated writing double underscores for language features.

Many C++ programmers tried hard to use these features, and most failed. Having the Managed Extensions turned out to be not significantly better for C++ than having no CLI support at all. However, the Managed Extensions did generate much direct real-world user experience with a shipping product about what kinds of CLI support did and didn't work, and why; and this experience directly informed C++/CLI.

About the Author

GORDON HOGENSON grew up in Fairbanks, Alaska, and retains the independent spirit and love of nature he learned there. Torn between a love of writing and a love of science, he wrote a fantasy novel in high school called *Phalshazhaln* and then went on to study chemistry at Harvey Mudd College, intern in chemical physics at the University of Oregon, and work toward a Ph.D. in physical chemistry at the University of Washington, when he published a paper with William P. Reinhardt in the Journal of Chemical Physics on computational methods combining quantum mechanics and thermodynamics, as well as an article on a meditation technique for the first issue of *The Resonance Project*, a journal for the psychedelic subculture.

Supported by fellowships from Connie Ringold and the U.S. Department of Energy, he studied quantum liquids and pursued attempts to bring together diverse ideas more appropriate for a natural philosopher than a modern scientist. He spent his free time studying the controversies at the edges of science and philosophy. In a moment of extreme distraction from his Ph.D. project, he even tried to learn ancient Greek and memorize parts of Homer's *The Iliad*. He later used his JCP paper as a master's thesis during his escape from the highly specialized world of academic science. He returned to more practical concerns in 1997 and began work at Microsoft testing Visual J++, C#, and C++, and later started work on software documentation, where he currently enjoys managing technical writing projects. Gordon met his wife, Jeni, while they searched the night sky near Mt. Rainier for signs of life beyond Earth as members of CSETI, an organization devoted to furthering our understanding of extraterrestrial life. His current pastimes include raising goats on his farm near Duvall, Washington, planning a permaculture garden, and dreaming of self-sufficiency on the land.

About the Technical Reviewer

DAMIEN WATKINS is a program manager on the Visual C++ team at Microsoft. His main area of interest is the design and implementation of component architectures. His first book, *Programming in the .NET Environment* (Addison-Wesley, 2003), coauthored with Mark Hammond and Brad Abrams, describes the architecture and goals of the .NET Framework. Prior to joining the Visual C++ Team, Damien was a member of the External Research Office at Microsoft Research Cambridge. Damien has presented tutorials, seminars, and workshops on COM/DCOM, CORBA, and the .NET Framework at numerous events, including ECOOP 2004, OOPSLA 2003, OOPSLA 2002, SIGCSE 2002, and the Microsoft Research Faculty Summit 2001.

Acknowledgments

This book would never have been possible had it not been for the constant support of Jeni, my lovely wife. I am very grateful to her for her patience with me during the project and for generally being such an inspiring presence in my life. I also want to heartily thank Damien Watkins, whose support, tough technical editing, humor, and encouragement all helped this text come together. I was also fortunate enough to have a technical review by Arjun Bijanki of the Visual C++ QA team, whose detailed knowledge of the C++/CLI language helped make the text much more accurate. The text also benefited greatly from feedback from many Microsoft employees who devoted their time and attention to pointing out an early draft's many flaws: Martin Chisholm, who printed and read the text very carefully while on a bike trip; John SvitaK, whose attention to detail really helped improve the polish; Kirill Kobelev, who pointed out errors and omissions in the radioactivity example; Thomas Petchel, who found several programming errors and had many other good suggestions; Yves Dolce, whose familiarity with developer problems helped make the book more practical; Peter-Michael Osera, who pointed out many subtleties and asked very good questions; Ron Pihlgren, who pointed out misleading statements and questionable assertions in Chapters 3 and 12; Bob Davidson, who despite his demanding schedule managed to provide feedback on the book; Ann Beebe, who allowed me to have a flexible work schedule so I could work on the text; and Chuck Bell, who had some great ideas on the exceptions discussion of Chapter 12. I also want to thank and Ewan Buckingham, Julie Smith, and Ami Knox at Apress for their patience and help getting this into print, and finally, Stan Lippman, whose idea this was and without whom none of this would ever have happened.

Introduction

Thank you for picking up this book. In it I present the new C++/CLI extensions to the C++ computer programming language, a significant development in the long history of the C and C++ programming languages.

Why extend C++? C++ has evolved over many years; it is used by millions of developers worldwide. The nature of C++ has been to grow as programming paradigms evolve. After all, it was the desire to extend the C language to support object-oriented concepts that prompted Bjarne Stroustrup and his colleagues at Bell Labs to develop "C with classes." Many of the new language features that have come along have been reflected in the C++ language, such as templates, runtime type information, and so on; they have enhanced the richness (and complexity) of the language. The features added to C++ by C++/CLI are no different. C++/CLI provides a new set of extensions to the C++ language to support programming concepts such as component-based software development, garbage collection, and interoperability with other languages that run on a common virtual machine, along with other useful features.

The CLI, or Common Language Infrastructure, is a standard adopted by ECMA International. The CLI defines a virtual machine and enables rich functionality in languages that target the virtual machine, as well as a framework of libraries that provide additional support for the fundamentals of programming against the CLI virtual machine. Collectively, these libraries and the platform constitute the *infrastructure* of the CLI. It's a *common language* infrastructure because a wide variety of languages can target that infrastructure.

The name "C++/CLI" refers to a standard that describes extensions to the C++ language that allow C++ programmers to program against a CLI virtual machine.

Microsoft's implementation of the CLI standard is called the CLR, or common language runtime, or the .NET Developer Platform (NDP). The libraries Microsoft provides that implement the CLI standard are collectively known as the .NET Framework, although the .NET Framework also includes other libraries that are not part of the CLI standard. There are several other implementations of the CLI, including the .NET Compact Framework (http://msdn.microsoft.com/netframework/programming/netcf), the Mono Project (http://www.mono-project.com), and dotGNU Portable.NET (http://dotgnu.org). Visual C++ 2005 is the first release of Visual C++ that supports C++/CLI.

First, let's address the issue of what the term "C++/CLI" means in the technical sense. C++ is a well-known language. While some might quibble over standards conformance, C++ is essentially the language design captured by the ANSI/ISO standard in the late 1990s. Purists will say that C++/CLI is a set of language bindings to the CLI standard, not a language in and of itself. ECMA has adopted C++/CLI as a standard itself, and it is in the process of being submitted to the appropriate ISO working group. The C++/CLI language is an approximate superset of the C++ language, so if you drop all the support for the CLI from the language, you're left with C++. This means that almost any C++ program is automatically supported as a C++/CLI program, just one that doesn't refer to any of the additional functionality provided by the CLI.

Why C++/CLI?

C++/CLI was created by Microsoft to be a more friendly programming language than its predecessor, Managed Extensions for C++. Microsoft had created the CLR, and the C++ team at Microsoft had devised a syntax that provided C++ programmers with a way to target the CLR. The first release of Visual Studio to support the CLR was Visual Studio .NET 2002. The syntax that was provided with Visual Studio .NET 2002 was constrained by the desire to adhere as much as possible to the existing C++ standard, the ISO C++ Standard. According to this standard, any extensions to a language had to conform to the rules for language extensions—among other constraints, this meant keywords had to begin with a double underscore (__). Thus, Managed Extensions for C++ provided a very clumsy syntax for targeting the CLR. In order to create a "managed" pointer (one that refers to an object that is garbage collected), one used syntax as follows:

```
int __gc * ptr;
```

The managed pointers were referred to as "__gc pointers." Similarly, in order to declare a managed class, one used the __gc keyword as a modifier:

```
__gc class C { ... };
```

and to declare an interface (a concept that does not exist as a specific language feature in C++), one had to use the syntax

```
__interface I { ... };
```

There were other cases of keywords added with double underscores as well. All in all, the syntax was cumbersome.

And not just because of the double underscores, but also because Managed Extensions for C++ did not provide natural support for several key concepts of the CLR, such as properties, events, automatic boxing, and so on. All this meant that C++ programmers did not enjoy programming in Managed Extensions for C++.

Programming should be fun. Language is more than just a utilitarian concept. After all, many people spend their entire day programming. Why should they hobble along with a difficult extension when they could be using a clean, crisp language that makes programming easy and fun? The C++ team at Microsoft recognized that in order to make C++ programming enjoyable and aesthetically pleasing, as well as to take full advantage of the CLR, the syntax had to change. And that meant taking the radical step of departing from the ISO C++ Standard.

However, Microsoft had made the decision to work through standards bodies, and if it was going to depart from the ISO C++ Standard, rather than being "nonstandard," it was felt that a new standard was needed. The C++/CLI standard was born.

The new language was designed with ease of use in mind and was intended to be a breath of fresh air. It should be a great relief to anyone who has tried to use Managed Extensions for C++.

Unlike Managed Extensions for C++, C++/CLI is designed to be a general-purpose programming language. It was not designed just for those who want to preserve an existing native code base and add a bit of managed code, although it's great for that and use of C++/CLI for such interoperability scenarios will certainly be a major way in which the language is used. The designers of C++/CLI had the advantage of looking at what works and what doesn't in the C# language, and planning the design of C++/CLI accordingly. For example, C++/CLI provides better and more predictable object cleanup more easily in the language. The bottom line is that now C++/CLI may well be the language of choice for programming against the CLI platform, for new applications as well as for extending existing native code bases.

About This Book

The purpose of this book is to show you the basics of the C++/CLI language. This book is not a general introduction to Visual C++ 2005; there are other features in Visual C++ 2005 that this book does not cover, such as the secure C runtime functions. I'd like this book to be used as a handy desktop reference, so if you have a question about how, say, an array is declared or how a ref class behaves, you can easily refer to this book. I am going to assume that you already "know C++," although the truth is that very few people know all there is to know about C++. However, I am assuming you know about as much as the majority of people who program in C++. I am assuming that you want to build on this existing knowledge, and may need the occasional refresher on the ins and outs of C++ as well. I do not assume any knowledge of the CLR, so if you have knowledge (perhaps from C# or Visual Basic .NET), you'll find a little bit of review. This book should be useful to professional developers getting started with C++/CLI, as well as to students, academic faculty, and hobbyists who want to learn the new language. In this text, we won't cover features of C++ that are not specifically C++/CLI extensions, even though C++/CLI does allow the use of nearly all of the C++ language. There are many good references available for classic C++.[1]

Also, this book is an introductory book. There are many complexities that are not fully explained, especially in dealing with interoperability between native C++ and C++/CLI. If you want to move on to more advanced material after reading this book, you may want to read *Expert C++/CLI* by Marcus Heege (Apress, forthcoming), and if you want more information about using the .NET Framework in C++/CLI, you should read *Pro Visual C++/CLI and the .NET 2.0 Platform* by Stephen R.G. Fraser (Apress, 2006).

One of the principles with which this book is written is that, to paraphrase Einstein, explanations should be as simple as possible, but no simpler. I shall try to give many code examples that can be understood at a glance. I hope you won't need to spend a long time poring over the text and code in this book, but that you can absorb the main point of each code example and apply it to your own project. But, like any principle, there are times when it must be violated, so this book also contains more extended code examples that are intended to give you a better feeling for how the language is used in more realistic programs and get you thinking about how to solve problems using C++/CLI.

In Chapter 1, I introduce some of the basic concepts behind the new language, culminating in a look at the classic "Hello, World" program in C++/CLI. Following that, you'll get a quick tour of the new language, using an example involving a simulation of radioactive decay to motivate the tour. You'll then look in Chapter 3 at some of the infrastructure outside of the programming language itself that you'll want to know about to program effectively in this environment, and in Chapter 4 you'll look at object semantics in the new language, as well as mixing native and managed objects. Chapter 5 covers the new C++/CLI features, starting with features of the CLI itself such as the String type and input/output, followed by enums and arrays. Chapter 6 describes classes and structs in C++/CLI. The text will then continue its treatment of classes in Chapter 7

---

1. Such as *C++ Primer, Fourth Edition* by Stanley B. Lippman, Josée Lajoie, and Barbara E. Moo (Addison-Wesley, 2005) and *The C++ Programming Language, Special Third Edition* by Bjarne Stroustrup (Addison-Wesley, 2000).

by looking at new elements of a class, such as properties, events, and operators. Chapter 8 describes inheritance in C++/CLI. In Chapter 9, I discuss interface classes, which provide an alternative to traditional multiple inheritance. You'll then have a chapter on other language features that covers exception handling, which is the fundamental mechanism for error handling in the CLR; attributes, which provide metadata for a type; and reflection, the C++/CLI equivalent of runtime type information. This is followed by a chapter on parameterized types and collection classes, and finally, I round out your introduction to C++/CLI in Chapter 12 with a closer look at the features of the language supporting interoperability with existing native C++ code and other .NET languages. Throughout the text, I encourage you to experiment with the code examples and work on your own programs as well as those in the text. Example code can be found online at http://www.apress.com, and you can try out C++/CLI for yourself for free by downloading Visual C++ Express from http://msdn.microsoft.com/vstudio/express. You can also visit my blog at http://blogs.msdn.com. I hope you learn much and enjoy reading this book.

CHAPTER 1

Introducing C++/CLI

This chapter introduces the C++/CLI language extensions to C++ and shows you the classic "Hello, World" example in C++/CLI. You'll learn just enough about the runtime environment that executes your C++/CLI programs to get started with your first program. You'll also learn some of the features available in that environment, including access to the .NET Framework (or the CLI class libraries), the common type system, and other helpful features such as garbage collection.

Garbage Collection and Handles

One convenience of a managed language is *garbage collection*—that you no longer have to keep track of all the objects you create. Your C++/CLI objects will be collected and destroyed by a background process called the *garbage collector*. Think about this analogy for a minute. When civilization in an area reaches a certain point, your household waste is collected conveniently at the curbside for burial, incineration, or recycling. As important as garbage collection is, the implications or benefits of the common language runtime (CLR) don't stop at garbage collection. In this analogy, a civilized environment has other implications as well. There is a government to contend with, which has its benefits and drawbacks. Taxes might be higher, but you get all kinds of services such as telephones, electricity, and a reliable water supply. Similarly, for your program, you might pay a performance penalty; however, you get a lot in return in terms of functionality that makes life easier as a programmer.

Remember that C++/CLI, unlike other languages that also target the CLR, doesn't replace standard C++ functionality. C++/CLI not only adds the ability to create managed objects, but also allows the creation of C++ objects, called *native objects*. But since both entities exist in the language, how are you to distinguish them? The answer is that instead of using pointers, you use tracking handles. Tracking handles are very similar to pointers, but they behave differently since they refer to managed objects, not native objects.

There are two entirely separate families of types in C++/CLI—the *native type system* exists fully intact alongside the *managed type system*. Objects or instances of native types can coexist in the same application with objects and instances of managed types. Whether a type is native or managed depends on whether it is declared with C++ syntax or with the C++/CLI syntax for managed types. Chapter 2 covers this in detail, but just to get started, instead of class, ref class is used for a managed reference class.

```
class N { ... };
ref class R { ... };
N* n = new N;     // standard C++ pointer to an object
R^ r = gcnew R;   // C++/CLI handle to an object
```

Recall that native objects, when created with the new statement (or malloc), are allocated on a large pool of memory called the *heap*. It's important to understand that there are actually two heaps in a C++/CLI application, the native heap and the managed heap. The *native heap* is used when you use the new statement, as usual, to create instances of your native classes. As in standard C++, you must explicitly manage the lifetime of the objects on this heap yourself. The *managed heap* is a separate pool of memory that is managed by the garbage collector. Instead of a normal pointer into the native heap, you use a *tracking handle* to point to objects in the managed heap. A tracking handle is expressed using the caret symbol (^), instead of the asterisk (*). Also, instead of new, the keyword gcnew is used. As you might have guessed, the "gc" stands for "garbage collected."

The reason these new pointer-like entities are called tracking handles is that in addition to freeing up unusable objects, the garbage collector also moves objects around in memory in order to organize the heap so that its operations can be carried out more efficiently. This is called *heap compaction*. This means that, unlike a native pointer, a tracking handle's address that tracks its object may change in the course of the program. For this reason, you don't normally access the address of a tracking handle. The runtime will update the address of any tracking handles if the garbage collector moves your object. From this point on, for brevity, I'll refer to them simply as *handles*.

There are certainly many parallels between pointers and handles; however, you must not assume that a handle is simply a "managed pointer." There are some subtle differences between the two, as you'll see in Chapter 4.

In general, the managed, garbage-collected environment makes for less detailed memory management work for developers, who no longer have to worry about making sure they free all allocated memory. Some might object that this makes programmers lazy. I recall that in Plato's dialogue *Critias*, the same argument arose among the ancient Egyptians over the Egyptian god Thoth's gift to mankind, the gift of writing. Some scholars at the time said that this was surely the end of memory, for the crutch of the written word would surely replace the need for memorization. All I can say is that some people's response to progress hasn't changed much in 6,000 years.

I'll refer to the C++ features that predate the C++/CLI extensions as *classic C++*. I'll use the word "managed" to describe anything governed by the CLR (or another implementation of the CLI): managed code, managed types, managed pointers, and so on. However, the term *managed C++* should not be used to describe the new language syntax. With a few exceptions, every feature of classic C++ is also a feature of C++/CLI, so it's not true to say that C++/CLI is only a managed language. The word "native" refers to the unmanaged world, hence I use the terms native types, native compilation, and so on. The term *native C++* could be used to refer to the C++ language without the extensions, but since the new language supports both managed and native types, I prefer the term *classic C++*.

The /clr Compiler Option

If you use Visual C++ 2005, you have to let the compiler know that you are targeting the CLR (and therefore want C++/CLI standard extensions enabled). You do this by using the /clr compiler option (or one of its variants, as discussed in Chapter 3). In the Visual C++ development environment, you would choose the appropriate type of project, and the option would be set appropriately for that project type. If you need to change the option later, you can set the Common Language Runtime support option in the General tab of the Project Properties dialog.

The Virtual Machine

C++/CLI applications execute in the context of the CLR. The CLR implements a *virtual machine*, which is a software implementation of an idealized, abstract execution environment. Programs that run on the CLR virtual machine use a language known as the *Common Intermediate Language* (CIL). Microsoft's implementation of CIL is often referred to as MSIL, or just plain IL. The CLR relies on a JIT (just-in-time) compiler to translate the CIL code on demand into machine code in order to execute the program.

The CLR virtual machine is Microsoft's implementation of the *Virtual Execution System* (VES), which is part of the ECMA standard. As processors change, you need only change the way in which the executable code is generated from the processor-independent layer, and you'll still be able to run the old programs written for the earlier processor. Pure IL generated by compilers targeting the CLR does not contain x86 instructions or any other object code that is configured to run on a particular processor. Compilers output MSIL code that can run on the virtual machine.

You'll see in Chapter 3 that there are several compilation modes available, ranging from native code to pure MSIL that is still machine-dependent, to verifiably safe code that is truly machine independent. Each of these modes has advantages and disadvantages. Later you'll learn in more detail when to use each option. For now, remember that there are many degrees of managed code. It is often assumed that once you transition to the CLR, all the problems (and freedoms) of the native code world are left behind. That is not true—you can run almost all classic C++ source code on the virtual machine just by recompiling it with the /clr option. The only difference is that your code is compiled to IL instead of assembler in between. Ultimately, it all boils down to machine code being executed by the processor.

The real benefits of the managed world come not with recompiling your existing classic C++ code, but by using the C++/CLI constructs that constitute a system of object types uniquely suited to do well in the managed world.

The CLR type system is mirrored in C++/CLI, so it's important to understand how it works.

The Common Type System

The CLR has a unified type system called the *common type system* (CTS). A unified type system has at its root a single type, often called Object, from which all types are derived. This is very different from the C++ type system, sometimes called a *forest*, in which there may arbitrarily be many independent type hierarchies.

The CTS represents a set of type relationships that many C++ programmers will find unfamiliar. There is no multiple inheritance, and only reference classes can be allocated on the managed heap and support inheritance and virtual functions. Chapter 2 will explain these differences. I'll use the term *managed type* to mean any type that is part of the CLR's type system. The C++/CLI type system for managed types is designed to allow the use of managed types in C++/CLI programs. Because all managed types must inherit (directly or indirectly) from the root type, Object, even the primitive types used in managed code (the managed versions of int, double, etc.) have a place in this type system, in the form of objects that wrap or "box" each primitive data type. The base class library defines a namespace called System, which contains fundamental types and other commonly used constructs. In fact, the CTS defines most primitive types in the System namespace with their own names, such as System::Int32. These names are common to all languages using the CLR. The primitive C++/CLI types such as int are synonyms for those types (e.g., int is synonymous with Int32), so that you have the convenience of referring to the type using the same name you'd use in C++. You can use two ways to refer to most primitive types. In Chapter 2, you'll learn how the primitive types in C++ map onto the CLI common type system.

Reference Types and Value Types

Every managed type falls into one of two categories: *reference types* or *value types*. The difference between value types and reference types is that value types have value semantics while reference types have reference semantics. *Value semantics* means that when an object is assigned (or passed as a parameter), it is copied byte for byte. *Reference semantics* means that when an object is assigned (or passed as a parameter), the object is not copied; instead, another reference to that same object is created.

Value types are used for objects that represent a value, like a primitive type or a simple aggregate (e.g., a small structure), especially one that is to be used in mathematical computations. Computations with value types are more efficient than with reference types because reference types incur an extra level of indirection; reference types exist on the heap and can only be accessed through the handle, while the value type holds its value directly. Value types actually live in a limited scope, either as an automatic variable at function scope or in the scope of another object as a field. They also do not have the overhead of an object header, as reference types do. However, value types are limited in many ways. Value types are often copied— for example, when used as a method parameter, a copy is automatically created—so they are not suitable for large objects; they also cannot be used in inheritance hierarchies, and they don't support more complex and powerful object operations such as copy constructors, nontrivial default constructors, assignment operators, and so on. Value types are useful for simple aggregates that are frequently passed around or used in computations, such as a complex number, a point, or a simple buffer.

Reference types are used wherever reference semantics are required and when modeling more complex objects for which the limitations of value types are too restrictive. They may inherit from another class and may in turn be inherited from. Thus they may be used to model complex objects. They are not copied byte for byte (for example, when passed as an argument to a function), rather, they are passed as references, so they may be large and not suffer a penalty from excessive copying. They can have special member functions such as default constructors, destructors, copy constructors, and the copy assignment operator (although neither type can have overloaded operators new and delete). The actual objects live on the managed heap. The handle itself is just an address that refers to the object's header (which is 8 bytes in size for the 32-bit CLR) on the heap.

Figure 1-1 shows the memory layout of a typical value type and a reference type.

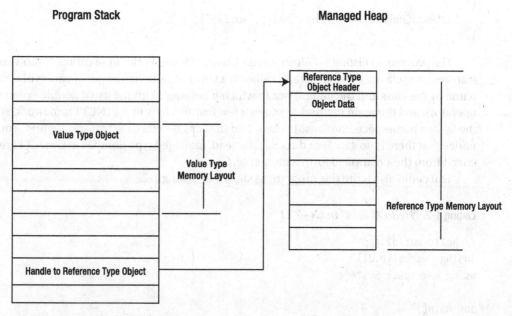

Figure 1-1. *Storage characteristics of reference types and value types. Value types are shown here on the stack (although they could also be a part of an object on the managed heap). Reference types involve a handle plus an object on the managed heap.*

The CLI and the .NET Framework

The CLI includes the VES and a standardized set of class libraries, often called the *base class library* (BCL), that provides support for fundamental programming. The .NET Framework is a large class library released by Microsoft that implements the base class library as well as additional functionality that isn't part of the ECMA standard. If you are using Visual Studio and targeting the CLR, you have access to the .NET Framework class libraries within your C++/CLI code. If you are using a different implementation of C++/CLI than Microsoft's, you still have the base class library. This book will not attempt to cover all that the .NET Framework, or even the base class library, allows you to do; however, it will cover basic input and output, the collection classes (Chapter 11), some of the exceptions, some of the metadata that can be applied to types, and ways of getting information on types at runtime (reflection), all in Chapter 10, as well as other useful aspects of the Framework as necessary.

The full .NET Framework contains support for database access, XML, web services, web pages, Windows application development, and so on.

"Hello, World"

Now let's look at our first program (Listing 1-1) and see how the language looks in actual code.

Listing 1-1. *"Hello, World" in Classic C++*

```
// hello_world1.cpp
int main()
{
    System::Console::WriteLine("Hello, World!");
}
```

The program in Listing 1-1 illustrates the classic "Hello, World" application. It shows several features from classic C++—a method call with a string argument, the qualification of a method name by the class and the namespace to which it belongs (with the usual double-colon scope operator), and the main method. It shows a few features new to the .NET Framework, such as the System namespace, the Console class, and the Console class's WriteLine method. You'll notice that there is no #include directive. Instead, managed type libraries in C++/CLI are referenced from their compiled form with #using.

You could also write this program as shown in Listing 1-2.

Listing 1-2. *"Hello, World" in C++/CLI*

```
// hello_world2.cpp
#using "mscorlib.dll"
using namespace System;

int main()
{
    Console::WriteLine("Hello World!");
}
```

The #using directive references the DLL file mscorlib.dll. The program also employs the using declaration in the classic C++ sense, which as you know is simply used to avoid having to use fully qualified names for program elements in the System namespace. The #using directive is a new C++/CLI concept used to reference the types contained in a DLL. This is very different from #include, which references types declared before compilation. The first example you saw works because the compiler automatically inserts #using "mscorlib.dll". This is convenient since nearly all CLI programs require the types that it defines. The DLL is a CLI assembly, which contains not just executable code but also metadata that exposes information about the types and program elements in the assembly. No header file is needed.

Listing 1-3 illustrates a few more features of the language.

Listing 1-3. *More C++/CLI Features*

```
// hello_world3.cpp

using namespace System;

ref class Hello
{
    String^ greeting;
```

```
    public:
    void Greet()
    {
        Console::WriteLine(greeting + "!");
    }

    void SetGreeting(String^ newGreeting)
    {
        greeting = newGreeting;
    }
};

int main()
{
    Hello^ hello = gcnew Hello();
    hello->SetGreeting("Hello World");
    hello->Greet();
    hello->SetGreeting("Howdy");
    hello->Greet();
}
```

This code creates a reference class, as indicated by the ref keyword. It's called Hello, with a method called Greet and another method called SetGreeting. The SetGreeting method takes a System::String parameter. The caret indicates that the parameter type is "handle to String." The String class is the CLI version of a (Unicode) character string. Unlike a native string, the String object is invariant, which means it cannot be changed without creating a brand new string. In Chapter 5, you'll see how to create a string that can be manipulated and changed.

■**Note** Actually, ref is not a keyword in exactly the same sense as a C++ keyword. For one thing, it is sensitive to the context in which it is used. Unlike keywords, context-sensitive keywords introduced in C++/CLI can be used as variable names without causing program errors. Also, keywords like ref class are considered *whitespaced keywords*, which obey certain special rules. See the appendix for information about context-sensitive keywords and whitespaced keywords.

Notice that the member variable greeting is initialized right at its point of declaration, which wouldn't be allowed for a nonconstant member in classic C++, but is conveniently allowed in C++/CLI. Also notice the Greet method uses a new C++/CLI method of concatenating strings using the + operator. Also, the SetGreeting method takes a String, but the code passes a string literal. The compiler creates a String object from the string literal passed in. You'll learn the details of how this works in Chapter 5, but for now just notice that you can use string literals in a natural way with the String type, without concerning yourself with the subtleties of whether it's a narrow or wide character string literal.

Just as in classic C++, the main method does not need to explicitly return a value, even though its return value is properly int, not void. This is because the compiler inserts return 0; automatically.

In the main method in Listing 1-3, you saw a very important pattern that is used throughout all C++/CLI code. The Hello class is a reference type, lives on the managed heap, is created with gcnew instead of new, and referred to using a handle, a named object that refers to the unnamed object on the managed heap. The indirection operator is used, just as if the handle were a pointer to the object.

I've demonstrated a simple reference type, but you may be wondering whether the Hello class could also be a value type. Indeed, it can be, because it has no explicit inheritance relationship with any other class (although, because it is a managed type, it implicitly inherits from Object); it has no special initialization that would require you to define a special default constructor; it has no other special member functions, and it contains no data. Listing 1-4 shows how the code would look with Hello as a value type.

Listing 1-4. *Using a Value Type*

```
// hello_world4.cpp
using namespace System;

value class Hello
{
    // This code is unchanged.
};

int main()
{
    Hello hello;
    hello.Greet("Hello World");
}
```

In the second version, hello is created as a local stack variable in the main function, rather than on the managed heap, which might result in some performance gain, although with only one object, this hardly matters. Also, a real value type would probably have member variables, perhaps as in Listing 1-5.

Listing 1-5. *A Value Type with Members*

```
value struct Greeting
{
    String^ greeting;
    Char punctuator;

    void PrintGreeting(String^ name)
    {
        Console::WriteLine(greeting + name + punctuator);
    }
};
```

As you can see, the code uses value struct in place of value class. Throughout this text, whenever I use the term *class*, I mean "class or structure." As in classic C++, the difference between a structure and a class is that structure members are public by default, and class members are private by default.

As you know, the main function, also known as the entry point, may take additional arguments that are passed in by the operating system: the number of arguments (traditionally called argc) and an array of the arguments as character arrays (traditionally called argv). This information is also available to C++/CLI programmers, but instead of using the traditional arguments, you use a managed array type. In this case, the array parameter is an array of handles to String, each string representing one of the supplied arguments. The managed array type is one of the many fundamental types defined by the CLR that has special language support in C++/CLI. These CLR analogs of C++ types provide bounds checking, but also are objects in and of themselves, and so provide features called *properties* (discussed in the next chapter), such as the Length property used in Listing 1-6, and useful methods. The old int parameter of classic C++'s main function, argc, isn't necessary since the Length property can be used to get the count of command-line arguments.

With this array of arguments, you can supply a person's name on the command line and print a greeting customized to that person, as demonstrated in Listing 1-6.

Listing 1-6. *Using Command-Line Arguments*

```cpp
// greeting.cpp
using namespace System;

value struct Greeting
{
    String^ greeting;
    Char punctuator;

    void PrintGreeting(String^ name)
    {
        Console::WriteLine(greeting + name + punctuator);
    }
};

int main(array<String^>^ args)
{
    Greeting greet;
    greet.greeting = "Hi ";
    greet.punctuator = '!';

    if (args->Length < 1)
    {
        Console::WriteLine("Enter names on the command line, like this:"
                           " greeting <name1> <name2> ...");
        Console::WriteLine("Use quotes around names with spaces.");
        return 1;
    }
```

```
    for (int i = 0; i < args->Length; i++)
    {
        greet.PrintGreeting(args[i]);
    }

    greet.greeting = "Hello, ";
    greet.punctuator = '.';

    for each (String^ s in args)
    {
        greet.PrintGreeting(s);
    }
}
```

As you can see, the type of the array elements is enclosed in angle brackets, and in this case it's a handle to String. Why a handle? Because String is a reference type. OK, but why are there two handle symbols? The array type is also a reference type, so the outer caret symbol indicates that the argument is a handle to an array.

Listing 1-6 also uses the for each statement. The for each statement is the semantic equivalent of the for loop above it. By eliminating the code for counting, bounds checking, and incrementing, the for each statement simplifies performing iteration of an array or other enumerable data structure. In Chapter 9, you'll see how to create data structures that allow the use of for each.

Also, notice that the program name is not part of the array, as it is in classic C++. The program name is consumed by the CLR, so it is not available to programs through the args array.

Summary

This chapter touched upon the basics of garbage collection and handles. You were introduced to a few terms, learned about the common type system, and saw a simple first program in C++/CLI. You looked closely at the new main function, with a brief preview of the managed array and the for each statement.

In the next chapter, you'll explore many more C++/CLI language features in a broad overview.

CHAPTER 2

■■■

A Quick Tour of the C++/CLI Language Features

The aim of this chapter is to give you a general idea of what C++/CLI is all about by providing a brief look at most of the new language features in the context of an extended example, saving the details for later chapters. By the end of this chapter, you'll have a good idea of the scope of the most important changes and will be able to start writing some code.

Primitive Types

The CLI contains a definition of a new type system called the common type system (CTS). It is the task of a .NET language to map its own type system to the CTS. Table 2-1 shows the mapping for C++/CLI.

Table 2-1. *Primitive Types and the Common Type System*

CLI Type	C++/CLI Keyword	Declaration	Description
Boolean	bool	bool isValid = true;	true or false
Byte	unsigned char	unsigned char c = 'a';	8-bit unsigned integer
Char	wchar_t	wchar_t wc = 'a' or L'a';	Unicode character
Double	double	double d = 1.0E-13;	8-byte double-precision floating-point number
Int16	short	short s = 123;	16-bit signed integer
Int32	long, int	int i = -1000000;	32-bit signed integer
Int64	__int64, long long	__int64 i64 = 2000;	64-bit signed integer
SByte	char	char c = 'a';	Signed 8-bit integer
Single	float	float f = 1.04f;	4-byte single-precision floating-point number

Table 2-1. *Primitive Types and the Common Type System (Continued)*

CLI Type	C++/CLI Keyword	Declaration	Description
UInt16	unsigned short	unsigned short s = 15;	Unsigned 16-bit signed integer
UInt32	unsigned long, unsigned int	unsigned int i = 500000;	Unsigned 32-bit signed integer
UInt64	unsigned __int64, unsigned long long	unsigned __int64 i64 = 400;	Unsigned 64-bit integer
Void	void	n/a	Untyped data or no data

In this book, the term *managed type* refers to any of the CLI types mentioned in Table 2-1, or any of the aggregate types (ref class, value class, etc.) mentioned in the next section.

Aggregate Types

Aggregate types in C++ include structures, unions, classes, and so on. C++/CLI provides managed aggregate types. The CTS supports several kinds of aggregate types:

- ref class and ref struct, a reference type representing an object

- value class and value struct, usually a small object representing a value

- enum class

- interface class, an interface only, with no implementation, inherited by classes and other interfaces

- Managed arrays

- Parameterized types, which are types that contain at least one unspecified type that may be substituted by a real type when the parameterized type is used

Let's explore these concepts together by developing some code to make a simple model of atoms and radioactive decay. First, consider an atom. To start, we'll want to model its position and what type of atom it is. In this initial model, we're going to consider atoms to be like the billiard balls they were once thought to be, before the quantum revolution changed all that. So we will for the moment consider that an atom has a definite position in three-dimensional space. In classic C++, we might create a class like the one in the upcoming listing, choosing to reflect the *atomic number*—the number of protons, which determines what type of element it is; and the *isotope number*—the number of protons plus the number of neutrons, which determines which isotope of the element it is. The isotope number can make a very innocuous or a very explosive difference in practical terms (and in geopolitical terms). For example, you may have heard of carbon dating, in which the amount of radioactive carbon-14 is measured to determine the age of wood or other organic materials. Carbon can have an isotope number of 12, 13, or 14. The most common isotope of carbon is carbon-12, whereas carbon-14 is a radioactive isotope. You may also have heard a lot of controversy about isotopes of uranium.

There's a huge geopolitical difference between uranium-238, which is merely mildly radioactive, and uranium-235, which is the principal ingredient of a nuclear bomb.

In this chapter, together we'll create a program that simulates radioactive decay, with specific reference to carbon-14 decay used in carbon dating. We'll start with a fairly crude example, but by the end of the chapter, we'll make it better using C++/CLI constructs. Radioactive decay is the process by which an atom changes into another type of atom by some kind of alteration in the nucleus. These alterations result in changes that transform the atom into a different element. Carbon-14, for example, undergoes radioactive decay by emitting an electron and changing into nitrogen-14. This type of radioactive decay is referred to as β⁻ (*beta minus* or simply *beta*) decay, and always results in a neutron turning into a proton in the nucleus, thus increasing the atomic number by 1. Other forms of decay include β⁺ (*beta plus* or *positron*) decay, in which a positron is emitted, or alpha decay, in which an alpha particle (two protons and two neutrons) is ejected from the nucleus. Figure 2-1 illustrates beta decay for carbon-14.

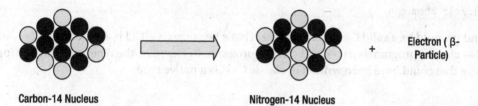

Figure 2-1. *Beta decay. Carbon-14 decays into nitrogen-14 by emitting an electron. Neutrons are shown in black; protons in gray.*

Listing 2-1 shows our native C++ class modeling the atom.

Listing 2-1. *Modeling an Atom in Native C++*

```
// atom.cpp
class Atom
{
    private:
        double pos[3];
        unsigned int atomicNumber;
        unsigned int isotopeNumber;

    public:
        Atom() : atomicNumber(1), isotopeNumber(1)
        {
            // Let's say we most often use hydrogen atoms,
            // so there is a default constructor that assumes you are
            // creating a hydrogen atom.
            pos[0] = 0; pos[1] = 0; pos[2] = 0;
        }
```

```
    Atom(double x, double y, double z, unsigned int a, unsigned int n)
      : atomicNumber(a), isotopeNumber(n)
    {
        pos[0] = x; pos[1] = y; pos[2] = z;
    }
    unsigned int GetAtomicNumber() { return atomicNumber; }
    void SetAtomicNumber(unsigned int a) { atomicNumber = a; }
    unsigned int GetIsotopeNumber() { return isotopeNumber; }
    void SetIsotopeNumber(unsigned int n) { isotopeNumber = n; }
    double GetPosition(int index) { return pos[index]; }
    void SetPosition(int index, double value) { pos[index] = value; }
};
```

You could compile the class unchanged in C++/CLI with the following command line:

```
cl /clr atom.cpp
```

and it would be a valid C++/CLI program. That's because C++/CLI is a superset of C++, so any C++ class or program is a C++/CLI class or program. In C++/CLI, the type in Listing 2-1 (or any type that could have been written in classic C++) is a native type.

Reference Classes

Recall that the managed types use ref class (or value class, etc.), whereas the native classes just use class in the declaration. Reference classes are often informally referred to as *ref classes* or *ref types*. What happens if we just change class Atom to ref class Atom to see whether that makes it a valid reference type? (The /LD option tells the linker to generate a DLL instead of an executable.)

```
C:\ >cl /clr /LD atom1.cpp
atom1.cpp(4) : error C4368: cannot define 'pos' as a member of managed 'Atom':
mixed types are not supported
```

Well, it doesn't work. Looks like there are some things that we cannot use in a managed type. The compiler is telling us that we're trying to use a native type in a reference type, which is not allowed. (In Chapter 12, you'll see how to use interoperability features to allow some mixing.)

I mentioned that there is something called a managed array. Using that instead of the native array should fix the problem, as in Listing 2-2.

Listing 2-2. *Using a Managed Array*

```
// atom_managed.cpp
ref class Atom
{
    private:
        array<double>^ pos;  // Declare the managed array.
        unsigned int atomicNumber;
        unsigned int isotopeNumber;
```

```
public:
    Atom()
    {
        // We'll need to allocate space for the position values.
        pos = gcnew array<double>(3);
        pos[0] = 0; pos[1] = 0; pos[2] = 0;
        atomicNumber = 1;
        isotopeNumber = 1;
    }
    Atom(double x, double y, double z, unsigned int atNo, unsigned int n)
        : atomicNumber(atNo), isotopeNumber(n)
    {
        // Create the managed array.
        pos = gcnew array<double>(3);
        pos[0] = x; pos[1] = y; pos[2] = z;
    }
    // The rest of the class declaration is unchanged.
};
```

So we have a ref class Atom with a managed array, and the rest of the code still works. In the managed type system, the array type is a type inheriting from Object, like all types in the CTS. Note the syntax used to declare the array. We use the angle brackets suggestive of a template argument to specify the type of the array. Don't be deceived—it is not a real template type. Notice that we also use the handle symbol, indicating that pos is a handle to a type. Also, we use gcnew to create the array, specifying the type and the number of elements in the constructor argument instead of using square brackets in the declaration. The managed array is a reference type, so the array and its values are allocated on the managed heap.

So what exactly can you embed as fields in a managed type? You can embed the types in the CTS, including primitive types, since they all have counterparts in the CLI: double is System::Double, and so on. You cannot use a native array or native subobject. However, there is a way to reference a native class in a managed class, as you'll see in Chapter 12.

Value Classes

You may be wondering if, like the Hello type in the previous chapter, you could also have created Atom as a value type. If you only change ref to value and recompile, you get an error message that states "value types cannot define special member functions"—this is because of the definition of the default constructor, which counts as a special member function. Thanks to the compiler, value types always act as if they have a built-in default constructor that initializes the data members to their default values (e.g., zero, false, etc.). In reality, there is no constructor emitted, but the fields are initialized to their default values by the CLR. This enables arrays of value types to be created very efficiently, but of course limits their usefulness to situations where a zero value is meaningful.

Let's say you try to satisfy the compiler and remove the default constructor. Now, you've created a problem. If you create an atom using the built-in default constructor, you'll have atoms with atomic number zero, which wouldn't be an atom at all. Arrays of value types don't call the constructor; instead, they make use of the runtime's initialization of the value type fields to zero, so if you wanted to create arrays of atoms, you would have to initialize them after constructing them. You could certainly add an Initialize function to the class to do that, but if some other programmer comes along later and tries to use the atoms before they're initialized, that programmer will get nonsense (see Listing 2-3).

Listing 2-3. *C++/CLI's Version of Heisenberg Uncertainty*

```
void atoms()
{
    int n_atoms = 50;
    array<Atom>^ atoms = gcnew array<Atom>(n_atoms);

    // Between the array creation and initialization,
    // the atoms are in an invalid state.
    // Don't call GetAtomicNumber here!

    for (int i = 0; i < n_atoms; i++)
    {
        atoms[i].Initialize( /* ... */ );
    }
}
```

Depending on how important this particular drawback is to you, you might decide that a value type just won't work. You have to look at the problem and determine whether the features available in a value type are sufficient to model the problem effectively. Listing 2-4 provides an example where a value type definitely makes sense: a Point class.

Listing 2-4. *Defining a Value Type for Points in 3D Space*

```
// value_struct.cpp
value struct Point3D
{
    double x;
    double y;
    double z;

};
```

Using this structure instead of the array makes the Atom class look like Listing 2-5.

Listing 2-5. *Using a Value Type Instead of an Array*

```
ref class Atom
{
    private:
        Point3D position;
        unsigned int atomicNumber;
        unsigned int isotopeNumber;
```

```
    public:
        Atom(Point3D pos, unsigned int a, unsigned int n)
            : position(pos), atomicNumber(a), isotopeNumber(n)
        { }

        Point3D GetPosition()
        {
            return position;
        }
        void SetPosition(Point3D new_position)
        {
            position = new_position;
        }

        // The rest of the code is unchanged.

};
```

The value type Point3D is used as a member, return value, and parameter type. In all cases you use it without the handle. You'll see later that you can have a handle to a value type, but as this code is written, the value type is copied when it is used as a parameter, and when it is returned. Also, when used as a member for the position field, it takes up space in the memory layout of the containing Atom class, rather than existing in an independent location. This is different from the managed array implementation, in which the elements in the pos array were in a separate heap location. Intensive computations with this class using the value struct should be faster than the array implementation. This is the sweet spot for value types—they are very efficient for small objects.

Enumeration Classes

So, you've seen all the managed aggregate types except interface classes and enumeration classes. The enumeration class (or *enum class* for short) is pretty straightforward. It looks a lot like a classic C++ enum, and like the C++ enum, it defines a series of named values. It's actually a value type. Listing 2-6 is an example of an enum class.

Listing 2-6. *Declaring an Enum Class*

```
// elements_enum.cpp

enum class Element
{
    Hydrogen = 1, Helium, Lithium, Beryllium, Boron, Carbon, Nitrogen, Oxygen,
    Fluorine, Neon
    // ... 100 or so other elements omitted for brevity
};
```

While we could have listed these in the order they appear in the Tom Lehrer song "The Elements" (a classic sung to the tune of "Major-General's Song"), we'll list them in order of increasing atomic number, so we can convert between element type and atomic number easily.

The methods on the enum class type allow a bit of extra functionality that you wouldn't get with the old C++ enum. For example, you can call the ToString method on the enum and use that to print the named value. This is possible because the enum class type, like all .NET types, derives from Object, and Object has a ToString method. The .NET Framework Enum type overrides ToString, and that implementation returns the enum named value as a String. If you've ever written a tedious switch statement in C or C++ to generate a string for the value of an enum, you'll appreciate this convenience. We could use this Element enum in our Atom class by adding new method GetElementType to the Atom class, as shown in Listing 2-7.

Listing 2-7. *Using Enums in the Atom Class*

```
ref class Atom
{
    // ...

    Element GetElementType()
    {
        return safe_cast<Element>( atomicNumber );
    }
    void SetElementType(Element element)
    {
        atomicNumber = safe_cast<unsigned int>(element);
    }
    String^ GetElementString()
    {
        return GetElementType().ToString();
    }
};
```

Notice a few things about this code. Instead of the classic C++ static_cast (or dynamic_cast), we use a casting construct that is introduced in C++/CLI, safe_cast. A *safe cast* is a cast in which there is, if needed, a runtime check for validity. Actually, there is no check to see whether the value fits within the range of defined values for that enum, so in fact this is equivalent to static_cast.

Because safe_cast is safer for more complicated conversions, it is recommended for general use in code targeting the CLR. However, there may be a performance loss if a type check must be performed at runtime. The compiler will determine whether a type check is actually necessary, so if it's not, the code is just as efficient as with another form of cast. If the type check fails, safe_cast throws an exception. Using dynamic_cast would also result in a runtime type check, the only difference being that dynamic_cast will never throw an exception. In this particular case (Listing 2-7), the compiler knows that the enum value will never fail to be converted to an unsigned integer.

Interface Classes

Interfaces are not something that is available in classic C++, although something like an interface could be created by using an abstract base class in which all the methods are pure virtual (declared with = 0), which would mean that they had no implementation. Even so, such a class is not quite the same as an interface. An interface class has no fields and no method implementations; an abstract base class may have these. Also, multiple interface classes may be inherited by a class, whereas only one noninterface class may be inherited by a managed type.

We want to model radioactive decay. Since most atoms are not radioactive, we don't want to add radioactivity methods to our Atom class, but we do want another class, maybe RadioactiveAtom, which we'll use for the radioactivity modeling. We'll have it inherit from Atom and add the extra functionality for radioactive decay. It might be useful to have all the radioactivity methods defined together so we can use them in another class. Who knows, maybe we'll eventually want to have a version of an Ion class that also implements the radioactivity methods so we can have radioactive atoms with charge, or something. In classic C++, we might be tempted to use multiple inheritance. We could create a RadioactiveIon class that inherits from both Ion and RadioactiveAtom. But we can't do that in C++/CLI (at least not in a managed type) because in C++/CLI managed types are limited to only one direct base class. However, a class may implement as many interface classes as are needed, so that is a good solution. An interface defines a set of related methods; implementing an interface indicates that the type supports the functionality defined by that interface. Many interfaces in the .NET Framework have names that end in "able," for example, IComparable, IEnumerable, ISerializable, and so on, suggesting that interfaces deal with "abilities" of objects to behave in a certain way. Inheriting from the IComparable interface indicates that objects of your type support comparison functionality; inheriting from IEnumerable indicates that your type supports iteration via .NET Framework enumerators; and so on.

If you're used to multiple inheritance, you may like it or you may not. I thought it was a cool thing at first, until I tried to write up a complicated type system using multiple inheritance and virtual base classes, and found that as the hierarchy got more complicated, it became difficult to tell which virtual method would be called. I became convinced that the compiler was calling the wrong method, and filed a bug report including a distilled version of my rat's nest inheritance hierarchy. I was less excited about multiple inheritance after that. Whatever your feelings about multiple inheritance in C++, the inheritance rules for C++/CLI types are a bit easier to work with.

Using interfaces, the code in Listing 2-8 shows an implementation of RadioactiveAtom that implements the IRadioactive interface.

Note the absence of the public keyword in the base class and interface list. Inheritance is always public in C++/CLI, so there is no need for the public keyword.

Listing 2-8. *Defining and Implementing an Interface*

```
// atom_interfaces.cpp

interface class IRadioactive
{
    void AlphaDecay();
    void BetaDecay();
```

```
        double GetHalfLife();
};

ref class RadioactiveAtom : Atom, IRadioactive
{
        double half_life;

        void UpdateHalfLife()
        {
                // ...
        }

public:
        // The atom releases an alpha particle
        // so it loses two protons and two neutrons.
        virtual void AlphaDecay()
        {
                SetAtomicNumber(GetAtomicNumber() - 2);
                SetIsotopeNumber(GetIsotopeNumber() - 4);
                UpdateHalfLife();
        }

        // The atom releases an electron.
        // A neutron changes into a proton.
        virtual void BetaDecay()
        {
                SetAtomicNumber(GetAtomicNumber() + 1);
                UpdateHalfLife();
        }

        virtual double GetHalfLife()
        {
                return half_life;
        }
};
```

The plan is to eventually set up a loop representing increasing time, and "roll the dice" at each step to see whether each atom decays. If it does, we want to call the appropriate decay method, either beta decay or alpha decay. These decay methods of the RadioactiveAtom class will update the atomic number and isotope number of the atom according to the new isotope that the atom decayed to. At this point, in reality, the atom could still be radioactive, and would then possibly decay further. We would have to update the half-life at this point. In the next sections, we will continue to develop this example.

The previous sections demonstrated the declaration and use of managed aggregate types, including ref classes, value classes, managed arrays, enum classes, and interface classes. In the next section, you'll learn about features that model the "*has-a*" relationship for an object: properties, delegates, and events.

Elements Modeling the "has-a" Relationship

One thing you've probably noticed by now in our Atom class is there are a lot of methods that begin with Get and Set to capture the "has-a" relationship between an object and the properties of the object. Some of the C++/CLI features were added simply to capture such commonly used patterns in the language. Doing this helps standardize common coding practices, which can help in making code more readable. Language features in C++/CLI supporting the "has-a" relationship include *properties* and *events*.

Properties

C++/CLI provides language support for properties. *Properties* are elements of a class that are represented by a value (or set of indexed values for indexed properties). Many objects have properties, and making this a first-class language construct, even if at first they might seem a trivial addition, does make life easier. Let's change all the Get and Set methods and use properties instead. For simplicity we'll return to the example without the interfaces (see Listing 2-9).

Listing 2-9. *Using Properties*

```
ref class Atom
{
    private:
        array<double>^ pos;

    public:

        Atom(double x, double y, double z, unsigned int a, unsigned int n)
        {
            pos = gcnew array<double>(3);
            pos[0] = x; pos[1] = y; pos[2] = z;

            AtomicNumber = a;
            IsotopeNumber = n;
        }

        property unsigned int AtomicNumber;
        property unsigned int IsotopeNumber;

        property Element ElementType
        {
            Element get()
            {
                return safe_cast<Element>(AtomicNumber);
            }
        }
```

```
        void set(Element element)
        {
            AtomicNumber = safe_cast<int>(element);
        }
    }

    property double Position[int]
    {
        // If index is out of range, the array access will
        // throw an IndexOutOfRange exception.
        double get(int index)            {
            return pos[index];
        }
        void set(int index, double value)
        {
            pos[index] = value;
        }
    }
};
```

We create four properties: AtomicNumber, IsotopeNumber, ElementType, and Position. We deliberately use three different ways of defining these properties to illustrate the range of what you can do with properties. The ElementType property is the standard, commonly used form. The property is named, followed by a block containing the get and set methods, fully prototyped and implemented. The names of the accessors must be get and set, although you don't have to implement both. If you implement only one of them, the property becomes read-only or write-only. The AtomicNumber and IsotopeNumber properties are what's known as trivial properties. *Trivial properties* have getter and setter methods created automatically for them: also notice that we remove the atomicNumber and isotopeNumber fields. They are no longer needed since private fields are created automatically for trivial properties. The third type of property is known as an *indexed property* or a *vector property*. Nonindexed properties are known as *scalar properties*. The indexed property Position is implemented with what looks like array indexing syntax. Vector properties take a value in square brackets and use that value as an index to determine what value is returned.

Also notice that we use the property names just like fields in the rest of the body of the class. This is what makes properties so convenient. In assignment expressions, property get and set methods are called implicitly as appropriate when a property is accessed or is assigned to.

```
AtomicNumber = safe_cast<int>(element); // set called implicitly
```

You can also use the compound assignment operator (+=, -=, etc.) and the postfix or prefix operators with properties to simplify the syntax in some cases. For example, consider the AlphaDecay method in the RadioactiveAtom class. It could be written as shown in Listing 2-10.

Listing 2-10. *Using Compound Assignment Operators with Properties*

```
virtual void AlphaDecay()
{
    AtomicNumber -= 2;
    IsotopeNumber -= 4;
    UpdateHalfLife();
}
```

Delegates and Events

Managed types may have additional constructs for events. Events are based on *delegates*, managed types that are like souped-up function pointers. Delegates are actually more than just a function pointer, because they may refer to a whole set of methods, rather than just one. Also, when referencing a nonstatic method, they reference both the object and the method to call on that object. As you'll see, the syntax, both for declaring a delegate and invoking one, is simpler than the corresponding syntax for using a function pointer or pointer to member. Continuing with the radioactivity problem, we'll now use delegates to implement radioactive decay. Atoms have a certain probability for decay. The probability for decaying during a specific interval of time can be determined from the half-life using the formula

probability of decay = ln 2 / halflife * timestep

The constant λ, known as the decay constant, is used to represent *ln 2 / halflife*, so this could also be just

probability of decay = λ* timestep

Listing 2-11 demonstrates creating a delegate type, in this case DecayProcessFunc. The RadioactiveAtoms class has a property named DecayProcess, which is of that delegate type. This property can be set to the beta decay function (here beta minus decay), the alpha decay function, or perhaps some other rare type of radioactive decay.

The delegate indicates both the object and the method. This is the main difference between a delegate and a pointer to member function in classic C++. Listing 2-11 provides the full code, with the delegate code highlighted. I've removed the interface that was used in Listing 2-8, as it is not central to the discussion now.

Listing 2-11. *Using a Delegate*

```
// radioactive_decay.cpp
using namespace System;

// This declares a delegate type that takes no parameters.
delegate void DecayProcessFunc();

enum class Element; // same as before
ref class Atom; // same as before, but without the position data
```

```cpp
ref class RadioactiveAtom : Atom
{

    public:
        RadioactiveAtom(int a, int n, bool is_stable, double half_life)
            : Atom(a, n)
        {
            IsStable = is_stable;
            HalfLife = half_life;
            Lambda = Math::Log(2) / half_life;
        }

        // The atom releases an alpha particle
        // so it loses two protons and two neutrons.
        virtual void AlphaDecay()
        {
            AtomicNumber -= 2;
            IsotopeNumber -= 4;
            Update();
        }

        // The atom releases an electron.
        void BetaDecay()
        {
            AtomicNumber++;
            Update();
        }

        property bool IsStable;
        property double HalfLife;
        property double Lambda;
        void Update()
        {
            // In this case we assume it decays to a stable nucleus.
            // nullptr is the C++/CLI way to refer to an unassigned handle.
            DecayProcess = nullptr;
            IsStable = true;
        }

        // Declare the delegate property. We'll call this when
        // an atom decays.
        property DecayProcessFunc^ DecayProcess;

}; // ref class RadioactiveAtom
```

```
void SimulateDecay(int a, int n, double halflife, int step,
                   int max_time, int num_atoms, int seed)
{
    array<RadioactiveAtom^>^ atoms = gcnew array<RadioactiveAtom^>(num_atoms);

    // Initialize the array.
    // We cannot use a for each statement here because the for each
    // statement is not allowed to modify the atoms array.
    for (int i = 0; i < num_atoms; i++)
    {
        atoms[i] = gcnew RadioactiveAtom(a, n, false, halflife);
        // Create the delegate.
        atoms[i]->DecayProcess =
            gcnew DecayProcessFunc(atoms[i], &RadioactiveAtom::BetaDecay);
    }

    Random^ rand = gcnew Random(seed);
    for (int t = 0; t < max_time; t++)
    {
        for each (RadioactiveAtom^ atom in atoms)
        {
            if ((!atom->IsStable) && atom->Lambda * step > rand->NextDouble())
            {
                // Invoke the delegate.
                atom->DecayProcess->Invoke();
            }
        }
    }
}

int main()
{
    // Carbon-14.  Atomic Number: 6  Isotope Number 14
    // Half-Life 5730 years
    // Number of atoms 10000
    // Maximum time 10000
    // Random number seed 7757
    SimulateDecay(6, 14, 5730, 1, 10000, 10000, 7757);
}
```

The delegate code consists of a delegate declaration, indicating what arguments and return types the delegated functions may have. Then, there is the point at which the delegate is created. A delegate is a reference type, so you refer to it using a handle, and you use gcnew to create the delegate. If the delegate is going to reference a nonstatic member function, call the delegate constructor that takes both an object pointer and the method to be called, using the address-of operator (&) and the qualified method name. If you're assigning the delegate to a static method, omit the object and just pass the second parameter, indicating the method, like this:

```
atoms[i]->DecayProcess =
          gcnew DecayProcessFunc(&RadioactiveAtom::SomeStaticMethod);
```

So far we've used delegates but not events. An *event* is an abstraction representing something happening. Methods called *event handlers* may be hooked up to events to respond in some way to the event. Events are of type delegate, but as you've seen, delegates themselves may be used independently of events. The delegate forms a link between the source of the event (possibly a user action, or some action initiated by other code) and the object and function that responds in some way to the action. In this case, the RadioactiveAtom class will have a Decay event, declared as in Listing 2-12.

Listing 2-12. *Declaring an Event*

```
ref class RadioactiveAtom
{
    // other code...

    // the event declaration
    event DecayProcessFunc^ Decay;

};
```

Instead of invoking the delegate directly, we call the event in the client code using function-call syntax. The code that hooks up the event looks the same as with the delegate property (see Listing 2-13).

Listing 2-13. *Hooking Up and Firing an Event*

```
// Hook up the event.
atoms[i]->Decay +=
          gcnew DecayProcessFunc(atoms[i], &RadioactiveAtom::BetaDecay);

// ...

// Fire the event.
a->Decay();
```

It is possible for an event to trigger multiple actions. You'll learn about such possibilities in Chapter 7.

You could certainly refine the design further. Perhaps you are bothered by the fact that every instance of RadioactiveAtom contains its own halflife and lambda properties. You might instead create a static data structure to store the half-life information for every type of isotope. What would this structure look like? It would require two indices to look up: both the atomic number and the isotope. However, a two-dimensional array would be a huge waste of space, since most of the cells would never be used. You might try implementing an isotope table as a *sparse array*—a data structure that can be used like an array but is a hashtable underneath so as to avoid storing space for unused elements. The implementation of such a collection type would probably be a template in classic C++. In C++/CLI, it could be a template or it could be another type of parameterized type, a generic type, which the next section describes.

Generics

While templates are supported in C++/CLI for both native and managed types, another kind of parameterized type has been defined in C++/CLI: *generics*. Generics fulfill a different purpose, providing runtime parameterization of types, whereas templates provide compile-time parameterization of types. You'll explore the implications of this difference in Chapter 11. The .NET Framework 2.0 supports generics and provides generic collection classes. One such class is the generic List, which is a dynamic array class that automatically expands to accommodate larger numbers of elements. The List class definition would look something like the code in Listing 2-14.

Listing 2-14. *Defining a Generic List Class*

```
generic <typename T>
ref class List
{
   public:
      T Add(T t) { /* ... */ }
      void Remove(T t) { /* ... */ }
      // other methods
};
```

This declaration indicates that List is a generic type with one type parameter, T. Returning to our example of treating isotopes of the chemical elements, the List class is a good choice to represent the isotopes of an element, since each element has a different number of isotopes. The generic List collection is exposed as a property in this class. When the List object is declared, an actual type (a handle to Isotope) is used as the parameter. Handles, rather than direct reference types, are allowed as type parameter substitutions. You can also use a value type without a handle. Listing 2-15 shows an ElementType class with the Isotopes property, which is a list of isotopes for a particular element.

Listing 2-15. *A Reference Class That Uses the Generic List As a Property*

```
ref class Isotope; // implementation omitted for brevity

ref class ElementType
{

   // other properties specifying the element name, atomic number, etc.

   property List<Isotope^>^ Isotopes;
};
```

Using this generic type is as easy as using the managed array type. The code in Listing 2-16 uses a for each statement to iterate through the generic List collection to look up an isotope by its number. Assume an Isotope class with an IsotopeNumber property.

Listing 2-16. *Iterating Through a Generic Collection*

```
ref class ElementType
{
    // omitting other members of the class

    // Find an isotope by number. If not found, return a
    // null handle (nullptr).
    Isotope^ FindIsotope(int isotope_number)
    {
        for each (Isotope^ isotope in Isotopes)
        {
            if (isotope->IsotopeNumber == isotope_number)
                return isotope;
        }
        return nullptr;
    }
};
```

A more complete discussion of generics and managed templates is the subject of Chapter 11. In the meantime, we will use the generic List class in examples throughout this book. You'll see in Chapter 11 how to define generic classes and functions.

Summary

In this chapter, you learned some of the important language constructs of C++/CLI. Of course, there are other significant features, and there is much more to say about each feature. You had a quick look at primitive types, various aggregate types, managed arrays, properties, delegates, events, and parameterized types. Later chapters will return to each of these aspects of the language in more detail.

Before doing that, though, let's look at compiling and building C++/CLI programs.

■■■

CHAPTER 3

Building C++/CLI Programs for the .NET Developer Platform with Visual C++

This chapter is a necessary distraction from your main purpose, which is to learn about the C++/CLI language. In this chapter, you'll find some important information that is not specifically related to the language syntax, but to the platform, compiler, and development tools. There's a great deal to the .NET Developer Platform (NDP); entire books have been written on the subject. This chapter can't begin to cover everything in detail, so it'll just touch upon some of the key concepts and give a few examples that will get you started.

While most of what this book covers will pertain to any implementation of the CLI, in this chapter I assume you are using Visual C++, the Microsoft implementation of the CLI, and your programs will run on the .NET Developer Platform. This chapter covers what you'll need to know about the NDP if you're using Visual C++. If you are already familiar with targeting the NDP in another language, such as C#, you'll find much of this chapter a review, except for the discussion of the C++/CLI #using statement and the discussion of the CLR compilation modes available in C++.

Also, this chapter discusses compilation modes available in Visual C++. The compilation modes produce different types of libraries and executables that are suited to different runtime environments, ranging from code that is compiled natively to the instruction set of the processor as previous generations of C++ compilers have always done, to verifiably safe managed code that can run in some of the most restrictive environments such as inside an Internet browser or inside a database engine such as Microsoft SQL Server 2005, where being certain that a program will not crash and corrupt the server's memory is crucial.

Targeting the .NET Developer Platform with Visual C++ 2005

If you are using Visual C++ 2005, you may use the compiler directly from the command line, perhaps using makefiles or a tool that ships with Visual Studio called MSBuild to build your applications. Or, you may prefer to use the Visual Studio IDE. Among many C++ programmers, the command line is still king. The examples in this book will all run from the command line.

It's sometimes better to learn how to use the compiler from the command line and then transfer that knowledge to the IDE.

Visual C++ 2005 Compilation Modes

Compilation modes produce code suited for different situations. The CLR compilation mode may be set in the IDE with the Common Language Runtime support property in the General tab of the Project Properties dialog.

Unless specifically noted, the examples in this book will compile with the /clr:pure and /clr:safe options.

Safe Mode (/clr:safe Compiler Option)

Code that is compiled with the /clr:safe compiler option is said to be verifiable, indicating that it can be proven that the code is maximally type safe, which in turn helps verify that it doesn't write into memory that it doesn't own, and so will not generate access violations, buffer overruns, and the like. Safe code is required when your assembly needs to run in a very restrictive environment. Most of the examples in this book will compile in safe mode, except for the code in Chapter 12, which deals specifically with unverifiable code, and code that uses specific constructs such as unsafe uses of static_cast. If you're familiar with C#, safe code is like C# code that doesn't have any unsafe blocks. In Visual Basic, it's not possible to use unsafe constructs, so Visual Basic code is the equivalent of the C++/CLI safe mode.

Safe code is also processor independent, which is useful if you need the same program code to run on both 32- and 64-bit implementations of the CLR.

Pure Mode (/clr:pure Compiler Option)

Pure mode produces code that uses IL instructions only, not machine instructions, but is not verifiably safe. It may use pointers or other features that result in code that could produce buffer overruns, access violations, and other memory corruption. If you're familiar with C#, pure code is like a C# program compiled with the /unsafe option. There is no equivalent in Visual Basic.

If you try to compile a native C++ application with /clr:pure, it will work only if the code being compiled has no constructs that generate machine-specific code. You can, however, link with native libraries. The linker will add the necessary hookups to call into native libraries in /clr:pure mode. For example, the program

```cpp
// message_box.cpp
#include <windows.h>

int main()
{
  ::MessageBox(0,"message","caption",MB_OK);
}
```

compiled with

```
cl /clr:pure message_box.cpp user32.lib
```

will produce an executable that runs as expected.

Prepackaged libraries may or may not support the pure option. For example, as of Visual C++ 2005, ATL and MFC don't support /clr:pure. It depends on whether or not they were compiled with the /clr:pure option. You may recompile your own native libraries as pure code, provided they meet certain restrictions, such as not using

- Inline assembly.

- __declspec(align).

- Any construct that brings in native code.

- Code that generates native exports (i.e., not using __dllexport to expose functions compiled in a pure assembly to native callers). This is because the calling convention used in pure assemblies (__clrcall) is incompatible with native code.

- #import to use a COM library.

- Intrinsics, unless the intrinsics have an MSIL implementation, such as certain C runtime or CRT functions.

Refer to the appendix for a table of what's available in which compilation mode.

If you're a library vendor, you might decide to ship a native and a pure version of the same library. This is what Microsoft does for the CRT and Standard C++ Libraries. Recent updates to the C Runtime Library and the Standard C++ Library allow programs to use the pure version of these libraries. If you compile with /clr or /clr:pure, the appropriate pure version of these standard libraries will be linked in. Using a separate pure version of a library can be advantageous if there are frequent calls to a library, since it's better if program execution remains mainly in either managed code or native code, rather than switching frequently between the two.

Mixed Mode (/clr Compiler Option)

In mixed mode, in addition to having the managed types and the .NET Framework available, you as a programmer in the C++ language with the C++/CLI extensions may use classic C++ code and libraries if needed. In fact, you can compile nearly all classic C++ code with the /clr option. The C++ language as extended by the C++/CLI language extensions is (for all practical purposes) a superset of the classic C++, so any C++ application is automatically a C++/CLI application—provided that you compile with the /clr option. Mixed mode lets you decide how much you want to transition your existing code to make use of the managed world. Your existing code will work in the managed world, and you are free to use managed constructs as needed and enjoy the benefits. Your mixed-mode assemblies are still capable of exporting native functions, importing COM libraries, using inline assembly, compiler intrinsics, and so on, which are not available in pure or safe mode.

Mixed-mode assemblies cannot be used with reflection (discussed in Chapter 10), because the reflection mechanism doesn't understand native types and functions. Pure mode does support reflection.

Managed Extensions Syntax (/clr:oldSyntax Compiler Option)

If you have code that was written with the managed extensions syntax, you can still compile it by using the /clr:oldSyntax option. You can link object files generated with this option with C++/CLI code or native code. You should avoid using the old syntax too heavily, though, since it is deprecated in the Visual C++ 2005 release.

None of the Above

Without /clr at all, of course, you are compiling native C++ in the classic way. If you try to use any of the C++/CLI language features, you will get compiler errors.

Caveats When Upgrading Code to Visual C++ 2005

Although we've said that preexisting code should compile in mixed mode just by turning on the /clr option, there are many changes to the standard libraries in Visual C++ 2005 that will cause compilation errors and warnings. For example, the C Runtime Library was updated to support more secure versions of many functions; by default, the unsafe versions of these functions will generate compiler warnings. Also, numerous changes were made to better conform with the C++ and C standards. Refer to the "What's New" section in the Visual C++ documentation for details on these changes and how to disable the warnings, if necessary.

Library changes aside, most code written for native C++, for example with Visual C++ 6.0, will work when compiled with the /clr option in Visual C++ 2005.

Architecture Dependence and 64-bit Programming

The CLR implements a layer that abstracts the processor architecture. The IL itself contained in managed assemblies is independent of any specific processor architecture. However, as you've seen, code compiled with /clr rather than /clr:pure or /clr:safe may contain platform-specific code. Also, even in pure mode, you can invoke platform-specific functions. If you want to produce an application that is capable of running on any implementation of the CLI, you should use the /clr:safe option. If you know you'll be using the Microsoft Windows platform, but want the output code to be neutral with respect to CPU architecture, then you can use /clr:safe. There are x64 and Itanium versions of the CLR, and these versions of the CLR will run the same platform-neutral assemblies compiled with /clr:safe, natively on the x64 architecture. If the x64 CLR is not available (for example if the 64-bit computer has only a 32-bit operating system installed), the code can be executed by the 32-bit CLR.

If you want to produce an application specific to a particular architecture that still runs under the CLR, use the /clr option but use the particular compiler (or cross-compiler) for that architecture. Visual C++ 2005 ships cross-compilers for x64 and Intel Itanium architectures, so you can generate code on an x86 computer that will execute natively on a 64-bit computer.

When compiling for 64-bit, there are some potential incompatibilities, since the size of a pointer is different, and so on. You can compile with the /Wp64 option to get warnings for many potential incompatibilities. Refer to the Visual C++ 2005 documentation for details.

Assemblies and Modules

The fundamental unit or packaging of code compiled for the CLI is the *assembly*. An assembly could be an executable (EXE), a dynamically linked library (DLL), or possibly a collection of files. The only difference between the two (other than the file name) is that an executable has an entry point (i.e., a main method). The similarity in file extension to native DLLs and EXEs hides the significant differences in the files themselves. Both assemblies and old-style DLLs and executables contain executable code, although assemblies contain IL code intended to be executed by the CLR.

The picture is a bit more complicated than just that assemblies contain IL code and native DLLs and executables contain native code. Assemblies can actually contain a mixture of native object code and IL. This feature is key for C++ programmers moving existing code to the managed environment, since code that compiles in classic C++ may actually be brought into the CLR fairly easily by recompiling your existing C++ in mixed mode to make an assembly. The actual file will be quite different.

Assemblies contain additional information called *metadata* that a traditional executable or DLL does not contain. The metadata is stored in assemblies along with the generated code. You can view the metadata using a tool called ILDasm.exe that ships with the .NET Framework, as explained in the upcoming section "Viewing Metadata with ILDasm.exe."

By default, Visual Studio Project packages all the source files in a project into a single assembly when the project is built. Similarly, the default behavior of a command-line compilation is to produce a single assembly. However, it is possible to change compiler options or project settings to omit the manifest required in an assembly. If you specify the /LN compiler option and the /NOASSEMBLY linker option, the resulting output is referred to as a *module* or *netmodule*. A .NET module has the extension .netmodule to distinguish it from an assembly. Where modules are useful is when you are planning to combine many modules from different compilations into a single assembly. You could compile the modules separately, and then link them all together with the linker (link.exe) or with something called the assembly linker (al.exe) to produce your final assembly. The common language runtime won't load modules that haven't been linked into an assembly since they don't have a manifest. The CLR makes use of the metadata in the manifest and cannot load code in a naked module without the metadata from its parent assembly.

The Assembly Manifest

The term *manifest* comes from the Latin *manifestus*, which means "blatant, obvious." It was later used in the shipping industry to mean the list of cargo and passengers on a ship or train. To find a particular passenger or to discover what cargo is contained on a train, you would consult the manifest. The assembly manifest serves the same purpose for an assembly. The runtime uses the manifest to find information about what types are in an assembly, and where to find those types in the assembly. Because of the information in the manifest, the assembly is said to be self-describing. This presents a significant advance from unmanaged executables and DLLs, which do not have such rich data describing themselves. This rich metadata makes it easier to dynamically load assemblies and start executing the code in them.

Viewing Metadata with ILDasm.exe

You can familiarize yourself with the basics of assemblies and metadata by compiling a simple C++/CLI program and looking at the resulting output using a tool called ILDasm.exe. ILDasm means *Intermediate Language Disassembler*. Consider the simple C++ program in Listing 3-1.

Listing 3-1. *A Simple C++/CLI Program*

```
// reftype.cpp
using namespace System;

ref class RefType
{
    String^ classname;

    public:

    RefType()
    {
        classname = gcnew String("RefType");
    }

    String^ GetMessage()
    {
        return String::Format("I am a " + classname);
    }
};

int main()
{
    RefType^ r = gcnew RefType();
    Console::WriteLine(r->GetMessage());
}
```

You must compile it (in Visual C++) with the /clr option, like this:

```
cl.exe /clr:safe reftype.cpp
```

This produces the executable reftype.exe. As in classic C++, you also have the option of producing an object file first, and then later linking to produce an executable. None of these basics have changed. In fact, the file name doesn't look any different. What has changed is that the resulting executable is an assembly with managed code, not a native executable. When it is executed, it will actually fire up the CLR and run in a managed context.

You can view the metadata for reftype.exe by running ILDasm.exe. You can find ILDasm.exe in your .NET Framework SDK *Bin* directory. You may want to add this directory to the PATH environment variable so you always have access to ILDasm, since it is so useful. For example, it might be C:\Program Files\Microsoft Visual Studio 8\SDK\2.0\Bin. Use the /text option if you just want text output to the console, instead of a GUI. Here's the output of the command line Ildasm.exe reftype.exe /text:

```
// Microsoft (R) .NET Framework IL Disassembler.  Version 2.0.50727.42
// Copyright (c) Microsoft Corporation.  All rights reserved.



// Metadata version: v2.0.50727
.assembly extern mscorlib
{
  .publickeytoken = (B7 7A 5C 56 19 34 E0 89 )                 // .z\V.4..
  .hash = (8B 15 F4 76 87 23 8A E0 94 A8 8B 19 BF 0F 87 C9     // ...v.#..........

          F0 97 3C C3 )                                        // ..<.
  .ver 2:0:0:0
}
.assembly reftype
{
  .hash algorithm 0x00008004
  .ver 0:0:0:0
}
.module reftype.exe
// MVID: {8C21FB19-23D0-45E2-87BD-20EC172CF3CA}
.imagebase 0x00400000
.file alignment 0x00000200
.stackreserve 0x00100000
.subsystem 0x0003       // WINDOWS_CUI
.corflags 0x00000001    // ILONLY
// Image base: 0x02EC0000



// =================== GLOBAL METHODS ===========================

.method assembly static int32  main() cil managed
{
  .entrypoint
  // Code size       19 (0x13)
  .maxstack  1
  .locals init (class RefType V_0)
  IL_0000: newobj     instance void RefType::.ctor()
  IL_0005: stloc.0
```

```
   IL_0006:  ldloc.0
   IL_0007:  call        instance string RefType::GetMessage()
   IL_000c:  call        void [mscorlib]System.Console::WriteLine(string)
   IL_0011:  ldc.i4.0
   IL_0012:  ret
} // end of global method main



// ================================================================


// =============== CLASS MEMBERS DECLARATION ====================

.class private auto ansi beforefieldinit RefType
       extends [mscorlib]System.Object
{
   .field private string classname
   .method public hidebysig specialname rtspecialname
           instance void  .ctor() cil managed
   {
     // Code size        18 (0x12)
     .maxstack  2
     IL_0000:  ldarg.0
     IL_0001:  call        instance void [mscorlib]System.Object::.ctor()
     IL_0006:  ldarg.0
     IL_0007:  ldstr       "MyRefType"
     IL_000c:  stfld       string RefType::classname
     IL_0011:  ret
   } // end of method RefType::.ctor


   .method public hidebysig instance string
           GetMessage() cil managed
   {
     // Code size        32 (0x20)
     .maxstack  2
     .locals init (string V_0,
              object[] V_1)
     IL_0000:  ldc.i4.0
     IL_0001:  newarr      [mscorlib]System.Object
     IL_0006:  stloc.1
     IL_0007:  ldstr       "I am a {0}"
     IL_000c:  ldarg.0
     IL_000d:  ldfld       string RefType::classname
     IL_0012:  call        string [mscorlib]System.String::Concat(string,
                                                                  string)
     IL_0017:  ldloc.1
     IL_0018:  call        string [mscorlib]System.String::Format(string,
```

object[])

```
    IL_001d:  stloc.0
    IL_001e:  ldloc.0
    IL_001f:  ret
  } // end of method RefType::GetMessage

} // end of class RefType


// ================================================================

// *********** DISASSEMBLY COMPLETE ***********************
```

You can see the generated Intermediate Language code for your RefType class and GetMessage method, the main method, and some metadata. You might want to read and understand this Intermediate Language. Even if you don't, you'll want to be able to use ILDasm.exe to view the classes and symbols defined in a particular assembly, and to examine the information in the manifest. You might try the same thing except instead of specifying /clr:pure, use just /clr. You'll notice a whole lot of other types and variables in addition to what was there before. This is the C runtime initialization plumbing. Because the CRT is not available in safe mode, you don't get that when you compile with /clr:safe.

Certain core classes of the .NET Framework are included in the assembly mscorlib.dll. There is not a direct correlation between namespaces and assemblies or DLL names. This can be confusing until you get used to it, since it's easy to forget. It's possible for members of a particular namespace to be distributed across many assemblies (DLLs).

The #using Directive

Like the classic C++ #include directive, the #using directive is used in a source code file to refer to an assembly (usually a DLL) that defines programming elements that you want to use in your program. The act of putting a #using directive for a particular assembly in your code is called *referencing the assembly*. Once an assembly is referenced in this way, you'll be able to use any publicly exposed classes, interfaces, and other program elements defined in that assembly.

The types in mscorlib.dll are referenced by default, so there is no need for the #using directive to reference anything in this assembly. If there's a question as to whether a particular type is in mscorlib.dll, use ILDasm.exe on mscorlib.dll (you can find mscorlib.dll in the .NET Framework installation folder).

In mixed code, ways of accessing native libraries remain the same. If COM libraries are used, use the #import directive as you would normally. Header files are not used for referencing managed types outside of the assembly where they live, but the #include directive is still used to reference headers written in classic C++ and for intra-assembly code (for example, in a Visual Studio project).

Types, assembly-level global functions, and other symbols are defined in assemblies and may or may not be accessible outside that assembly, depending on accessibility modifiers declared on the symbol. Accessibility modifiers are slightly different in C++/CLI, as you'll see in Chapter 6. For now just know that you can use public or private on types and assembly-global functions to control whether the program element is accessible to other assemblies or internal to the assembly.

Listing 3-2 shows a typical use of the #using directive. The Windows Forms APIs are not in the mscorlib.dll assembly, so they must be referenced via the #using directive. The #using directive should not be confused with the using statement. The using namespace statement following this directive is optional, and merely allows us to avoid typing the fully qualified name System::Windows::Forms::MessageBox.

Listing 3-2. *Using the #using Directive*

```
// using_directive.cpp
#using "System.Windows.Forms.dll"

using namespace System::Windows::Forms;

int main()
{
    MessageBox::Show("Hello World!");
}
```

There are times when you may want to omit the using namespace statements, and simply use the fully qualified name. You will introduce ambiguities if you use two or more namespaces that define the same identifiers. To disambiguate these, you need to fully qualify the names using the scope operator (::), as in Listing 3-3.

Listing 3-3. *Using the Scope Operator*

```
// using_directive2.cpp
#using "System.Windows.Forms.dll"

int main()
{
    System::Windows::Forms::MessageBox::Show("Hello World!");
}
```

The rule is the same as in classic C++, but I mention it here to emphasize the #using directive is distinct from the using namespace directive, and you may often use both.

If you are used to .NET programming in C# or Visual Basic .NET, you are used to providing references on the compile command line or in the Visual Studio project system. If you are using C++, you don't need to reference the assembly on the command line if you reference the assembly via the #using directive. However, you can use the /FU (Force Using) compiler option to reference assemblies via the command line without a #using directive in the code.

```
cl.exe mycode.cpp /FUmylibrary.dll
```

You can also set the /FU compiler option in the Visual C++ development environment. The name of the property is Force #using in the Advanced section of the C/C++ property pages.

Referencing Assemblies and Access Control

You will want to separate your code into different dynamically linked libraries. Let's look at how to use types from one assembly in another in the simplest possible example.

Compile the code in Listing 3-4 using the /LD option to generate a DLL. This DLL is a CLR assembly just as was the executable created in a previous section.

Listing 3-4. *A Trivial Public Class*

```
// file1.cpp

public ref class R
{
};
```

As mentioned, we must add the keyword public at the class level to make this type visible in another assembly (see Listing 3-5).

Listing 3-5. *Using Our Trivial Class from Another Assembly*

```
// file2.cpp
#using "file1.dll"

// We'll define a function, so we can see it in the metadata later.
void F()
{
    R r;
}

int main()
{}
```

Without the keyword public, the type R will not be visible to the code in file2.cpp. Compile file2.cpp with the usual options for managed code (just /clr or /clr:pure will do) to generate an executable assembly file2.exe.

Friend Assemblies

It's possible to set up a special relationship between assemblies that is rather like the friend class in classic C++. Such assemblies are called *friend assemblies*. To reference a friend assembly, use the as_friend modifier in the #using directive.

```
#using "myfriend.dll" as_friend
```

The assembly that's referenced needs to have an assembly attribute. You'll read about attributes in detail in Chapter 10, but for now you can just add the following line anywhere in the assembly source code (let's say this is in the source code for myfriend.dll). Typically, this would go in the AssemblyInfo.cpp file in a Visual Studio project:

```
[assembly:InternalsVisibleTo("friend_assembly_filename")];
```

This line means that an assembly called `friend_assembly_filename.dll` or `friend_assembly_filename.exe` is allowed to use the `as_friend` modifier when referencing `myfriend.dll`.

When an assembly has the special friend relationship, all types at global scope, and any global functions, are accessible to the friend assembly.

Assembly Attributes

The `InternalsVisibleTo` attribute is an example of an *assembly attribute*. As you saw in Chapter 2, attributes in general specify metadata that can be applied to program elements. If the word assembly is specified in square brackets, the attribute applies to the entire assembly. Most of the metadata in the manifest can be set via assembly attributes.

The Linker and the Assembly Linker

Both the assembly linker and the traditional linker are important tools that do different things. They are both called by the Visual C++ project system, and both can be used from the command line or in build scripts. You should refer to the product documentation for full information on these tools, but I will describe briefly what role these tools play so you will know when you need them. If you just use Visual Studio and let these be called for you, you'll see them referenced in the build output. When debugging build problems or configuring a new build, it's necessary to know the distinct roles that they have.

The linker, `link.exe`, is still a very useful tool in CLR programming. The linker normally runs automatically when you compile, whether you are compiling for native or CLR code. You can run it explicitly if you need to. The linker will create native DLLs and executables if given native object files. It will create managed assemblies if given managed object files as input. If given both managed and native input, it produces a mixed-mode assembly that links together both the managed and native object code. Linker command-line options provide additional control. For example, suppose you are linking object files with different compilation modes, where some were compiled in pure mode, and some in safe mode. By default, the output will be considered to be the lowest level of verifiability, in this case pure instead of safe. You can also control the linker to reduce the level of verifiability if that's what you need. Refer to the Visual C++ documentation for details if you require such behavior.

The assembly linker, or `al.exe`, is a tool used to create assemblies from .NET modules. In other words, it adds assembly manifests to module files. The assembly linker can be run at the command line; it will take any modules specified on the command line and create an assembly that links together these modules. You can also use the assembly linker to specify assembly-level metadata in the assembly's manifest, such as the version of the assembly, your company name, description, and so on. Most of these can also be set via assembly attributes; if there is a conflict, the values set by `al.exe` override those in source.

Resources and Assemblies

The term *resources*, as in classic Visual C++ applications, refers to constant data such as strings, images, audio data, and the like. The .NET Framework provides extensive support for managing resources. If your code requires resources, you can use the linker to embed those resources into the output assembly using the /ASSEMBLYRESOURCE command-line option. You can access both Windows resources, for example an .RC file, and managed resources in .resources files. The assembly linker allows you to add managed resources to assemblies, but not operating system resources. Refer to product documentation for details on how to create these files and access these resources from code.

Signed Assemblies

The linker and assembly linker also provide support for applying security features to an assembly. The process is referred to as signing an assembly. Signing assemblies is covered in detail in *Expert Visual C++/CLI* by Marcus Heege (Apress, forthcoming).

Multifile Assemblies

Assemblies can also consist of more than one file. The manifest for an assembly may actually be a separate file. The manifest actually contains information that specifies all the files that make up an assembly. Since this is an introductory text, it won't cover how to create and work with multifile assemblies.

Summary

In this chapter, we've looked at the difference between programming in classic C++ vs. managed code. We looked at Microsoft's Visual C++ 2005 and in particular the compilation modes available with Visual C++ 2005, including /clr:pure, /clr:safe, /clr:oldSyntax, /clr, and none of the above. We briefly discussed how to target 64-bit architectures with Visual C++ 2005. You also learned what an assembly is, looked at how to build one, examined what's in an assembly, saw how to reference other assemblies in a C++/CLI program, including how to control access to types in other assemblies, and briefly looked at the difference between the linker and the assembly linker. You also briefly saw some of what else there is to know about working with assemblies. There is much more that can be learned about assemblies in the CLR, but you now have enough for the purposes of working through the rest of this book.

In the next chapter, you'll learn about objects and their semantics.

CHAPTER 4

■■■

Object Semantics in C++/CLI

This chapter gets back into the language itself and covers how objects behave in C++/CLI. You'll learn a bit more about value types and reference types, including some of the implications of having a unified type system. You'll also see how to work with objects on the managed heap as though they were automatic variables, complete with the assurance that they will be cleaned up when they go out of scope. You'll look at tracking references and object dereferencing and copying. You'll also explore the various methods of passing parameters in C++/CLI and look at how to use C++/CLI types as return values.

Object Semantics for Reference Types

Variables of reference types, whether declared as a handle or not, are not the objects themselves; they are only references that may point to an actual object or may be unassigned. When a handle is first declared, it need not be assigned a value immediately. If not assigned, it is assigned the "value" nullptr, which is essentially an equivalent way of saying NULL or 0 in classic C++. Because handles can be null, functions that take reference types as parameters must always check to see whether the handle is null before using the object. Any attempt to access the nonexistent object will result in a NullReferenceException being thrown.

References can be assigned using the assignment operator (=), so more than one handle may be created to the same object. Unlike value types, the assignment operator does not copy the object; only the handle (internally a heap address) is copied. Over the lifetime of an object, the number of handles to it may become quite large. The number of handles increases whenever an assignment occurs and decreases as reference variables go out of scope or are redirected to other objects. There is nothing special about the original handle that created the object—it could go out of scope, but as long as there is at least one handle to an object, it is still considered a live object. There may come a time, finally, when the object has no remaining handles. At that point, it is an orphaned object. It still exists, but there's no way it can be accessed again in the program. The garbage collector is designed to eventually free up the memory for that object. The garbage collector runs on a separate background thread and has its own algorithm for determining when an object will be cleaned up. There is no way to be sure of when the object will be cleaned up relative to the execution of your program. If you need to explicitly control object cleanup, there is a way, which Chapter 6 will explain.

Object Semantics for Value Types

Value types are rather like primitive types in many ways. When assigned to another variable, the full object is copied byte for byte. For this reason, it is not a good idea to use a value type for a large object or a resource. Value types generally represent a small aggregate of data that represents a quantity or a small amount of information. They are generally not to be used for abstractions and generally provide few member functions. They also are not involved in inheritance hierarchies. I use the word "generally" because there are no hard-and-fast rules for when to use value types and when to use reference types; there is certainly a gray area where either a value type or a reference type will do well.

Value types can always be "boxed up" and used like a reference type, for example, if passed to a function that takes a handle to an object (Object^) as a parameter, as described in the next section. The term *boxing* refers to the fact that an object is created on the heap to contain the value type instance.

Implications of the Unified Type System

As stated in Chapter 1, the managed type system is unified. Every managed type directly or indirectly inherits explicitly or implicitly from a single type called Object. This includes all reference types and the boxed form of all value types, and even the built-in primitive types, considering the aliases for those types such as Int32, Char, Double, etc. In Chapter 2, you saw how the array type is an object type, complete with properties, such as Length, and methods. These methods are part of the System::Array class. In fact, there are also methods defined on the Object class that every managed type has. Listing 4-1 is what the declaration of the Object type would look like, showing the available public methods (there are some protected methods as well, not shown here).

Listing 4-1. *The Object Type*

```
ref class Object
{
    public:
        virtual Type^ GetType();
        virtual String^ ToString();
        virtual bool Equals(Object^);
        static bool Equals(Object^, Object^);
        static bool ReferenceEquals(Object^);
        virtual int GetHashCode();

};
```

The unified type system enables us to create functions that can operate on objects of any type, simply by taking a handle to Object as a parameter. The function can then figure out the type of the object and do something appropriate for that object. Or, in the case of a collection class, a single collection type with object handles as its elements could be used for objects of any type, although you'll see in Chapter 11 that a generic collection would be better. A very simple example of a function that might be useful is one that displays the type of an object along with a string representation of the object. Something like the function in Listing 4-2 might serve as a useful debugging tool.

Listing 4-2. *Displaying an Object As a String*

```
// debug_print.cpp
using namespace System;

void DebugPrint(Object^ obj)
{
    // For debugging purposes, display the type of the object
    // and its string conversion.

    System::Type^ type = obj->GetType();
    Console::WriteLine("Type: {0} Value: {1}", type->ToString(),
        obj->ToString() );

}
```

This function could be called with any managed type, but also any of the primitive types. It may seem strange that you could call these methods on a primitive type, like int, so it is worthwhile to delve into how this is possible.

Implicit Boxing and Unboxing

In classic C++, the primitive types don't inherit from anything. They're not classes, they're just types. They're not objects and can't be treated as such—for example, you can't call methods on them. And they certainly don't have all the members of the base class Object. In the managed world, the primitive types may be wrapped in an object when there is a need to represent them as objects. This wrapping is referred to as *boxing*. Boxing is used whenever a value type (which could be a primitive type) is converted into an object type, either by being cast to an object handle, or by being passed to a function taking a handle to an Object as a parameter type, or by being assigned to a variable of type "handle to Object." When a variable of a type that does not explicitly inherit from Object, such as an integer, is implicitly converted to an Object in any of the preceding situations, an object is created on the fly for that variable. The operation is slower than operations involving the naked value type, so it is good to know when it is taking place. Because boxing takes place implicitly, it is possible to treat all primitive types, in fact all managed types, as if they inherit from Object whenever the need arises. Consider the calls to DebugPrint in Listing 4-3.

Listing 4-3. *Boxing an Integer Type*

```
int i = 56;
DebugPrint(i);

String^ s = "Time flies like an arrow; fruit flies like a banana.";
DebugPrint(s);
```

Unboxing occurs when an object type is cast back to a primitive type, as shown in Listing 4-4.

Listing 4-4. *Unboxing an Object to an Integer*

```
// unboxing.cpp
using namespace System;

Object^ f(Object^ obj)
{
    Console::WriteLine("In f, with " + obj->ToString() + ".");
    return obj;
}

int main()
{
    int i = 1;
    int j = safe_cast<int>( f(i) );   // Cast back to int to unbox the object.

}
```

The output of Listing 4-4 is as follows:

```
In f, with 1.
```

In Listing 4-4, the object returned is not needed after the integer is extracted from it. The object may then be garbage collected, because all handles to it are gone. I view boxing as a welcome convenience that allows all types to be treated in the same way; however, there is a performance price to pay. For a function like DebugPrint, which has to deal with all kinds of types, it makes a lot of sense to rely on boxing because it's likely not a performance-critical function. For performance-critical code, you would want to avoid unnecessary boxing and unboxing since the creation of an object is unnecessary overhead.

Boxing takes place whenever a value type is converted to an object, not just in the context of a function call. A cast to Object, for example, results in a boxing conversion.

```
int i = 5;
Object^ o = (Object^) i;   // boxing conversion
```

Aside from conversions, even literal values can be treated as objects and methods called on them. The following code results in a boxing conversion from int to Object:

```
Console::WriteLine( (100).ToString() );
```

To summarize, implicit boxing and unboxing of value types allows value types to be treated, just like reference types. You might wonder if there's a way of treating a reference type like a value type, at least in some respects. One aspect of value types that may be emulated by reference types is their deterministic scoping. If they are members of a class, they are cleaned up and destroyed when the function scope ends. For various reasons that I will describe, you might want your reference types to exhibit this behavior. In the next section you'll see how this is done.

Stack vs. Heap Semantics

As you know, in a C++ program, variables may be declared *on the stack* or *on the heap*. Where they live is integral to the lifecycle of these objects. You just saw how value types can be treated as heap objects, and in fact are wrapped up in objects that are actually on the heap. This begs the question of whether the opposite could be true. Could a reference type live on the stack? Before we go too far, let's work through an example that will help you understand why you would need this behavior.

In the following example, we have a botany database. This is a large database of information on plants. For plant lovers, such as myself, this database is an incredible treasure trove of knowledge on the botany and cultivation requirements of thousands of trees, shrubs, vines, fruits, vegetables, and flowers. It also happens to be a very heavily accessed database that's used by thousands of people, and there is a hard limit on the number of simultaneous connections to that database. One of the key pieces of code that hits that database is in a class, CPlantData, that serves up the information on plants. It's our job to rewrite this class using C++/CLI as part of the new managed access code to this database (see Listing 4-5). There is a static function called PlantQuery that handles requests for data. As a native class, it creates a DBConnection object on the stack, uses the connection to query the database, and then allows the destructor to close the connection when the function exits.

Listing 4-5. *Accessing the Botany Database*

```cpp
// PlantQuery.cpp

class Recordset;

class DBConnection
{
    public:
        DBConnection()
        {
            // Open the connection.
            // ...
        }
        void Query(char* search, Recordset** records)
        {
            // Query the database, generate recordset.
            // ...
        }
        ~DBConnection()
        {
            // Close the connection.
            // ...
        }
};
```

```
class PlantData
{
    public:
      static void PlantQuery(char* search, Recordset** records)
      {
          DBConnection connection;
          connection.Query( search, records);
      } // destructor for connection called
};
```

A bit of a philosophical perspective is in order here. The stack and the heap have a historical origin in terms of how programming languages and memory models were implemented and evolved. There are significant lifecycle differences between stack and heap objects. Stack objects are short-lived and are freed up at the end of the block in which they are declared. They are fundamentally local variables. Heap objects could live for a lot longer and are not tied to any particular function scope. The design of C++/CLI is shaped by the idea that the notion of the semantics of a stack variable or a heap variable can be separated from the actual implementation of a given variable as actual memory on the stack or heap. Another way of looking at it is that because we have reference types that cannot live on the stack, we'd like a way to have our cake and eat it, too. We'd like reference types with the semantics of stack variables. With this in mind, consider the managed version of the preceding example.

If you went ahead and implemented the native classes DBConnection and PlantData as managed types using a literal transliteration of the code, your code would look something like Listing 4-6.

Listing 4-6. *Accessing the Botany Database with Managed Classes*

```
// ManagedPlantQuery.cpp
using namespace System;

ref class Recordset;

ref class DBConnection
{
    public:
      DBConnection()
      {
          // Open the connection.
          // ...
      }
      Recordset^ Query(String^ search)
      {
          // Query the database, generate recordset,
          // and return handle to recordset.
          // ...
      }
```

```
    ~DBConnection()
    {
        // Close the connection.
        // ...
    }
};

ref class PlantData
{
    public:
        static Recordset^ PlantQuery(String^ search)
        {
            DBConnection^ connection = gcnew DBConnection();
            return connection->Query( search );
        }
};
```

If you were to use this code in production, you would run into a problem in that the large botany database with the limited number of connections frequently runs out of available connections, so people have trouble accessing the database. Depending on the database and data access implementation, this could mean connections are refused, or a significant delay enters the system as data access code is blocked awaiting a connection. And all this because the destruction of managed objects happens not when the function exits, but only when the garbage collector feels like cleaning them up. In fact, you will find that the destructor never gets called at all in the preceding code even when the object is finally cleaned up. Instead, something called the *finalizer* gets called by the garbage collector to take care of the cleanup, if one exists. You'll learn more about that in Chapter 6.

The ability to control when a variable goes out of scope and is destroyed is clearly necessary. Objects that open database connections or block a communication channel such as a socket should free up these resources as soon as they're no longer needed. For native C++ programmers, the solution to this problem might be to create the variable on the stack and be assured that its destructor, which frees up the resources, would be called at the end of the function. What can be done in the managed environment, when reference types cannot be created on the stack at all?

There are several ways of solving the problem. In the code for Listing 4-6, for example, we could have inserted an explicit delete, as in Listing 4-7.

Listing 4-7. *Using an Explicit Delete*

```
static Recordset^ PlantQuery(String^ search)
    {
        DBConnection^ connection = gcnew DBConnection();
        Recordset^ records = connection->Query( search );
        delete connection;
        return records;
    }
```

This would work, but now we find ourselves having to remember to call delete. Another possibility is to have DBConnection be a value type. Value types are created in a specific scope, not on the heap, so that is a possible solution that would mean the object would be cleaned up automatically when the enclosing scope (perhaps a stack frame or enclosing object) terminates. However, value types cannot define their own constructors and destructors, so this won't work in this case and in fact is too limited to be a general solution. What we really would like is a way to have a reference type with a deterministic lifetime.

If you're a C# programmer, you'll know that the way to provide a reference type with a deterministic lifetime in that language is the using statement. The using statement in C# involves the creation of a block and defines the scope of an object as local to the block. When the block exits, a cleanup method gets called on the object that acts like a destructor and frees any resources. This works fine, except that in order to be used in a using statement, objects must implement an interface, IDisposable, and a method, Dispose, which performs the cleanup. The Dispose method gets called when the block exits. The main drawback of the C# method is that programmers forget to implement IDisposable, or do it incorrectly..

C++ programmers are already familiar with creating an object that gets destroyed at the end of a function. So instead of requiring that you implement an interface and define a block for everything that is to be destroyed, the C++/CLI language allows you to use reference types with stack semantics. Using variables as if they were on the stack is so integral to C++ programming methodology that C++/CLI was designed with the ability to create instances of managed objects (on the heap) but treat them as if they were on the stack, complete with the destructor being called at the end of the block.

In Listing 4-8, we are opening a connection to a database of botanical information on various plants and creating the DBConnection class using stack semantics, even though it is a reference type on the heap.

Listing 4-8. *Treating an Object on the Heap Like One on the Stack*

```cpp
// ManagedPlantQuery2.cpp
using namespace System;

ref class Recordset;

ref class DBConnection
{
    public:
        DBConnection()
        {
            // Open the connection.
            // ...
        }
        Recordset^ Query(String^ search)
        {
            // Query the database, generate recordset,
            // and return pointer to recordset.
            // ...
        }
}
```

```
        ~DBConnection()
        {
            // Close the connection.
            // ...
        }
};

ref class PlantData
{
    public:
        static Recordset^ PlantQuery(String^ search)
        {
            DBConnection connection;
            return connection.Query( search);
        }
};
```

If you use stack semantics, you are working with an object that is actually on the heap, but the variable is not used as a handle type. What the compiler is doing here could be called sleight of handle, if you'll pardon the expression. The actual IL code emitted with stack semantics and heap semantics doesn't differ much—from the perspective of the runtime, you are manipulating a reference to a heap object in both cases. What is different is the syntax you use and, critically, the execution of the destructor at the end of the function. To sum up, the heap-allocated object is immediately deleted at the end of the block, rather than lazily garbage collected, and, as a consequence, the destructor is called immediately upon deletion.

Pitfalls of Delete and Stack Semantics

Stack semantics works for reference types, but not String or array types. Both of these are built-in special types that are not designed to be used in this way. Consider Listing 4-9.

Listing 4-9. *Misconstruing Stack Semantics*

```
// string_array_stack_semantics.cpp

using namespace System;

int main()
{
    String s = "test"; // error
    array<int> a;  // error
}
```

The output of Listing 4-9 is as shown here:

```
Microsoft (R) C/C++ Optimizing Compiler Version 14.00.50727.42
for Microsoft (R) .NET Framework version 2.00.50727.42
Copyright (C) Microsoft Corporation.  All rights reserved.

string_array_stack_semantics.cpp
string_array_stack_semantics.cpp(7) : error C3149: 'System::String' :
cannot use this type here without a top-level '^'
string_array_stack_semantics.cpp(8) : error C3149: 'cli::array<Type>' :
cannot use this type here without a top-level '^'
        with
        [
            Type=int
        ]
```

There is a risk of misusing these semantics, especially if you use the % operator to get the underlying handle to your stack semantics variable. You must be careful that there are no handles to the stack object that are retained after the function terminates. If you do retain a handle to the object and then try to access the object, you may silently access a destroyed object. The same dangers exist in calling delete on managed objects. You should try to use delete only when you can be sure that there are no others holding handles to the object you are deleting.

The Unary % Operator and Tracking References

Suppose you'd like to use stack semantics, but you still have a function that takes a handle type. Let's say we have to call a method Report in the PlantQuery function, and that method takes a handle to the DBConnection object. Now that we're using stack semantics, we don't have a handle type, we have a bare object. Listing 4-10 is the function we'd like to call.

Listing 4-10. *A Method Requiring a Handle*

```
void Report(DBConnection^ connection)
{
    // Log information about this connection.
    // ...
}
```

In order to call this method, you need to pass a handle, not the instance variable, as the connection parameter. You'll have to use the unary % operator to convert the instance variable to a handle, for example, to pass the variable to a function that takes a handle (see Listing 4-11). The % operator is like the address-of operator for managed types that returns a handle to the object, just as the address-of operator (&) in classic C++ returns a pointer to the object. The address-of operator (&) is used for primitive types, such as int, although you can still assign to a tracking reference. The % operator is used instead of the address-of operator for instances of reference and value types.

Listing 4-11. *Using the % Operator*

```
public ref class PlantData
{
    public:
      static Recordset^ PlantQuery(String^ search)
      {
          DBConnection connection;
          Report(%connection);
          return connection.Query( search);
      }
};
```

You can certainly see that the % operator is the managed analog of the & operator for native types. The analogy extends also to the other use of the & symbol to represent a reference. Rather like a tracking handle, you can use % to declare a tracking reference. Like a handle, a tracking reference is updated whenever the garbage collector moves the object it is referencing. Tracking references are somewhat more limited in use than native references. They can be used in function arguments and declared on the stack, but they cannot be declared as a member of a class. They can be used to refer to handles, value types, or value type members, but they cannot be used to refer to objects of reference type directly (as opposed to through a handle). The declaration and assignment to a variable might look like this:

```
int i = 110;
int% iref = i;
R r;
R% r_ref = r;
```

Just like a classic C++ reference, the tracking reference is another reference to the existing object, so if you change the value of the object through the reference and access the object through another means (such as the variable i itself in the foregoing example), the value is changed. There is still only one value. Figure 4-1 shows what's happening in memory.

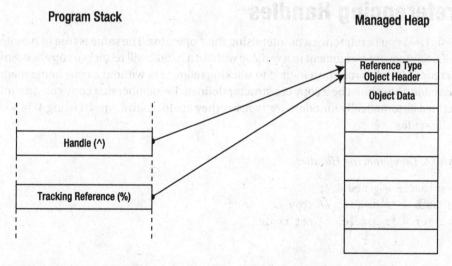

Figure 4-1. *A handle and a tracking reference designating the same object on the managed heap*

With tracking references, we could have returned a handle as a parameter rather than using the return value. Since a function can only have one return value, this is useful. In classic C++, you might have used a double indirection to accomplish the same thing. The code in Listing 4-12 shows the use of a tracking reference to a handle, which allows the handle to be set in the function and retain its new value outside the function.

Listing 4-12. *Using a Tracking Reference*

```
void Query(String^ search, Recordset^% records)
{
    // Query the database, generate recordset,
    // and set the records handle to point to it.
    records = gcnew Recordset();
}
```

The function would be called as in Listing 4-13.

Listing 4-13. *Calling a Function with Tracking References*

```
static Recordset^ PlantQuery(String^ search)
{
    DBConnection connection;
    Recordset^ records;
    connection.Query( search, records );
    return records;
}
```

This example is a very typical use of tracking references. Without the tracking reference, you could change the object in the function and have those changes preserved, but you would not be able to make the handle reference a different object entirely or assign it to a newly created object.

Dereferencing Handles

In classic C++, you dereference a pointer using the * operator. The same is true of handles in C++/CLI. Subsequent assignment to a variable without a handle will result in a copy being made. Dereferenced handles may be assigned to tracking references without a copy being made. If a copy is made, there must be a copy constructor defined. Remember that copy constructors are not defined automatically for reference types as they are for native types. Listing 4-14 shows the basic syntax.

Listing 4-14. *Dereferencing Handles*

```
R^ r_handle = gcnew R();
R r_auto = *r_handle; // copy ctor used
R% r_ref = *r_handle; // not copied
```

Copy Constructors

Copy constructors take a tracking reference (%) as a parameter, as shown in Listing 4-15.

Listing 4-15. *Using Tracking References with Copy Constructors*

```
// passing_with_copy_ctor.cpp
using namespace System;

ref class R
{
   int val;
   String^ str;

   public:

   property int Value
   {
      int get() { return val; }
      void set(int i) { val = i; }
   }
   property String^ Label
   {
      String^ get() { return str; }
      void set(String^ s) { str = s; }
   }

   R(int val_in, String^ label) : val(val), str(label)
   { }

   R(const R% r)
   {
      // Copy the elements of R.
      // Value is a value type, so it gets copied.
      val = r.val;
      // Strings are immutable, so
      // a reference copy will work here even
      // in a copy ctor.
      str = r.str;
   }
};
```

Unlike in classic C++, there is no default copy constructor generated for a managed class, so you need to define one explicitly in order to use this method of parameter passing. The parameter to a copy constructor is normally declared const, although the language does not enforce this. If you do use a const reference as a parameter, you cannot use properties in the copy constructor, since properties take nonconstant parameters. The solution is to use the fields directly in the body of the copy constructor, as in Listing 4-15.

Lvalues, GC-lvalues, Rvalues, and GC-rvalues

When working with tracking references, handle dereferencing, and so on, you'll find it much easier to understand how it all works if you know how the compiler understands whether a given expression may be on the left or the right of an assignment. In classic C++, expressions that are addressable may appear on the left side of an assignment. An addressable entity is one that has a memory address associated with it, into which a value may be placed. Such an entity is called an *lvalue* (see Listing 4-16). Other expressions, which may not be assigned to, are referred to as *rvalues*. They may be used on the right side of an assignment, but not the left.

Listing 4-16. *Using Lvalues*

```
// lvalues.cpp

int main()
{
    int i;
    int j = 10;    // "int j" is an lvalue.
    i = 15;        // "i" is an lvalue.

    15 = 10;       // Error: 15 is NOT an lvalue!
}
```

C++/CLI introduces the concept of a *gc-lvalue*, an lvalue that has a managed heap address. All gc-lvalues are lvalues, but not all lvalues are gc-lvalues. In practical terms, this means that you can always use a gc-lvalue to represent either managed or native data, but that you cannot use an ordinary lvalue to represent managed data. gc-lvalues are different from lvalues in general because the address of the value may be changed, since it could be moved around by the garbage collection process; the ordinary lvalue is incapable of tracking this. Thus, to ensure type safety, the compiler does not allow lvalues to represent addresses on the managed heap. A *gc-rvalue* is an entity that can be the addressee of a managed heap address—these can appear on the right side of assignment expressions where the left side is a gc-lvalue.

A native reference or native pointer cannot be used to refer to a gc-lvalue; instead, a handle or tracking reference must be used to represent a gc-lvalue. Because value types may live on the stack or may live inside a managed heap object, whether they are considered gc-rvalues depends on where they are stored.

Listing 4-17 illustrates the various cases.

Listing 4-17. *GC-lvalues and GC-rvalues*

```
// gc_lvalues.cpp

value struct V
{
    int i;
};
```

```
ref class R
{
    public:

    V m_v;

};

R^ GetRHandle() { return gcnew R(); }

int main()
{
    // i is an lvalue, 12 is an rvalue.
    int i = 12;

    // An lvalue i2; i is used here as an rvalue.
    // Lvalues can always be used as rvalues.
    int i2 = i;
    V v; // value type on the stack
    R r; // reference type (on the managed heap but with stack semantics)

    int& i3 = i;  // native reference: an lvalue
    int% i4 = i;  // Tracking reference: lvalues can be assigned gc-rvalues.
    int& i5 = v.i; // OK: v.i is a stack-based object.
    int& i6 = r.m_v.i; // Illegal: r is a managed heap-based object.
    i4 = v.i;  // OK: i4 is a gc-lvalue.

    R^ r1, ^r2;    // r1 and r2 are gc-lvalues.
    // gcnew R() is a gc-rvalue.
    r1 = gcnew R();
    // GetRHandle() is a gc-rvalue, too.
    r2 = GetRHandle();

    R% r3 = *r1; // A gc-lvalue r3 is assigned to the gc-rvalue *r1.
}
```

Compiling Listing 4-17 gives the following error:

```
Microsoft (R) C/C++ Optimizing Compiler Version 14.00.50727.42
for Microsoft (R) .NET Framework version 2.00.50727.42
Copyright (C) Microsoft Corporation.  All rights reserved.

gc_lvalues.cpp
gc_lvalues.cpp(32) : error C2440: 'initializing' : cannot convert from 'int' to
'int &'
        An object from the gc heap (member of a managed class) cannot be
converted to a native reference
```

There is one interesting and useful variation on how you can hold references to objects that you'll want to know about: auto_handle, which is used for managed types that you want treated like automatic variables that are not created in the function, but rather come from the result of a function call.

auto_handle

Let's say you want to use stack semantics, but you also need to get the instance back from a function call rather than creating it yourself. A typical example would be if a function call (sometimes referred to as an *object factory*) is used to create instances and return a handle to them.

You can do this with an auto_handle, which is a handle that acts like an automatic variable. auto_handle is a "managed template"—a template applied to a reference type. You'll read more about managed templates in Chapter 11. The auto_handle template takes one parameter: the type of the handle. Listing 4-18 shows an example.

Listing 4-18. *Using auto_handle*

```cpp
// auto_handle.cpp
#include <msclr\auto_handle.h>

using namespace System;
using namespace msclr;

ref class DBConnection
{
    public:
      bool Open()
      {
          // Open a database connection (actual code omitted).
          // ...
          return true;
      }
      void Close()
      {
          // Close the database connection.
          // ...
      }
};

ref class PlantData
{
      DBConnection^ connection;
      int id;
```

```
        PlantData(int i) : id(i)
        {
            if (connection->Open() == true)
            {
                Console::WriteLine("Opened connection for id {0}.", id);
            }
        }

    public:

        static PlantData^ GetPlantData(int id)
        {
            return gcnew PlantData(id);
        }

        void Use()
        {
            Console::WriteLine("Using id {0}.", id);
            // Query database.
            // Update records, etc.
        }

        ~PlantData()
        {
            connection->Close();
            Console::WriteLine("Closing connection for id {0}.", id);
        }
};

// Using stack semantics: destructor called.
void f_stack(int i)
{
    auto_handle<PlantData> data = PlantData::GetPlantData(i);
    data->Use();
}

int main()
{
    f_stack(1);
}
```

The output verifies that the destructor is called when the auto_handle goes out of scope:

```
Opened connection for id 1.
Using id 1.
Closing connection for id 1.
```

So far in this chapter, you've seen reference types and value types, and the many different ways of referring to objects in code. You've learned the semantic differences between these methods, including objects with heap and stack semantics, tracking references, dereferencing handles, copying objects, lvalues, and the auto_handle template. Now focus will turn to how objects are passed to functions. As in classic C++, there are many ways to pass parameters, and it's important to know the semantic differences between all of them.

Parameter Passing

Just like classic C++, C++/CLI supports passing parameters by value and by reference. Let's review how this works in classic C++, as in Listing 4-19. Passing a parameter by value means that the function gets a copy of the value, so any operations don't affect the original object. Passing a parameter by reference means that the object is not copied; instead, the function gets the original object, which may consequently be modified. In C++, parameters passed with a reference (&) to an object are passed by reference. That is to say, the object is not copied, and any changes made to the object in the function are reflected in the object after the function returns.

Listing 4-19. *Passing by Value and by Reference in Classic C++*

```
// parameter_passing.cpp

void byvalue(int i)
{
    i += 1;
}
void byref(int& i)
{
    i += 1;
}
int main()
{
    int j = 10;
    System::Console::WriteLine("Original value: " + j);
    byvalue(j);
    System::Console::WriteLine("After byvalue: " + j);
    byref(j);
    System::Console::WriteLine("After byref: " + j);
}
```

The output of Listing 4-19 is

Original value: 10
After byvalue: 10
After byref: 11

---

because only the version that passes the parameter by reference actually affects the value of j in the enclosing scope.

Figure 4-2 shows the basic characteristics of passing by value and by reference.

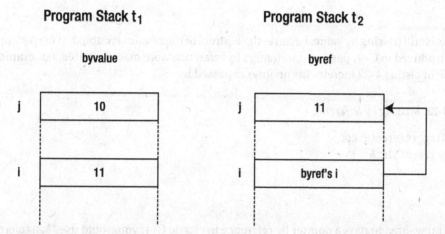

Figure 4-2. *The left side shows the objects in the main method; the right side shows the copies of those values in the function byvalue, and the native reference to the original value in the function byref.*

Where pointers are involved, the rules are the same, but thinking about them can be a bit trickier. Let's turn the clock back to the time when the C programming language reigned supreme. Consider a somewhat dangerous C function, shown in Listing 4-20, that takes a pointer as a parameter.

Listing 4-20. *A Dangerous C Function*

```
void stringcopy(char* dest, char* src)
{
    while (*dest++ = *src++);
}
```

The pointer src is modified within the function, but that does not affect the value outside the function because the pointer is passed by value. In those cases where you need a pointer to be modified, in C, you would use a double pointer (see Listing 4-21).

Listing 4-21. *Using a Double Pointer in C*

```
// double_pointer.cpp
#include <malloc.h>

int newstring(void** new_buffer)
{
    *new_buffer = malloc( 1024 );
    if (! *new_buffer) return -1;
    return 1;
}
```

This is still passing by value, because the address of the pointer is copied. When references were introduced in C++, passing parameters by reference were made possible. For example, the code in Listing 4-22 increments an integer passed in.

Listing 4-22. *Passing by Reference*

```
// passing_reference.cpp
void increment(int& i)
{
    i++;
}
```

If you wanted to pass a pointer by reference in classic C++, you would use *&, a reference to a pointer.

```
void modify_pointer(CClass*& ptr);
```

These constructs have equivalents in the C++/CLI managed world. The handle symbol in the parameter list is used for objects passed by reference.

```
void g(R^ r);
```

This is the normal way of passing reference types. This default makes sense for several reasons. First, passing by value is expensive for larger objects. Primitive types and value types are generally small, and the overhead of passing by value is not large, so value types are usually passed by value, like this:

```
void f(V v);
```

Figure 4-3 shows the typical case of value types and reference types being passed to functions. Because the local data is freed up when the function exists, any changes to the local data, either the local value type or the local handle, are not reflected outside the function. A copy is created of a value type passed to a function, in this case declared as f(V v_local), and a value passed in with the expression f(v). Figure 4-3 also shows a reference type that was passed to a function declared as g(R^ r_local) and a handle passed in with the expression g(r). The local handle in g refers to the same object on the managed heap.

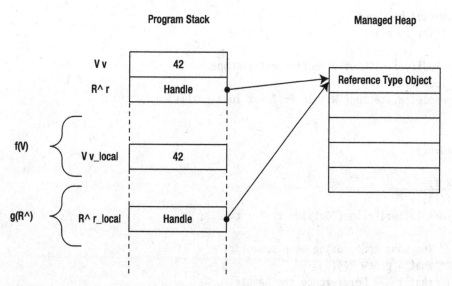

Figure 4-3. *Value types and reference types being passed to functions*

Passing Reference Types by Value

To pass reference type objects by value, omit the handle symbol, as shown in the declaration of the function h in Listing 4-23. While this is normal for a value type, it is also possible for a reference type as long as the reference type has a copy constructor.

Listing 4-23. *Passing a Reference Type by Value*

```
// pass_by_value.cpp
using namespace System;

ref struct R
{
    R()
    {
        val = 1;
    }

    // copy constructor
    R( R% r)
    {
        val = r.val;
    }

    property int val;
};
```

```cpp
// R passed by value (no ^)
void f(R r_local)
{
    // Modify r without affecting outer scope.
    r_local.val = 2;
    Console::WriteLine("Within f: " + r_local.val);
}

int main()
{
    R r;
    f(r);
    Console::WriteLine("Outside f: " + r.val);

    // The same code, using heap semantics
    R^ rhat = gcnew R();
    f(*rhat);   // Dereference the handle.
    Console::WriteLine("Outside f: " + rhat->val);
}
```

The output of Listing 4-23 is as follows:

```
Within f: 2
Outside f: 1
Within f: 2
Outside f: 1
```

Figure 4-4 shows what's happening in memory for this type of parameter passing.

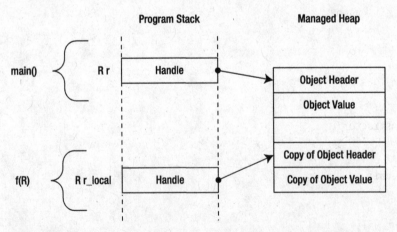

Figure 4-4. *The main method declares R r and passes by value to f(R r_local). The copy constructor is invoked, creating another copy of the reference type object on the managed heap.*

Passing Value Types by Reference

Parameters normally passed by value (such as primitive types and value types) may be passed by reference using the % symbol in the parameter declaration. This is useful if you want to write a function that changes a value type, such as in Listing 4-24.

Listing 4-24. *Changing a Value Type in a Function*

```cpp
// pass_by_ref.cpp
using namespace System;

value class Pair
{
  public:
    int x;
    int y;
};

void swap_values(Pair% pair)
{
    int temp = pair.x;
    pair.x = pair.y;
    pair.y = temp;
}

int main()
{
    Pair p;
    p.x = 5;
    p.y = 3;
    Console::WriteLine("{0} {1}", p.x, p.y);
    swap_values(p);
    Console::WriteLine("{0} {1}", p.x, p.y);
}
```

The output of Listing 4-24 is shown here:

```
5 3
3 5
```

Figure 4-5 shows the memory layout for the preceding example.

Program Stack

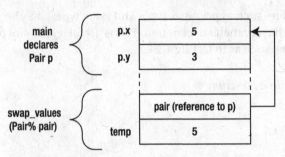

Figure 4-5. *The swap_values method contains a reference pair to main's copy of p as well as a local integer variable to hold a temporary value.*

Temporary Handles

In Listing 4-12, you saw how you could pass a handle by reference using the ´^% indirection. In Listing 4-25, you see that a reference type object with stack semantics isn't affected by a function that takes a reference to a handle if you use the tracking reference operator (%) to create a handle to the object. This is because the handle obtained with the % operator is a different, temporary handle. As a result, an object with stack semantics always represents the original object, so you can be assured that the correct object is cleaned up at the end of the block.

Listing 4-25. *C++/CLI Stack Semantics*

```cpp
// pass_by_ref2.cpp
// This example illustrates that a stack semantics
// reference type can't be redirected by a function
// that operates on references to handles.
using namespace System;

ref struct R
{
    property int A;
    R(int a) { this->A = a; }
};

// Takes a reference to a handle
void reset_handle(R^% r)
{
    r = gcnew R(5);
}

int main()
{
    R r(2); // stack semantics
    reset_handle(%r);  // Use % to create a handle.

    // The output is 2, since the handle passed to f
```

```
    // was a temporary one, so it didn't get changed by
    // the function f.

    Console::WriteLine("Value: {0}", r.A);
}
```

It's worth having a solid understanding of the semantics of parameter passing. Using what you've seen so far, see if you can predict the output of Listing 4-26.

Listing 4-26. *What Does This Output?*

```
// pass_by_ref3.cpp
// This example requires some careful thought.
// Can you figure out what the final output
// will be?
using namespace System;

ref struct R
{
    property int A;
    R(int a) { this->A = a; }
};

// Takes a reference to a handle. This function
// sets the property value on the object, then
// overwrites the object!
// Will the object in the calling scope
// have the value 3, or 5, or will it retain its
// original value?
void reset_handle(R^% r)
{
    r->A = 3;
    r = gcnew R(5);
}

int main()
{
    R r_stack(1); // stack semantics
    R^ r_heap = gcnew R(2); // heap semantics

    reset_handle(%r_stack);  // Use % to create a handle.
    reset_handle(r_heap);

    Console::WriteLine("Final value, stack semantics: {0}", r_stack.A);
    Console::WriteLine("Final value, heap semantics: {0}", r_heap->A);
}
```

The stack semantics variable is converted to a handle using the unary % operator before being passed into the function. The function operates on a reference to the handle. Changing the object through this handle does affect the object, since the object itself is never copied. The subsequent action to reset the object handle does affect the heap handle, since it is passed in directly, but it does not affect the temporary handle to the stack object created using the unary % operator. Thus, the stack variable still points to the original object, with the property value set to 3, but the heap variable points to a new object with the property value 5. So the output of Listing 4-26 is as follows:

```
Final value, stack semantics: 3
Final value, heap semantics: 5
```

Passing Value Types As Handles

Value classes may also be used in a parameter list as a handle. If you use a handle to a value class as a parameter, you also use the unary % operator to pass the value. This creates a temporary copy that the function uses. If you modify the object in the function, the changes do not persist outside the function (see Listing 4-27).

Listing 4-27. *Using a Handle to a Value Type*

```cpp
// handle_to_valuetype.cpp

using namespace System;

value struct V
{
    int a;
    int b;
};

// function taking a handle to a value type
void f(V^ v)
{
    v->a = 10;
    v->b = 20;
}

int main()
{
    V v;
    v.a = 1;
    v.b = 2;
    f(%v);  // creates a copy of v
    Console::WriteLine("{0} {1}", v.a, v.b);
}
```

The output of Listing 4-27 is

---

1 2

---

showing that the original value type was not changed by the function call.

The way to think of this is that both reference and value types support parameter passing using handles or using objects. For reference types, there is a real difference between the two. When passed as a handle, they are passed by reference. When passed as an object, they are passed by value. Value types, on the other hand, are passed by value regardless of whether the syntax involves the use of handles or objects (or even references to handles). However, they can be passed by reference using a tracking reference parameter type, as Listing 4-28 shows.

Listing 4-28. *Passing a Value Type by Reference*

```cpp
// valuetype_trackingref.cpp
using namespace System;

value struct V
{
    int a;
    int b;
};

void f(V% v)
{
    v.a = 10;
    v.b = 20;
}

int main()
{
    V v;
    v.a = 1;
    v.b = 2;
    f(v);
    Console::WriteLine("{0} {1}", v.a, v.b);
}
```

The output of Listing 4-28 is as follows:

---

10 20

This distinction will be important later when you look at generics, since it is possible for a generic class to use either a reference or a value type, and it's important to be aware of the different semantics that each has, particularly when you don't know whether one or the other will be used as the type parameter of a generic type.

Summary of Parameter-Passing Semantics

Table 4-1 summarizes the semantics of parameter passing.

Table 4-1. *Parameter-Passing Semantics*

Function Signature	Argument Type	Use This Syntax in Calling Code	Semantics
f(R r)	Handle to reference type (R^ handle)	f(*handle)	Object copied (requires copy constructor).
f(R r)	Reference type with stack semantics (R obj)	f(obj)	Object copied (requires copy constructor).
f(R^ r)	Handle to reference type (R^ handle)	f(handle)	Object not copied; handle copied.
f(R^ r)	Reference type with stack semantics (R obj)	f(obj)	Object not copied.
f(R^% r)	Handle to reference type (R^ handle)	f(handle)	Handle not copied.
f(R^% r)	Reference type with stack semantics (R obj)	f(%obj)	Handle copied.
f(V v)	Value type	f(obj)	Object copied.
f(V^ v)	Value type	f(%obj)	Object copied.
f(V^% v)	Value type	f(%obj)	Object copied.
f(V% v)	Value type	f(obj)	Object not copied.

Do's and Don'ts of Returning Values

Handles may be used as return values, just as pointers can be. Tracking references may also be used as return values, as long as you take care not to return a reference to a temporary variable. Objects that are to be destroyed at the end of a function call, such as reference types declared using stack semantics, should not be returned as a tracking reference, since they will be destroyed when the function scope ends. If the return type is an object type (not a handle), then it must have a copy constructor. Listing 4-29 illustrates several return value scenarios.

Listing 4-29. *Returning Values*

```cpp
// return_values.cpp
using namespace System;

ref class R
{
    bool destroyed;
  public:
    R() { }
    R(const R% r) { }  // copy constructor

    R% GetTrackingRefMF();
    void PrintR()
    {
       if (destroyed)
          Console::WriteLine("Using destroyed object!");
       else
          Console::WriteLine("R");
    }

    ~R() { destroyed = true; }
};

value struct V
{
   int a;
   int b;
};

// Handle return value: OK
R^ GetHandle()
{
   // Create a new R.
   R^ r = gcnew R();
   // Return it.
   return r;
}

// Return reference to local variable.
// -- avoid
R% GetTrackingRef()
{
   // Create a new R.
   R^ r = gcnew R();
   return *r; // compiler warning
}
```

```
// Return reference to local variable.
// -- avoid
R% GetTrackingRef_Bad()
{
    R r;
    return r; // compiler warning
}

// OK: return a nontemporary reference.
R% R::GetTrackingRefMF()
{
    return *this;
}

// Value type return value: OK
V GetValue()
{
    V v;
    v.a = 100;
    v.b = 54;
    // Value gets copied.
    return v;
}

// Return value with stack semantics.
// Requires copy constructor
R GetR()
{
    R r;
    return r; // requires copy constructor
}


int main()
{
    // Valid uses:
    R^ r1 = GetHandle();  // OK
    R% r2 = r1->GetTrackingRefMF();  // OK
    V v1 = GetValue();  // OK
    Console::WriteLine("{0} {1}", v1.a, v1.b);

    R r3 = GetR(); // OK only if R has a copy constructor
```

```
// Using a tracking reference in the GetTrackingRef function works,
// but a handle would work as well and would eliminate the compiler
// warning in the function declaration.
R% r4 = GetTrackingRef();
r4.PrintR();

// Using the tracking reference here is not OK
// since the destructor was called.
R% r5 = GetTrackingRef_Bad();
r5.PrintR();

}
```

The output of Listing 4-29 is shown here:

```
100 54
R
Using destroyed object!
```

This code illustrates several return value possibilities using handles, references, and value types. Just as it is not a good idea to return references to local variables in classic C++, returning tracking references to local variables is not a good idea in C++/CLI since the destructor is called for local variables, leaving the caller with a reference to a destructed object. Instead, create a permanent object (with gcnew) and return a handle. This is particularly important for C# programmers since C# allows references to be returned from functions. This works in C# since C# doesn't have the concept of stack semantics for reference types.

Summary

In this chapter, you looked at reference types and value types and at the many different ways of referring to objects in code. You saw the semantic differences between these methods, including objects with heap and stack semantics, tracking references, dereferencing handles, copying objects, gc-lvalues, and the auto_handle template. You also looked at passing parameters in various ways, the behavior of C++/CLI handles and tracking references as function parameters, and using handles and references as return values.

Now you'll learn about some fundamental, but special, types: strings, arrays, and enums.

CHAPTER 5

Fundamental Types: Strings, Arrays, and Enums

In this chapter, you'll learn about some special types in the C++/CLI type system. I have been using the term *primitive* type to refer to the built-in integral and floating-point types. Other types, such as those discussed in this chapter, are built upon these primitive types and are fundamental to any program. Each of these types is a .NET version of a classic C++ concept, and each of these has special language support in addition to being a bona fide .NET Framework object type. The chapter will go into some detail not just on the syntax and mechanics of the types themselves, but also some of the commonly used .NET Framework library functionality related to these types.

My primary aim in this book is to focus on the C++/CLI language itself, not the .NET Framework. However, input and output is so fundamental to any language that it's worth discussing on its own, and what better place to discuss it than in the context of strings? Input and output of text are necessary for almost any application, not just an old-style console application. You might need to output text to a string for display in a user interface or for a formatted file. Output usually involves manipulating strings, so this chapter first looks in depth at the String type. The String type is the one that actually provides much of the formatting capability needed in output, whether it's to the console or a web application or a graphical user interface.

Strings

The String type is a reference type that consists of a sequence of Unicode characters representing text. The class has many useful instance methods and many static methods that support copying and manipulation of strings. The String class represents an immutable sequence of characters; methods that manipulate strings do not modify them in-place, they create new, modified versions of the strings. Even those methods that suggest that they modify the string (such as Insert, Remove, Replace, etc.) create new strings. If you need a string that is modifiable in-place, use the StringBuilder class.

Let's start with a few basics. To create a simple string, write code like the following:

```
String^ str = gcnew String("Text");
String^ str1 = "Text";
```

In the first statement, we explicitly spell out the String constructor with a string literal argument. In the second statement, the right side is a string literal. Historically, in Visual C++, if you use the prefix L in front of the string, the string literal is interpreted as Unicode. C++/CLI interprets string literals as narrow 1-byte characters or wide 2-byte Unicode characters depending on the context. If a string literal is immediately assigned to a String, it is interpreted as a wide character string literal even without the L prefix. In any event, the String class always refers to a Unicode string, and an automatic conversion from a string literal is defined in C++/CLI, so when the string literal is assigned to a string handle, the result is a handle to a Unicode string. Because of the context-dependent nature of string literals, it is sometimes said that the type of a string literal is inexpressible in the language. In practical terms, it simply means that you can use string literals without a lot of fussing about the types involved.

To concatenate two strings, use the static method String::Concat, as follows:

```
String^ str = String::Concat(str1, str2);
```

What this does is create a new String object, str, that is the concatenation of str1 and str2. The str1 and str2 objects themselves are left unmodified.

To get at a single character in a string, use the Chars indexed property, as follows:

```
char c = str1->Chars[5];
```

You'll read more about indexed properties in Chapter 7; the indexed property Chars allows array-indexing syntax to be used on the property.

To copy a string, you can either make another reference to the same string or copy the string. Depending on your application, one or the other might make the most sense. The assignment operator creates another reference to the same string. This is what is meant by a *shallow copy*. The Copy member function creates a new string, which is known as a *deep copy*. Since String objects cannot be modified, multiple references to the string will retain the correct value; thus it is usually not necessary to copy the string.

However, to compare strings, you must be aware of whether you're comparing the reference (testing for reference equality) or the characters of the strings themselves. The equality operator (==) is equivalent to the Equals method, and both test for equality of a string's value. The example in Listing 5-1 demonstrates this.

Listing 5-1. *Comparing Strings*

```
// string_equality.cpp
using namespace System;

int main()
{
    String^ str1 = "1";
    String^ str2 = "1";
    String^ str3 = str1;
```

```
    // All of the following tests result in True, since
    // the == operator is equivalent to the Equals method.
    if (str1 == str2)
    {
        Console::WriteLine(" str1 == str2" );
    }
    if (str1 == str3)
    {
        Console::WriteLine(" str1 == str3" );
    }
    if (str1->Equals(str2))
    {
        Console::WriteLine(" str1 Equals str2" );
    }
    if (str1->Equals(str3))
    {
        Console::WriteLine(" str1 Equals str3");
    }

    // ReferenceEquals compares the handles, not the actual
    // string. The results are implementation dependent,
    // since if the compiler creates a single-string representation
    // for both string literals, as is the case here, this will resolve
    // true.
    if (String::ReferenceEquals(str1, str2))
    {
        Console::WriteLine(" str1 ReferenceEquals str2");
    }
    if (String::ReferenceEquals(str1, str3))
    {
        Console::WriteLine(" str1 ReferenceEquals str3");
    }
}
```

The output of Listing 5-1 is as follows:

```
str1 == str2
str1 == str3
str1 Equals str2
str1 Equals str3
str1 ReferenceEquals str2
str1 ReferenceEquals str3
```

To get the string as an array of characters, you can convert it to a character array using the ToCharArray method, as shown in Listing 5-2. Unlike the Chars property, this creates a new array of System::Char that contains a copy of each character in the string. System::Char is also known as wchar_t, the Unicode character type.

Listing 5-2. *Converting a String to a Character Array*

```cpp
// string_tochararray.cpp
using namespace System;

int main()
{
    String^ str = "A quick sly fox jumped over the lazy brown dog.";

    array<Char>^ character_array = str->ToCharArray();

    // Print the original string.
    Console::WriteLine( str);

    // Modify characters in the character array.
    for (int i = 0; i < character_array->Length; i++)
    {
        if ( character_array[i] >= L'a' && character_array[i] <= 'z')
        {
            character_array[i] -= (L'a' - L'A');
        }
    }

    // Convert back to a String using the String constructor
    // that takes a Unicode character array.
    str = gcnew String(character_array);

    // Print the modified string:
    // A QUICK SLY FOX JUMPED OVER THE LAZY BROWN DOG.
    Console::WriteLine( str);
}
```

The output of Listing 5-2 is shown here:

```
A quick sly fox jumped over the lazy brown dog.
A QUICK SLY FOX JUMPED OVER THE LAZY BROWN DOG.
```

Or, if you need to iterate over characters in a string, use the for each statement, as in Listing 5-3.

Listing 5-3. *Looping Through a String*

```cpp
// string_foreach.cpp
using namespace System;
```

```
int main()
{
    String^ str1 = "Ode on a Grecian Urn";

    for each (Char ch in str1)
    {
        Console::Write(ch);
    }
    Console::WriteLine();
}
```

Here's the output of Listing 5-3:

```
Ode on a Grecian Urn
```

This code works because first, the String class implements the interface IEnumerable, and second, the GetEnumerator function returns a CharEnumerator, a class that implements IEnumerator. IEnumerator includes a property, Current, which in the case of CharEnumerator, returns a Char (which, as mentioned earlier, is the same as wchar_t).

String Operators

C++/CLI supports, for convenience, the use of the + operator on strings, string literals, and other entities that can be converted to strings (which includes any managed type, since Object defined the ToString method that other objects inherit). The result is the concatenation of the strings. In this way you can build up an output string using concatenation, rather than using the format string. This is not generally a good idea for applications that must be localized into other languages, since the different word order of different languages may mean that the order of concatenation is language dependent.

Listing 5-4 shows the use of the string concatenation operator.

Listing 5-4. *Concatenating Strings*

```
// string_operator_plus.cpp
using namespace System;

int main()
{
    String ^hrs = "Hours", ^mins = "Minutes";
    wchar_t separator = ':';
    int minutes = 56, hours = 1;

    Console::WriteLine( hrs + separator + " " + hours + "\n" + mins +
                        separator + " " + minutes);
}
```

The output of Listing 5-4 is as follows:

```
Hours: 1
Minutes: 56
```

The addition operator works from left to right, so as long as the first operand is a string, each operand in the series will be converted to a string, even if some part of the expression could also be interpreted as another type of addition (such as adding integers). The ToString function is used to convert types to strings. The string concatenation operator works with all managed types, since all managed types inherit the ToString operator from System::Object. Strings that are editable (also called *mutable*) should be instances of StringBuilder rather than String. You'll learn more about StringBuilder strings later in this chapter.

Comparing Strings

Strings implement IComparable, so they support the CompareTo method to compare to another string. You can also use the static method, Compare, to compare two strings. The version of the Compare static method that takes only two strings as parameters and the CompareTo method use the same comparison algorithm, but the Compare static method is overloaded and has several variations that allow the comparison to be customized. The CompareTo method, for any object that implements IComparable, returns a value representing one of three possibilities. A negative return value indicates that the first object is less than the second. A zero return value indicates that the two objects are equal. A positive return value indicates that the first object is greater than the second. For the CompareTo method, the first object is the object whose instance method is being called; for the static method, the first object is the first argument. Listing 5-5 shows the basic use of string comparison.

Listing 5-5. *Comparing Strings with CompareTo*

```cpp
// string_compare.cpp
using namespace System;

int main()
{
   String^ str1 = "cat";
   String^ str2 = "cab";

   if (str1->CompareTo( str2 ) < 0)
   {
       Console::WriteLine(str1 + " is less than " + str2);
   }
      // For variety, use the static method.
   else if ( String::Compare(str1, str2) > 0 )
   {
       Console::WriteLine("{0} is less than {1}", str2, str1);
   }
```

```
    else if ( str1->CompareTo( str2 ) == 0)
    {
        Console::WriteLine("The strings are both equal, with value {0}.", str1);
    }
}
```

Here is the output of Listing 5-5:

```
cab is less than cat
```

Implementing the IComparable interface allows strings to be used in all sorts of container classes where comparison is a requirement. For example, in Chapter 11, you'll see how to define a generic collection class that has a constraint indicating that any class used in the generic collection must implement IComparable. This allows the author of the generic class to assume certain functionality, such as the existence of the CompareTo method.

The CompareTo method alone isn't rich enough to support all the factors that might be relevant in comparing strings in real-world code. Sometimes comparison must be case sensitive, other times comparison must be case insensitive. Additionally, comparison in some applications must be sensitive to culture, since alphabets and alphabetical order are dependent on locale. The CompareTo method also includes overloads that support comparison of substrings. There's also a CompareOrdinal method that is useful if the strings represent numbers and you want a comparison of the number.

Formatting Strings

The Format methods format a string for output. The .NET Framework formatting support is very rich, supporting a highly customizable output format and providing an extensible framework for defining your own custom formats as well. The same formatting rules are used for the Console class's WriteLine method for output to the console.

The string used to specify the desired formatting and that acts as a template for the output is called the *format string*. The format string contains placeholders that are numbered starting with zero and surrounded by curly braces, as in the following string:

```
Console::WriteLine("The population of {0} is {1}.", "Pleasantville", 500);
```

This code substitutes Pleasantville for the {0} and 500 for the {1}. The type of the argument need not be supplied, as the language contains enough type information without any further specification.

The number in curly braces is referred to as the *index*. It is followed, optionally, by a comma and number specifying the minimum width of the field. The sign of the number specifies the justification (positive for right-justification, negative for left-justification). One can also append a colon and a formatting string that is used to customize the output format. The available formatting strings are dependent on the type. A variety of formatting codes exists for formatting numeric output, as well as date, time, and currency output, which is dependent on the locale. The following sections provide detailed examples.

The Width Field (or Alignment Specifier)

Listing 5-6 provides some examples of formatting using the width field, including a negative width indicating left justification, and a currency formatting string—the c2 following the colon in the Price column, which is ignored when used with a string.

Listing 5-6. *Formatting Strings Using the Width Field*

```cpp
// string_alignment_specifier.cpp
using namespace System;

int main()
{
    // The format string is interpreted as follows:
    // { 0, -30 } 30 characters in width, left-justified.
    // { 1, 10 } 10 characters in width, right-justified.
    // { 2, 10:c2 } 10 characters in width, currency with 2 decimal places.
    String^ format = "{0,-30}{1,10}{2,10:c2}";
    String^ header = String::Format(format, "Item", "Quantity", "Price");
    String^ str1 = str1->Format(format, "Matches, Strike Anywhere", 10, 0.99);
    String^ str2 = str2->Format(format, "Gloves", 1, 12.50);
    String^ str3 = str3->Format(format, "Iodine", 1, 4.99);

    Console::WriteLine(header);
    Console::WriteLine(str1 + "\n" + str2 + "\n" + str3);
}
```

The output of Listing 5-6 on U.S. English systems is as follows:

Item	Quantity	Price
Matches, Strike Anywhere	10	$0.99
Gloves	1	$12.50
Iodine	1	$4.99

Numeric String Formatting

Formatting in C runtime functions such as printf involves the use of formatting characters for various data types and, in particular, certain formatting characters for decimal or hexadecimal output, exponential format, and so on. The usual numeric formatting characters from C are supported, as well as additional formats for currency, and a special round-trip format specifically to ensure accurate results when reading the data back in using the Read or ReadLine methods. The code in Listing 5-7 shows the typical use of these formats. The formatting specifier follows the colon after the index (and optional alignment specifier specifying the width of the field) in the format string. In the following example, the alignment specifier is not used, and the index is always zero since we only have one variable to format.

Listing 5-7. *Formatting Numeric Strings*

```cpp
// string_numerical_formatting.cpp
using namespace System;

int main()
{
    String^ str;
    int i = -73000;
    double dbl = 1005.01;

    // Formats for floating-point types:

    str = String::Format("Currency format: {0:c2}", dbl);
    Console::WriteLine(str);

    str = String::Format("Scientific format: {0:e6}", dbl);
    Console::WriteLine(str);

    str = String::Format("Fixed-point format: {0:f6}", dbl);
    Console::WriteLine(str);

    str = String::Format("General format: {0:g6}", dbl);
    Console::WriteLine(str);

    str = String::Format("Number format: {0:n6}", dbl);
    Console::WriteLine(str);

    str = String::Format("Percent format: {0:p6}", dbl);
    Console::WriteLine(str);

    str = String::Format("Round-trip format: {0:r6}", dbl);
    Console::WriteLine(str);

    // Formats for integral types:

    str = String::Format("Decimal format: {0:d6}", i);
    Console::WriteLine(str);

    str = String::Format("General format: {0:g6}", i);
    Console::WriteLine(str);

    str = String::Format("Number format: {0:n0}", i);
    Console::WriteLine(str);

    str = String::Format("Hexadecimal format: {0:x8}", i);
    Console::WriteLine(str);
}
```

Here is the output of Listing 5-7:

```
Currency format: $1,005.01
Scientific format: 1.005010e+003
Fixed-point format: 1005.010000
General format: 1005.01
Number format: 1,005.010000
Percent format: 100,501.000000 %
Round-trip format: 1005.01
Decimal format: -073000
General format: -73000
Number format: -73,000
Hexadecimal format: fffee2d8
```

StringBuilder

For manipulation and editing of strings in-place, you need to use StringBuilder rather than String. StringBuilder contains methods for appending, inserting, removing, and replacing elements of a string (see Listing 5-8). StringBuilder maintains an internal buffer with a given capacity and expands this capacity as the size of the string increases.

Listing 5-8. *Using StringBuilder*

```cpp
// stringbuilder.cpp

using namespace System;
using namespace System::Text;

int main()
{
    // Construct a StringBuilder string with initial contents
    // "C" and initial capacity 30.
    StringBuilder^ sb = gcnew StringBuilder("C", 30);

    sb->Append(gcnew array<Char>{'+','+'});

    sb->Append("/CLI.");

    sb->Insert(0, "I love ");

    sb->Replace(".","!");

    Console::WriteLine( sb->ToString() );
}
```

The output of Listing 5-8 is as follows:

I love C++/CLI!

Refer to the documentation for the .NET Framework or CLI Base Class Library for further information.

Conversions Between Strings and Other Data Types

You've seen many examples of rendering primitive types as strings. What about converting from a string to a primitive type? System::String implements IConvertible, which means it supports conversions to a variety of types using functions such as ToBoolean, ToInt32, and so on. Also, the object wrappers for the primitive types support the ability to parse strings. There are static methods called Parse on the classes for the primitive types that take a string to be parsed as a parameter and return an object of the numeric type. Listing 5-9 provides some examples.

Listing 5-9. *Converting Strings to Primitive Types*

```
// convert_and_parse.cpp

using namespace System;

int main()
{
    String^ str1 = "115";
    String^ str2 = "1.4e-12";

    // Parse the string to get the integer value.
    int i = Int32::Parse( str1 );

    // Get the double value.
    double x = Double::Parse( str2 );

    // Use Convert class to convert the value.
    int j = Convert::ToInt32( str1 );
    double y = Convert::ToDouble( str2 );

    // Exception handlers may be used to catch parse failures and overflows.

    try
    {
        int k = Int32::Parse("bad format");
    }
    catch(FormatException^ e)
    {
        Console::WriteLine("Exception occurred! {0}", e->Message );
    }
}
```

The output of Listing 5-9 is as follows:

```
Exception occurred! Input string was not in a correct format.
```

Input/Output

The System::Console class supports basic input and output to the console.

Basic Output

The CLI Library (or .NET Framework) provides the System::Console class for performing most simple I/O functions. You've been using the WriteLine method for quite some time now. WriteLine has an overload that uses the same format string and variable argument list as String::Format. All the formatting rules described earlier for String::Format apply to Console::WriteLine and, incidentally, to Console::Write, which is just like WriteLine except that it does not automatically append a newline to its output.

Other overloads of WriteLine and Write omit the format parameter and simply output a representation of the object rendered as text in the default format. Write and WriteLine contain overloads that take all of the primitive types as well as arrays of Char (wchar_t).

Listing 5-10 uses various overloads of Write and WriteLine.

Listing 5-10. *Using Write and WriteLine*

```cpp
// writeline.cpp

using namespace System;

int main()
{
    // output without newline
    Console::Write("a");
    Console::Write("b");
    Console::Write("c");

    // newline alone
    Console::WriteLine();

    // output with format string
    Console::WriteLine("Fourscore and {0} years ago.", 7);

    // output with direct types
    Console::WriteLine(7);
    Console::WriteLine( 1.05);
    Console::WriteLine('A');
}
```

The output of Listing 5-10 is as follows:

```
abc
Fourscore and 7 years ago.
7
1.05
65
```

Out, Error, and In

The Console class exposes the Out, Error and In properties as abstractions for the standard filestreams stdout, stderr, and stdin. Out, Error, and In are represented as objects of the System::IO::TextWriter and TextReader classes.

Basic Input with Console::ReadLine

Use Console::ReadLine to read from standard input (stdin). When the end of input is reached, ReadLine returns nullptr, as shown in Listing 5-11.

Listing 5-11. *Reading from Standard Input*

```cpp
// to_upper.cpp
// Convert text read from stdin to uppercase and write to stdout.
using namespace System;

int main()
{
    String^ str;
    while ((str = Console::ReadLine()) != nullptr)
    {
        Console::WriteLine( str->ToUpper() );
    }
}
```

Reading and Writing Files

StreamWriter is the class used for output to files. StreamWriter supports the Write and WriteLine methods, and StreamReader supports the Read and ReadLine methods for input and output to files in a variety of formats. These classes allow you to specify the encoding of the output file, so you can write easily to ASCII or Unicode UTF-8, UTF-16, and other encodings.

A StreamWriter may be opened with a file name or the File class, which has static methods for creating or opening files (see Listing 5-12).

Listing 5-12. *Using StreamWriter*

```
StreamWriter^ sw = gcnew StreamWriter("textfile.txt");
sw->WriteLine("Can code be poetry?");
sw->Flush();
sw->Close();

// The File class's CreateText static method is used to
// create a text file.
StreamWriter^ sw2 = File::CreateText("newtextfile.txt");
```

To read text, use the StreamReader class (see Listing 5-13).

Listing 5-13. *Using StreamReader*

```
StreamReader^ sr = gcnew StreamReader("textfile.txt");
String^ line;
// Read each line and write it out to the console.
while ((line = sr->ReadLine()) != nullptr)
{
    Console::WriteLine(line);
}
```

Whenever you deal with files, of course, you cannot neglect proper error handling. The .NET Framework classes throw exceptions of type System::IO::IOException to indicate error conditions, so you would normally use a try/catch block around any attempt to work with a file. This code is a typical example: the exception has a Message property that contains an informative error message, as in Listing 5-14.

Listing 5-14. *Using an Exception's Message Property*

```
String^ filename = "textfile.txt";
try
{
    // Another way of creating a StreamReader class is with
    // static methods of the File class.
    StreamReader^ sr2 = File::OpenText(filename);

    String^ line;
    // Read each line and write it out to the console.
    while ((line = sr2->ReadLine()) != nullptr)
    {
        Console::WriteLine(line);
    }
}
catch(IOException^ e)
{
    Console::WriteLine("Exception! {0}", e->Message );
}
```

I've only scratched the surface here, to give you some of the simplest examples. Refer to the documentation for the .NET Framework for all the methods of the File, StreamWriter, StreamReader, and related classes to learn more.

Reading and Writing Strings

StringWriter and StringReader provide support for writing and reading strings using the same interfaces used for writing to streams and files. The use of this class is straightforward, as demonstrated in Listing 5-15, which uses some of my wife's poetry, this one inspired by Seattle's Pike Place market.

Listing 5-15. *Writing Poetry with StringWriter*

```cpp
// stringwriter.cpp

// The Windows Forms namespace lives in a different
// assembly, which is not referenced by default as is
// mscorlib.dll, so we must use #using here.
#using "System.Windows.Forms.dll"

using namespace System;
using namespace System::IO;
using namespace System::Text;
using namespace System::Windows::Forms;

int main()
{
    StringWriter^ sw = gcnew StringWriter();
    sw->WriteLine("Pike Place");
    sw->WriteLine("Street of Dreams");
    sw->WriteLine("(C) 2006 Jeni Hogenson");
    sw->WriteLine();

    sw->Write("Walking with bare feet\n");
    sw->Write("Seattle streets, gospel beat,\n");
    sw->Write("She's got magic\n");
    sw->WriteLine();

    sw->WriteLine("Bag of black upon her back\n" +
                  "A sensual blend, soul food that is;\n" +
                  "Local color.");
    sw->WriteLine();

    String^ jambo = "jambo";
    String^ s = String::Format("Open the bag, {0}, {1}.", jambo, jambo);
    sw->WriteLine(s);
    sw->Write("Make a wish, {0}, {0}.", jambo);
    sw->WriteLine();
```

```
    s = "Feel it, grab it, grope it.\n";
    String::Concat(s, "Follow every curve.\n");
    String::Concat(s, "Can you wait to find it?\n");
    String::Concat(s, "Do you have the nerve?");
    sw->WriteLine(s);

    sw->WriteLine("A drop of oil, jambo, jambo.");
    sw->WriteLine("Whisper in her ear,");
    sw->WriteLine("Ask the question in your heart");
    sw->WriteLine("that only you can hear");
    sw->WriteLine();

    StringBuilder^ sb = gcnew StringBuilder();
    sb->Append("Fingers now upon your ears,\n");
    sb->Append("Waiting for the space\n");
    sb->Append("An answer if you're ready now\n");
    sb->Append("From the marketplace\n");
    sw->WriteLine(sb);

    sw->WriteLine("The call of a bird, jambo, jambo.");
    sw->WriteLine("The scent of a market flower,");
    sw->WriteLine("Open wide to all of it and");
    sw->WriteLine("Welcome back your power");
    sw->WriteLine();

    sw->WriteLine("Jambo this and jambo that,");
    sw->WriteLine("Walking with bare feet.");
    sw->WriteLine("No parking allowed when down under,");
    sw->WriteLine("Keep it to the street.");
    sw->WriteLine();

    sw->WriteLine("Dead people rising,");
    sw->WriteLine("Walking with bare feet,");
    sw->WriteLine("No parking allowed when down under,");
    sw->WriteLine("Keep it to the street.");

    // The resulting string might be displayed to the user in a GUI.
    MessageBox::Show(sw->ToString(), "Poetry", MessageBoxButtons::OK);
}
```

System::String and Other I/O Systems

Still prefer the trusty C runtime function printf? Unless you're compiling with safe mode (the /clr:safe compiler option), you can still use the C Runtime (CRT) Library or the iostream library if that's what you prefer, although the resulting code will not be verifiably safe from memory corruption problems. Most CRT functions taking a variable argument list will work with System::String, as in Listing 5-16. Note that as of Visual C++ 2005, it is recommended that you use the more secure variants of the standard CRT functions. While these are not yet part of the ANSI standard, they have been proposed as extensions to the standard.

Listing 5-16. *Using printf*

```
// cli_printf.cpp

using namespace System;
#include <stdio.h>

int main()
{
    String^ str = "managed string";

    // The string is automatically converted to a
    // char array for printf_s.
    printf_s("%s", str );
}
```

The output of Listing 5-16 is shown here:

---

managed string

The conversion for printf_s (and printf) is due to the String class's ability to be converted via a variable argument list and not a general conversion to const char *. For example, the following line:

```
printf_s(str);
```

produces an error:

```
cli_printf.cpp(12) : error C2664: 'printf_s' : cannot convert parameter 1 from '
System::String ^' to 'const char *'
        No user-defined-conversion operator available, or
        Cannot convert a managed type to an unmanaged type
```

Using cout with System::String is a bit more complicated. The string must be marshaled as a native data type that the overloaded shift operator (<<) supports, and because we are getting a native pointer to managed data (which could be moved by the garbage collector) it must be artificially fixed in memory during the time that the native data type is active. We accomplish this by declaring a pinning pointer (pin_ptr), as shown in Listing 5-17. The first step is to use PtrToStringChars (defined in vcclr.h) to get a pointer into the underlying wide character array that represents the string, and assign that to a pinning pointer that fixes the data it points to as long as the pinning pointer is in scope. This pinning pointer must in turn be converted to a type that the shift operator supports, so we use static_cast to convert it to const wchar_t* and pass that to the expression involving wcout, the wide character version of cout.

Listing 5-17. *Using a Pinning Pointer*

```cpp
// string_wcout.cpp
#include <vcclr.h>
#include <iostream>

using namespace std;
using namespace System;

int main()
{
    String^ s = "Testing String conversion to iostream.";

    pin_ptr<const wchar_t> ptr = PtrToStringChars(s);
    wcout << static_cast<const wchar_t*>( ptr ) << endl;
}
```

The output of Listing 5-17 is as follows:

```
Testing String conversion to iostream.
```

Listing 5-17 is just a taste of the concerns you have to deal with in mixing native and managed libraries. Using CLR types with classic C++ libraries is an example of C++ interop, which is discussed in greater detail in Chapter 12.

The preceding sections looked in detail at the String type, including its methods, support for the + operator, and the Format method in detail, including specific formatting rules for numeric output. You also saw the StringBuilder class for manipulating strings in-place, and the Console class for input and output to the console or command-line window, including a discussion of the In, Out, and Error representations of stdin, stdout, and stderr. I covered the Write and WriteLine methods, the Read and Readline methods, and file I/O using the StreamWriter and StreamReader classes, and corresponding functionality for string I/O in the StringWriter and StringReader classes. Now let's look at another fundamental type: the array.

Arrays

The C++/CLI managed array provides the functionality of a classic array and is also an object type complete with methods. The methods simplify common tasks such as getting the length of the array, sorting, and handling thread synchronization.

A managed array is declared as follows:

```cpp
array< type, rank >^ array_name;
```

This is read as "array_name is a handle to a managed array of some type and number of dimensions (rank)." Here are some examples of declarations of managed arrays:

```
array<int>^ array_of_ints; // a 1D array of int
array<double, 2>^ array_2D_of_doubles;  // a 2D array of doubles
array<String^>^ array_of_string_handles; // a 1D array of strings
```

The preceding declarations produce a null handle, that is, one that doesn't point to anything. We create an array with both a long and a short form, as follows:

```
array_name = gcnew array< type >( length );
```

```
array_name = gcnew array< type, rank>( length1, length2, ... );
```

The rank is the number of dimensions of the array (not the number of elements); it is optional for a one-dimensional array.

Here are some examples of managed arrays:

```
array<int>^ array_of_ints; // a 1D array of int
array<double, 2>^ array_2D_of_doubles;  // a 2D array of doubles
```

```
// Declare and create a new 1D array of int with 100 elements.
array<int>^ array_of_ints = gcnew array<int>(100);
```

```
// Declare and create a 1D array of references to Strings with 4 elements.
array<String^>^ array_of_strings = gcnew array<String>(4);
```

Also, the array type is always used with the handle symbol (^). This serves as a reminder that the array references an object on the heap. However, these handles cannot be dereferenced like a pointer to get at an object. The address of the array is the address of the handle; it is not the same as the address of the first element of the array.

Element access for managed arrays is done using square brackets, although for arrays of more than one dimension, commas are used as shown here:

```
element2_2 = native_2D_array[2][2];  // native 2D array
element2_2 = managed_2D_ array[2, 2]; // managed 2D array
```

Indices are zero-based in both native and managed arrays; that is, the first index is 0 and the last is $N - 1$ where N is the length of the array.

Initializing

Native and managed arrays may be initialized when they are created using array initialization syntax. An array initializer consists of a list of values separated by commas. Unlike the initializer for native arrays, the equal sign is not used in the managed array initializer. If the array is multidimensional, curly braces are nested. Listing 5-18 illustrates various initializers, showing the native and managed equivalents side by side.

Listing 5-18. *Initializing Arrays*

```cpp
// arrays_initializing.cpp
int main()
{

    // Declare, create, and initialize a 1D native array.
    int native_array[2] = { 10, 20 };

    // Declare, create, and initialize a 1D managed array.
    array<int>^ managed_array = gcnew array<int>(2) { 10, 20 };

    // Declare, create, and initialize a 2D native array.
    int native_array_2D[2][2] = { { 1, 0 }, { 0, 1 } };

    // Declare, create, and initialize a 2D managed array.
    array<int, 2>^ managed_array_2D = gcnew array<int, 2>(2, 2)
                    { { 1, 0 }, { 0, 1 } };

}
```

If an initializer is present, the size of the dimensions may be omitted. In this case, the number of elements in the initializer determines the size of the array. You can also use an initializer by itself on the right side of an assignment operator, without gcnew, to create a new array. You can use variables in an initializer, as for array_int3 in Listing 5-19.

Listing 5-19. *Initializing an Array Without gcnew*

```cpp
// arrays_initializing2.cpp
int main()
{
    // initialization without gcnew

    array<int>^ array_int1 = { 0, 1, 2 };

    // Initialization with gcnew (no equal sign is used).
    // Here, the size is omitted and determined by the three
    // elements in the initializer list.
    array<int>^ array_int2 = gcnew array<int> { 0, 1, 2 };

    // You can use variables in the initializer list.

    int i = 1, j = 2, k = 3;
    array<int>^ array_int3 = { i, j, k };
}
```

As in the C++ new expression, the default constructor (the constructor with no arguments) is called to initialize the elements of the array. You can use gcnew in the array initializer to call a specific constructor, as in Listing 5-20.

Listing 5-20. *Initializing Array Elements with Constructors*

```cpp
// arrays_nondefault_ctor.cpp
using namespace System;

ref class C
{

   public:
      C(int i) { Value = i; }

      property int Value;
};

int main()
{
   array<C^>^ array_C = { gcnew C(0), gcnew C(1), gcnew C(2)};

   Console::WriteLine( " {0}, {1}, {2} ", array_C[0]->Value,
               array_C[1]->Value, array_C[2]->Value);
}
```

The output of Listing 5-20 is as follows:

```
0, 1, 2
```

Array Length

An array is a CLI object and has some self-knowledge that can be accessed using its properties and methods. For example, you can use the Length property to get the length of an array, as in Listing 5-21.

Listing 5-21. *Getting the Length of an Array*

```cpp
// arrays_length.cpp
using namespace System;

int main()
{
   array<String^>^ string_array =
         gcnew array<String^>(2) { "first", "second" } ;

   for (int i = 0; i < string_array->Length; i++)
   {
      Console::WriteLine( string_array[i] );
   }
}
```

Here is the output of Listing 5-21:

```
first
second
```

If you use a size greater than the number of elements provided, the uninitialized elements are included in the length, as in Listing 5-22.

Listing 5-22. *Initializing Only Part of an Array*

```cpp
// arrays_uninitialized_elements.cpp
using namespace System;

int main()
{
    array<String^>^ stringArray = gcnew array<String^>(5)
        { "one", "two" };

    for (int i = 0; i < stringArray->Length; i++)
    {
        Console::WriteLine( stringArray[i] );
    }

    Console::WriteLine("End.");
}
```

The uninitialized elements are null String handles, which are rendered as extra blank lines:

```
one
two



End.
```

Listing 5-23 shows the syntax for creation and element access of a managed one-dimensional array alongside the classic C++ equivalent.

Listing 5-23. *Creating One-Dimensional Arrays*

```cpp
// arrays_managed_native_comparison.cpp
#include <iostream>
using namespace std;
```

```
int main()
{
    // native 1D array
    int native_array_1D[10];

    // managed 1D array
    array<int>^ managed_array_1D = gcnew array<int>(10);

    for (int i = 0; i < 10; i++)
    {
        native_array_1D[i] = i*i;
        cout << native_array_1D[i] << " ";
        managed_array_1D[i] = native_array_1D[i];
        cout << managed_array_1D[i] << " ";
    }

    cout << endl;
}
```

Here is the output of Listing 5-23:

0 0 1 1 4 4 9 9 16 16 25 25 36 36 49 49 64 64 81 81

Navigating Arrays

Another feature of native arrays is that, to some extent, arrays and pointers are interchangeable. The name of a native array is the starting address of the array. The square bracket array-index syntax is always equivalent to a pointer-offset syntax. That is, the following are equivalent for a native array:

```
native_array[i]
*(native_array + i)
```

Although this is not possible with managed arrays, you can navigate through an array using iterators, and you can also use interior pointers to navigate an array. Iterators are special classes that point to elements of arrays or another collection and can be incremented to step through a collection. You could think of them as smart pointers. Listing 5-24 shows how to walk through an array using iterators.

Listing 5-24. *Using Iterators to Traverse an Array*

```
// arrays_iterators.cpp
using namespace System;
using namespace System::Collections;
```

```cpp
int main()
{
   array<DateTime^>^ dateArray = gcnew array<DateTime^>(2);

   dateArray[0] = gcnew DateTime(1970, 12, 18);
   dateArray[1] = gcnew DateTime(1990, 1, 5);

   IEnumerator^ enumerator1 = dateArray->GetEnumerator();
   while ( enumerator1->MoveNext() )
   {
      DateTime^ current = (DateTime^) enumerator1->Current;
      Console::WriteLine( current->ToString("MM/dd/yyyy") );
   }

}
```

The output of Listing 5-24 is shown here:

```
12/18/1970
01/05/1990
```

The for each statement may be used to iterate through an array, as Listing 5-25 shows.

Listing 5-25. *Using for each to Traverse an Array*

```cpp
// arrays_foreach.cpp
using namespace System;

int main()
{
   array<String^>^ stringArray = gcnew array<String^>
      { "one", "two", "three", "four", "five" };

   for each (String^ str in stringArray)
   {
      Console::WriteLine(str);
   }
}
```

The output of Listing 5-25 is as follows:

```
one
two
three
four
five
```

Interior pointers are another way of navigating an array that allows you to use pointer arithmetic. The interior pointer is a pointer to some part of a managed object, in this case an array. Interior pointers get updated, just as handles do, when the objects they point to get moved around by the garbage collection process. Chapter 12 will discuss them in more detail. Listing 5-26 is a preliminary example of using an interior pointer to navigate a managed array.

Listing 5-26. *Using an Interior Pointer to Traverse an Array*

```cpp
// arrays_interior_ptr.cpp
using namespace System;

ref class Buf
{
    // ...
};

int main()
{
    array<Buf^>^ array_of_buf = gcnew array<Buf^>(10);

    // Create a Buf object for each array position.
    for each (Buf^ bref in array_of_buf)
    {
        bref = gcnew Buf();
    }

    // Create an interior pointer to elements of the array.
    interior_ptr<Buf^> ptr_buf;

    // Loop over the array with the interior pointer.
    // using pointer arithmetic on the interior pointer
    for (ptr_buf = &array_of_buf[0]; ptr_buf <= &array_of_buf[9]; ptr_buf++)
    {
        // Dereference the interior pointer with *.
        Buf^ buf = *ptr_buf;
        // use the Buf class
    }
}
```

What happens when you run off the end of the array? If you attempt to access an index that doesn't exist in the array, an IndexOutOfRangeException will be thrown, as shown in Listing 5-27.

Listing 5-27. *Going Past the End of an Array*

```cpp
// array_exception.cpp
using namespace System;

int main()
{
    int i;
    array<int>^ array1 = { 0, 1, 2};

    try
    {
        i = array1[3];
    }
    catch(IndexOutOfRangeException^ e)
    {
        Console::WriteLine( "{0}, {1}" , e->ToString(), e->Message);
    }
}
```

The output of Listing 5-27 is as follows:

```
System.IndexOutOfRangeException: Index was outside the bounds of the array.
   at main(), Index was outside the bounds of the array.
```

Differences Between Native and Managed Arrays

If you're familiar with arrays in classic C++, you know that a native 2D array is an array of arrays. This is not the case for managed arrays.

The size of a managed array is not part of its type; only its rank is. For classic C++ arrays, every dimension except the last is part of its type. This makes it a bit easier to define functions that take managed arrays of unknown sizes, but a known number of dimensions.

There are some important differences in the way in which native and managed arrays behave at runtime. Managed arrays are created on the managed heap, and as such have a lifetime just like other objects. A native array declared as a local variable is created on the stack, and so is destroyed at the end of the block. Native arrays created with new are created on the native heap.

There are some restrictions on native types that can be used in managed arrays. You can create a managed array of managed types (either reference or value types, or any of the primitive types) or native pointers. You cannot create a managed array with native aggregate types such as native arrays, classes, and structures. Table 5-1 outlines differences between native arrays and managed arrays.

Table 5-1. *Differences Between Native and Managed Arrays*

Difference	Native Array	Managed Array
Underlying representation?	A native array is a pointer to a block of memory.	A managed array is an object with properties and methods.
What's in the type?	Rank, and size of each dimension except the last.	Rank, not size.
Stack or heap?	Arrays are created on the stack.	Arrays are created on the managed heap.
Allowed element types?	Native types.	Managed types, primitive types, or native pointers.

Arrays As Parameters

Using arrays as parameters and return values requires special care in C++, because the type of the array includes the length of the last dimension, but not any others, as you can see by considering that the code in Listing 5-28 is legal in C++. An array with a dimension unequal to that specified in the function signature is accepted by the function g, and in fact the size of dimensions other than the last do not even need to be specified in the function signature, as in the signature for f.

Listing 5-28. *Passing an Array of Inconsistent Size*

```
// array_dimension_type.cpp

void f(int a[][2]) { }

void g(int a[5][2]) { }

int main()
{
    int native_2d_array[5][2];
    int native_2d_array2[15][2];

    f(native_2d_array);
    f(native_2d_array2);
    g(native_2d_array);
    g(native_2d_array2);
}
```

For managed arrays, the rank (number of dimensions) is part of the type, but not the length of the dimensions.

Arrays are passed by reference, not by value. Managed arrays are passed by reference, like any reference type, so this behavior is the same. Listing 5-29 shows how to use a managed array as a function parameter.

Listing 5-29. *Using an Array As a Parameter*

```
// arrays_parameter.cpp
using namespace System;

// using an array as an argument

void set_to_one(int i, array<int>^ array_arg)
{
    // Change the array inside this function.
    array_arg[i] = 1;
}

int main()
{
    array<int>^ array1 = { 0, 1 };
    set_to_one(0, array1);

    // The output here is " 1 1", indicating that the array
    // change is made to the same array.
    Console::WriteLine(" {0} {1}", array1[0], array1[1]);

}
```

Arrays may be used as return values just as any reference type.

Copying an Array

If you use the assignment operator with arrays, you'll create another reference to the same array. In other words, the assignment operator is a shallow copy, just as you saw with String. If you want a deep copy, you need to use the static Array::Copy method. Listing 5-30 shows how.

Listing 5-30. *Making Copies of an Array*

```
// arrays_copy.cpp
using namespace System;

int main()
{
    array<int>^ array1 = { 0, 1, 2};
```

```
  // Shallow copy creates another name for the array.
  array<int>^ array2 = array1;

  array2[0] = 100;

  // This prints "100" since array2 is a synonym of array1.
  Console::WriteLine( "{0}", array1[0] );

  array<int>^ array3 = gcnew array<int>(3);
  Array::Copy(array1, array3, array1->Length);

  // Change a value in the new copy of the array.
  array3[0] = 200;

  // This prints "100 1 2" since the old array was not affected.
  Console::WriteLine( "{0} {1} {2}", array1[0], array1[1], array1[2]);
}
```

Here is the output of Listing 5-30:

```
100
100 1 2
```

Managed Array Class Members

A managed array is actually an instance of the class System::Array. System::Array inherits from System::Object and implements IList. All managed arrays have the members shown in Tables 5-2 and 5-3.

Table 5-2. *Some Public System::Array Properties*

Property	Description
Length	Returns the number of elements in all the dimensions of the array
LongLength	Returns lengths greater than the maximum 32-bit integer, $2^{31} - 1$
Rank	Returns the number of dimensions in the array
SyncRoot	Returns an object which can be used for thread synchronization

Table 5-3. *Some Public System::Array Methods*

Name of Method	Type of Method	Description
AsReadOnly	generic, static	Returns a read-only IList generic wrapper class, ReadOnlyCollection<T>, for the array.
BinarySearch (various overloads)	static	Locates an element in a sorted 1D array.
Clear	static	Sets elements of an array to 0, NULL, or false, depending on the element type.
Clone		Creates a shallow copy of the array.
ConstrainedCopy	static	Copies a range of elements in an array, and undoes changes if the copy fails.
generic ConvertAll	generic, static	Returns a new array with every element converted to a new type.
Copy	static	Creates a deep copy of the array.
CopyTo		Copies elements from one 1D array to another 1D array or another position in the array.
CreateInstance	static	Creates an array with specified rank and size.
Equals		Tests for equality (inherited from Object). Tests reference equality, not whether elements are equal.
generic Exists	generic, static	Returns true if an array contains an element that meets the specified criteria.
generic Find	generic, static	Returns the first element in an array that matches the specified criteria.
generic FindAll	generic, static	Returns all the elements in an array that match the specified criteria.
generic FindIndex	generic, static	Like Find, but returns the index of the element, not the element itself.
generic FindLast	generic, static	Like Find, but returns the last element matching the criteria.
generic FindLastIndex	generic, static	Like FindLast, but returns the index, not the element.
generic ForEach	generic, static	Executes a specified action on each element of an array.
GetEnumerator		Returns an enumerator for iterating over the array.
GetHashCode		Returns hash code. Inherited from Object.
GetLength		Returns the length of the specified dimension of the array.
GetLongLength		Like GetLength, but supports lengths up to $2^{63} - 1$.

Table 5-3. *Some Public System::Array Methods*

Name of Method	Type of Method	Description
GetLowerBound		Returns the starting index if the array starts at an index other than zero.
GetType		Gets a Type object for this type (inherited from Object).
GetUpperBound		Gets the last index of the array.
GetValue		Gets the value of an element.
IndexOf	static	Gets the index of the first occurrence of an element in a 1D array, starting from a specified index.
Initialize		For value type arrays, initializes the array by calling the default constructor of that value type.
LastIndexOf	static	Like IndexOf, but searches from the end of the array or specified index.
generic Resize	generic, static	Changes the size of the array.
Reverse	static	Reverses the order of a 1D array (or portion of the array).
SetValue		Sets an element to the specified value.
Sort	static	Sorts a 1D array.
ToString		Returns a String representing the type. Inherited from Object.
TrueForAll	generic, static	Determines whether a condition is true for all elements in an array.

The methods implemented by the System::Array class implement the most common array operations. For example, you can sort an array by calling its Sort method. This is possible for any fundamental type or any element type that defines IComparable. Once an array is sorted, you can use some of the search functions, such as BinarySearch. Listing 5-31 shows the use of the Array methods to sort and search.

Listing 5-31. *Sorting and Searching Arrays*

```cpp
// arrays_sort_search.cpp
using namespace System;

int main()
{
    array<int>^ array1 = gcnew array<int>(10)
        { 122, 87, 99, 6, 45, 12, 987, 115, 0, 10 };
```

```
Array::Sort(array1);

for each (int i in array1)
{
    // Output is sorted.
    Console::Write("{0} ", i);
}

Console::WriteLine();

// Search for one of the values
int index = Array::BinarySearch( array1, 115);

if (index >= 0 )
    Console::WriteLine( "Found {0} at position {1}.", array1[index], index );
else
    Console::WriteLine(" Not Found. ");
}
```

The output of Listing 5-31 is as follows:

```
0 6 10 12 45 87 99 115 122 987
Found 115 at position 7.
```

Array Equality

The Equals method or the == operator tests for reference equality only. Listing 5-32 is an example of two arrays being tested for element equality by various methods, element by element.

Listing 5-32. *Testing Array Equality*

```
// array_equality_test.cpp
using namespace System;

// This function tests the equality of two 1D
// arrays of int.
bool ReallyEquals(array<int>^ a, array<int>^ b)
{
    if (a->Length != b->Length)
        return false;

    // Element-by-element comparison
    for (int i = 0; i < a->Length; i++)
    {
        if (a[i] != b[i]) return false;
    }
```

```
    return true;
}

int main()
{
    array<int>^ ai1 = gcnew array<int> { 1, 2 };
    array<int>^ ai2 = gcnew array<int> { 1, 2 };

    // Are these arrays equal?
    if ( ai1 == ai2 )
    {
        Console::WriteLine("The arrays are equal using the == operator.");
    }
    if (ai1->Equals(ai2) )
    {
        Console::WriteLine("The arrays are equal using the Equals method.");
    }
    if (ReallyEquals(ai1, ai2))
    {
        Console::WriteLine(
        "The arrays are equal using element-by-element comparison.");
    }
}
```

Here is the output of Listing 5-32:

```
The arrays are equal using element-by-element comparison.
```

Parameter Arrays

Variable argument lists are necessary whenever a function needs to handle an unknown number of optional parameters, such as an I/O function that will be passed an unknown number of variables. An array is used for these parameters, and a special syntax is used for such functions, as in Listing 5-33.

Listing 5-33. *Using Parameter Arrays*

```
// param_array.cpp
using namespace System;

// Total takes at least one int and a variable
// number of subsequent integers that are wrapped
// into a managed array.
```

```
int Total( int a, ... array<int>^ varargs)
{
    int tot = a;
    for each ( int i in varargs)
    {
        tot += i;
    }
    return tot;
}

int main()
{
    int sum1 = Total(100, 200, 350);
    Console::WriteLine("First total: {0}", sum1);

    int sum2 = Total(1, 2, 3, 4, 5, 6, 7, 8);
    Console::WriteLine("Second total: {0}", sum2);
}
```

The output of Listing 5-33 is shown here:

```
First total: 650
Second total: 36
```

Arrays in Classes

Arrays are often used as private data inside a class. Usually you will want to control access to your internal array to make sure the data it contains retains integrity. It's a bad idea to return an internal instance of an array. If you do, you lose control over the data in your array.

You may also want to create a class that can be used as an array. In classic C++ you could define the indirection operator (operator[]). In C++/CLI, you can still do that, and you can also use what's called a default indexed property, which you'll learn more about in Chapter 7.

Beyond Arrays: ArrayList

There are times when a fixed-size array will not meet your needs. Similarly, there are times when you need a data structure that you can insert items into or delete items from. Inserting and deleting items in the middle of an array is not possible without moving all the subsequent elements. For efficient deletion and insertion, use an ArrayList (see Listing 5-34). An ArrayList is like an array that supports list-like functionality. An ArrayList can grow to an undetermined length as needed.

Listing 5-34. *Using an ArrayList*

```cpp
// arraylist.cpp
using namespace System;
using namespace System::Collections;

int main()
{
   ArrayList^ array_list = gcnew ArrayList();

   array_list->Add("apple");
   array_list->Add("banana");

   // Iterate using the for each operator.
   for each (String^ s in array_list)
   {
       Console::WriteLine( s );
   }

   // Iterate using indexing.

   for (int i = 0; i < array_list->Count; i++)
   {
       Console::WriteLine("{0} {1}", i, array_list[i]);
   }
}
```

The output of Listing 5-34 is as follows:

```
apple
banana
0 apple
1 banana
```

The problem with the ArrayList class is that it represents an untyped collection. Unlike an array, which forces its elements to be of the specified type, the ArrayList used in the previous example has no such enforcement. Fortunately, there is a solution in the form of the generic ArrayList class. As you saw briefly in Chapter 2, it is possible in C++/CLI to use a generic class that contains an unknown type parameter. In the .NET Framework generic List class, in the namespace System::Collections::Generic, the element type is the generic type parameter. Using this generic List class, you can have a strongly typed version of the ArrayList (see Listing 5-35). For more information on generics, see Chapter 11.

Listing 5-35. *Using a Generic List*

```cpp
// list_generic.cpp
using namespace System;
using namespace System::Collections::Generic;

int main()
{
   List<String^>^ list = gcnew List<String^>();

   list->Add("apple");
   list->Add("banana");

   // Iterate using the for each operator.
   for each (String^ s in list)
   {
       Console::WriteLine( s );
   }

   // Iterate using indexing.

   for (int i = 0; i < list->Count; i++)
   {
       Console::WriteLine("{0} {1}", i, list[i]);
   }
}
```

The output of Listing 5-35 is also

```
apple
banana
0 apple
1 banana
```

The preceding sections reviewed the classic C++ array and compared that construct to the new C++/CLI array construct. You saw the syntax for creating and initializing arrays, and learned about copying arrays, using arrays as parameters and return values, and the usefulness of some of the functionality that C++/CLI arrays inherit from System::Array, including sorting and searching.

Next, you'll get a look at another fundamental .NET type used in C++/CLI—the Enum type (represented by System::Enum).

Enumerated Types

C++/CLI supports an enumerated type. Of course, classic C++ also supports enumerated types. There are some interesting differences between the managed enum class type and C++ enums.

In classic C++, an enum is an integer type. In C++/CLI, the enum class is also treated as an integral type but, rather like int can be boxed into an object type, and array types inherit implicitly System::Array, enum objects inherit implicitly from System::Enum, and methods available on System::Enum may be called. This inheritance relationship doesn't preclude them from being treated as integers for efficiency, however, since, like any other value type, they are only boxed into the relevant object type when needed, for example, to call a method.

The Enum Class

Enumerated types are supported in C++/CLI using the enum class (or enum structure). Enum classes have a series of static named fields that have a fixed integral value. There is no operative difference between an enum structure and class.

You saw in Chapter 2 that the enum class is used to define an enumerated type. Enumerated types are value types. The enum variable may be a handle, in which case it's a boxed value type, or it may be created on the stack. It could also be a member of a class and be part of the layout of the enclosing class. The example in Listing 5-36 shows the basic syntax for declaring and using an enum class.

Listing 5-36. *Using an Enum*

```
// enum.cpp

enum class Flavor
{
    Vanilla,
    Chocolate,
    Strawberry
};

int main()
{
    // The enum variable may be a handle
    // or a stack variable. If used as a handle,
    // it's a boxed value type.

    // The enum value, Vanilla, is
    // scoped by the enum class name.
    Flavor^ flavor_handle = Flavor::Vanilla;
    Flavor flavor_stack = Flavor::Vanilla;
}
```

Note the differences between the usage of enum class values and classic C++ enum values. Enum class values are scoped with the name of the enum class; classic C++ enum values are not scoped with the name of the enum.

Enumerated Types and Conversions

Another difference between C++/CLI enum class types and classic C++ enums is in how they are handled in conversions. The classic C++ enum is readily converted to an int. In fact, it is an int in disguise. This can be very useful, and many programming idioms use this conversion liberally. The C++/CLI enum is also an integral type in disguise, but by contrast, enum class objects must be converted to integer types explicitly.

```
// Try to convert an enum class value to int.
   int i = Flavor::Vanilla;  // Error!
```

The conversion must be made explicit with a cast, like so:

```
int i = (int) Flavor::Vanilla;
```

Stylistically, a safe_cast is preferred:

```
int i = safe_cast<int>(Flavor::Vanilla);
```

The Underlying Type of an Enum

The enum class has an underlying integral type. C++/CLI provides a way to specify this underlying type. The syntax is rather like the syntax for inheritance, in that the underlying type is used after a colon, rather like specifying a base type (see Listing 5-37).

Listing 5-37. *Specifying the Underlying Type of an Enum*

```
// enum_type_specified.cpp
using namespace System;

enum class Ordinal : char
{
    zero, one, two, three, four, five, six, seven, eight, nine, ten,
    eleven, twelve, thirteen, fourteen, fifteen, sixteen, seventeen,
    eighteen, nineteen, twenty
};

int main()
{
    char c1 = 13;
    char c2 = 156;
    Ordinal ord1 = safe_cast<Ordinal>(c1);
    Console::WriteLine(ord1.ToString());
}
```

Here is the output of Listing 5-37:

```
thirteen
```

The Flags Attribute

A typical use of enums is to define a set of independent binary values, known as *flags*, that can be combined by using the bitwise OR operator (|). The Flags attribute is intended to be used on enum classes that can be treated as a series of flags, as in Listing 5-38.

Listing 5-38. *Using the Flags Attribute*

```cpp
// enum_flags.cpp
using namespace System;

[ Flags ]
enum class FontFormat
{
    None = 0,  // No flags set.
    BOLD = 1,  // The values are set to powers of 2
    ITALIC = 2,  // so that in binary, each represents one bit position.
    UNDERLINE = 4,
    STRIKETHROUGH = 8,
    RED = 16,
    FLASHING = 32,
    BOLD_ITALIC = BOLD | ITALIC  // combination of two values
};

ref class Font
{
    public:

        property String^ Name;

        Font(String^ s) { Name = s; }
};

ref class Display
{
    public:

    static void SetFont(Font^ font, FontFormat format)
    {
        // Testing the bits of a Flags enum using the bitwise and operator (&)
        // requires a cast to int.
        if (safe_cast<int>(format) & safe_cast<int>(FontFormat::BOLD))
        {
            // Use a bold font.
        }
```

```
            if (safe_cast<int>(format) & safe_cast<int>(FontFormat::ITALIC))
            {
                // Use italics.
            }
            // etc.
        };

};

int main()
{
    // The bitwise or operator (|) combines the flag values.
    Display::SetFont(gcnew Font("Times New Roman"),
        FontFormat::BOLD | FontFormat::RED );

    Display::SetFont(gcnew Font("Helvetica"),
        FontFormat::ITALIC | FontFormat::FLASHING );
}
```

Enum Values As Strings

The enumeration value can be obtained easily as a string. An enumeration value may be passed to any of the string formatting functions, such as the Format method in the String class, or a Write or WriteLine method. The format character used after the colon determines whether it is displayed as a name, decimal number, or hex number. Possible format characters include D or d, G or g, F or f, X or x. The G or g format indicates "general," and causes the formatting to resolve to the name of the enumeration value. If the FlagsAttribute is used on the enumeration, the formatted value is a delimiter-separated list of flag names. The F or f format is similar except that the enumeration is interpreted as a flag regardless of whether the FlagsAttribute was used on the enum declaration. The other formatting characters specify numeric output in decimal (D or d) or hexadecimal (X or x). For all these formats, the case of the formatting character is ignored. You can also use the ToString method on the enumeration object. The ToString method takes the same formatting string as a parameter. Listing 5-39 provides some examples.

Listing 5-39. *Formatting Enum Values*

```
// enum_format.cpp
using namespace System;

enum class Color
{
    Red = 1,
    Blue = 2,
    Green = 3
};
```

```cpp
int main()
{
    Console::WriteLine("Colors: {0}, {1}, {2}", Color::Red, Color::Blue,
        Color::Green);
    Console::WriteLine("Colors: {0:d}, {1:d}, {2:d}", Color::Red, Color::Blue,
        Color::Green);

    Color c = Color::Red;

    String^ s1 = c.ToString("X"); // Specify the hex representation.
    Console::WriteLine( s1 );

    // Use the Format method of the Enum class.
    String^ s2 = Enum::Format( Color::typeid, c , "G");

    Console::WriteLine(s2 );
}
```

The output of Listing 5-39 is shown here:

```
Colors: Red, Blue, Green
Colors: 1, 2, 3
00000001
Red
```

This example also illustrates the use of the Format method of the System::Enum class, which is implicitly inherited by every enumeration in C++. The first argument of the Format method is the Type object for the desired enumeration type. The second argument is the enumeration value, and the third is the format specifier, which is interpreted in the same way as described for the String::Format family of methods.

For an example of how formats work with an enum with the Flags attribute specified, consider Listing 5-40, a modified version of Listing 5-39.

Listing 5-40. *Enum Formatting with the Flags Attribute*

```cpp
// enum_format2.cpp
using namespace System;

// Use the FlagsAttribute.
[ Flags ]
enum class Color
{
    Red = 1,
    Blue = 2,
    Green = 4    // Use powers of 2.
};
```

```
int main()
{
    Console::WriteLine("Colors: {0}, {1}, {2}", Color::Red, Color::Blue,
        Color::Green);
    Console::WriteLine("Colors: {0:d}, {1:d}, {2:d}", Color::Red, Color::Blue,
     Color::Green);

    // Use the bitwise OR operator to combine flags.
    Color c = Color::Red | Color::Blue;

    String^ s1 = c.ToString("X"); // Specify the hex representation.
    Console::WriteLine( s1 );

    // Use the Format method of the Enum class.
    String^ s2 = Enum::Format( Color::typeid, c , "G");

    Console::WriteLine(s2 );
}
```

The output changes to the following:

```
Colors: Red, Blue, Green
Colors: 1, 2, 4
00000003
Red, Blue
```

Summary

In this chapter, you looked at the .NET Framework special types that also have language support in C++/CLI and that are the modern versions of classic C++ types: String for character strings, .NET arrays, and .NET enumerated types. You also learned about related functionality in the .NET Framework and C++/CLI language for each of these types, such as stream I/O, the use of parameter arrays to implement variable argument lists, and the use of enums as flags.

In the next chapter, you'll study other types, classes, and structs.

CHAPTER 6

■■■

Classes and Structs

Since you already know the basics of how classes (and structs) are handled in C++, this chapter will focus on the differences between native classes and managed classes. Because the C++ type system exists intact alongside the managed type system in C++/CLI, you should keep in mind that the C++ behavior is still true and valid in C++/CLI native types.

Structs are the same as classes except that in a struct, the members are public by default, and in a class, they are private. Also, inheritance is public by default for structs, but private by default for classes. To avoid needless repetition, I will just use the term *class*, and it shall be understood to refer to both.

At a glance, the major differences are that there is more than one category of class, and that these categories of classes behave differently in many situations. Chapter 2 has already discussed this feature. There are reference types and there are value types. Native types would make a third category.

Another key difference is the inheritance model. The inheritance model supported in C++ is multiple inheritance. In C++/CLI, a restricted form of multiple inheritance is supported for managed types involving the implementation of multiple interfaces, but not multiple inheritance of classes. Only one class may be specified as the direct base type for any given class, but (for all practical purposes) an unlimited number of interfaces may be implemented. The philosophy behind this difference is explained more thoroughly in Chapter 9.

C++/CLI classes also benefit from some language support for common design patterns for properties and events. These will be discussed in detail in Chapter 7.

Due to the nature of the garbage collector, object cleanup is different in C++/CLI. Instead of just the C++ destructor, C++/CLI classes may have a destructor and/or a finalizer to handle cleanup. You'll see how these behave, how destructors behave differently from C++ native destructors, and when to define destructors and finalizers.

Also in this chapter, you'll look at managed and native classes and how you can contain a native class in a managed class and vice versa. You'll also explore a C++/CLI class that plays a Scrabble-like game to illustrate classes along with the fundamental types discussed in Chapter 5.

Much of the information in this chapter applies to value classes as well as reference classes. Value classes do not participate in inheritance, and they have different semantics when copied (as discussed in Chapter 2) and when destroyed, but otherwise they behave in a similar manner to reference types. Other than the differences mentioned in this paragraph and in Table 6-1, you should assume that the information applies equally to both value types and reference types unless stated otherwise. For reference, the differences between reference types and value types are shown in Table 6-1.

Table 6-1. *Differences Between Value Types and Reference Types*

Characteristic	Reference Type	Value Type
Storage location	On the managed heap.	On the stack or member in a structure or class.
Assignment behavior	Handle assignment creates another reference to the same object; assignment of object types copies the full object if a copy constructor exists.	Copies the object data without using a constructor.
Inheritance	Implicitly from System::Object or explicitly from exactly one reference type.	Implicitly from System::ValueType or System::Enum.
Interfaces	May implement arbitrarily many interfaces.	May implement arbitrarily many interfaces.
Constructors and destructors	A default constructor and destructor are generated, but no copy constructor (unlike native types). You can define a default constructor or constructors with parameters. You can define a default destructor.	A default constructor and destructor are generated, but no copy constructor. You cannot define your own default constructor or copy constructor. You can define constructors with parameters. You cannot define a default destructor.

Constructors and Initialization

Constructors in managed types work essentially the same way as constructors for native types. There are a few differences worth mentioning. In the constructor, you normally initialize members of the class. However, experience has taught programmers some limitations of the C++ language support for construction and initialization. For example, a lot of initialization was really class-level initialization, not instance-level initialization. C++/CLI addresses this by adding support for static constructors, which run once before a class is ever used. They are never called from code, but they are called by the runtime sometime prior to when the class is first used.

You'll also see in this chapter two new types of constant values. The first is a literal field. Literal fields are very much like static const values in a class. In this chapter, I will explain why literal fields are preferable to static const values in managed types. The second type of constant is an initonly field. An initonly field is only considered a constant value after the constructor finishes executing. This allows you to initialize it in the constructor but enforces the constancy of the variable in other code.

Value types act as if they have a default constructor, and always have a default value that is the result of calling the default constructor. In reality, the value type data is simply zeroed out. There is no actual constructor function body generated for a value type. The default constructor is created automatically, and in fact, if you try to create one, the compiler will report an error. Reference types need not implement a default constructor, although if they do not define any constructors, a default constructor is created implicitly, just as in classic C++. This constructor does not actually do any real work; the CLR automatically zeroes out any managed object upon creation without an actual constructor call.

Static Constructors

A *static constructor* or *class constructor* is a static method in a class that is called prior to when the class is first accessed. A static constructor handles any class-level initialization.

In classic C++, if you want code to run when a class is first loaded, for example, when an application starts up, you would probably define a class with a constructor and make that class a static member of another class. The static initialization for the enclosing class will invoke the constructor of the member, as in Listing 6-1.

Listing 6-1. *Using a Static Initialization*

```
// startup_code.cpp
#include <stdio.h>

class Startup
{
    public:
    Startup()
    {
        // Initialize.
        printf("Initializing module.\n");
    }
};
class N
{
    static Startup startup;

    N()
    {
        // Make use of pre-initialized state.
    }
};
```

Alternatively, you might have a static counter variable that is initialized to zero, and have code in the class constructor that checks the counter to see whether this class has ever been used before. You need to be careful about thread safety in such a function, taking care to ensure that the counter is only modified by atomic operations or locking the entire function. You could then choose to run some initialization code only when the first instance is created. C++/CLI provides language support for this common design pattern in the form of static constructors, as demonstrated in Listing 6-2.

Listing 6-2. *Using a Static Constructor*

```cpp
// static_constructor.cpp
using namespace System;

ref class C
{
  private:
    static String^ data;

  static C()
  {
      Console::WriteLine("C static constructor called.");
      data = "Initialized";
  }

public:

  C()
  {
      Console::WriteLine("C Constructor called.");
      Console::WriteLine(data);
  }

};

int main()
{
    Console::WriteLine("main method");
    C c1;
    C^ c2 = gcnew C();
}
```

Here is the output for Listing 6-2:

```
C static constructor called.
main method
C Constructor called.
Initialized
C Constructor called.
Initialized
```

The static constructor should be private and cannot take any arguments, since it is called by the runtime and cannot be called by user code.

You cannot define a static destructor; there is no such animal. This makes sense because there is no time in a program when a type is no longer available when it would make sense to call a default destructor.

Copy Constructors for Reference and Value Types

Unlike native types, reference types do not automatically get a copy constructor and an assignment operator. They may be created explicitly if required. These functions don't always make sense for reference types, which normally don't represent a value that can be copied or assigned. Value types can be copied and assigned automatically. They behave as if they have copy constructors and assignment operators that copy their values.

Literal Fields

In managed classes, const fields are not seen as constant when invoked using the #using directive. You can initialize constant values that will be seen as constants even when invoked in that way by declaring them with the literal modifier. The literal field so created has the same visibility rules as a static field and is a compile-time constant value that cannot be changed. It is declared as in Listing 6-3.

Listing 6-3. *Declaring Literals*

```
ref class Scrabble
{
    // Literals are constants that can be initialized in the class body.
    literal int TILE_COUNT = 100;   // the number of tiles altogether
    literal int TILES_IN_HAND = 7;  // the number of tiles in each hand

    // ...

};
```

A literal field is allowed to have an initializer right in the class declaration. The value initialized must be computable at compile time. literal is added as a modifier in the same position that static would appear, that is, after other modifiers (see Listing 6-4) but before the variable name; literal is considered a storage class specifier.

Listing 6-4. *Initializing a Literal*

```
// literal.cpp
using namespace System;

ref class C
{
    literal String^ name = "Bob";

    public:
```

```
    C()
    {
        Console::WriteLine(name);
    }

    void Print()
    {
        Console::WriteLine(name);
    }
};

int main()
{
    C^ c = gcnew C();
    c->Print();
}
```

You can use literal values (e.g., 100 or 'a'), string literals, compile-time constants, and previously defined literal fields in the initialization of literal fields. Literal fields are not static; do not use the keyword static for them. However, because they are not instance data, they may be accessed through the class like a static field, as in Listing 6-5.

Listing 6-5. *Accessing Literals*

```
// literal_public.cpp
using namespace System;

ref class C
{
    public:

    literal String^ name = "Bob";

    C()
    {
        Console::WriteLine(name);
    }

    void Print()
    {
        Console::WriteLine(name);
    }
};
```

```
int main()
{
    C^ c = gcnew C();
    c->Print();

    // Access through the class:
    Console::WriteLine( C::name );
}
```

Literal fields are needed because of a limitation in how the compiler is able to interpret static constant fields that are imported into an application from a compiled assembly with the #using statement. The compiler is unable to consider static constant fields compile-time constants. Literal fields are marked in a different way in the assembly and are identifiable as compile-time constants, so they are allowed wherever a compile-time constant value is needed, such as in nontype template arguments and in native array sizes. Listing 6-6 shows a simple class in which both a static constant and a literal member are declared and initialized, and Listing 6-7 shows how they differ in behavior when used in another assembly.

Listing 6-6. *Defining Static Constants and Literals*

```
// static_const_vs_literal.cpp
// compile with: cl /clr /LD static_const_vs_literal.cpp

public ref class R
{
    public:
        static const int i = 15;
        literal int j = 25;
};
```

Listing 6-7. *Compiling Static Constants and Literals*

```
// static_const_main.cpp

#using "static_const_vs_literal.dll"

template<int i>
void f()
{ }

int main()
{
    int a1[R::i]; // Error: static const R::i isn't considered a constant.
    int a2[R::j]; // OK

    f<R::i>();  // Error
    f<R::j>();  // OK
}
```

As you can see, the static constant value is not interpreted as a compile-time constant when referenced in another assembly.

```
Microsoft (R) C/C++ Optimizing Compiler Version 14.00.50727.42
for Microsoft (R) .NET Framework version 2.00.50727.42
Copyright (C) Microsoft Corporation.  All rights reserved.

static_const_main.cpp
static_const_main.cpp(13) : error C2057: expected constant expression
static_const_main.cpp(13) : error C2466: cannot allocate an array of constant si
ze 0
static_const_main.cpp(13) : error C2133: 'a1' : unknown size
static_const_main.cpp(16) : error C2975: 'i' : invalid template argument for 'f'
, expected compile-time constant expression
        static_const_main.cpp(5) : see declaration of 'i'
```

On the other hand, if you include the same code as source rather than reference the built assembly, static const is interpreted using the standard C++ rules.

initonly Fields

Now suppose we have a constant value that cannot be computed at compile time. Instead of marking it literal, we use initonly. A field declared initonly can be modified only in the constructor (or static constructor). This makes it useful in situations where using const would prevent the initialization code from compiling (see Listing 6-8).

Listing 6-8. *Using an initonly Field*

```
// initonly.cpp
using namespace System;

ref class R
{
   initonly String^ name;

   public:

   R(String^ first, String^ last)
   {
       name = first + last;
   }
```

```
    void Print()
    {
        name = "Bob Jones";        // Error!
        Console::WriteLine(name);  // OK
    }
};

int main()
{
    R^ r = gcnew R("Mary", "Colburn");
    r->Print();
}
```

The compilation output is for Listing 6-8 is as follows:

```
Microsoft (R) C/C++ Optimizing Compiler Version 14.00.50727.42
for Microsoft (R) .NET Framework version 2.00.50727.42
Copyright (C) Microsoft Corporation.  All rights reserved.

initonly.cpp
initonly.cpp(17) : error C3893: 'R::name' : l-value use of initonly data member
is only allowed in an instance constructor of class 'R'
```

An initializer is allowed if the initonly field is static, as demonstrated in Listing 6-9.

Listing 6-9. *Initializing a Static initonly Field*

```
// initonly_static_cpp
using namespace System;

ref class R
{
    public:

    static initonly String^ name = "Ralph";  // OK
    // initonly String^ name = "Bob"; // Error!

    // rest of class declaration
};
```

The initonly modifier can appear before or after the static modifier.

Const Correctness

In classic C++, a method can be declared const, which enforces that the method does not affect the value of any data in the object, for example:

```
class N
{
    void f() const { /* code which does not modify the object data */}
};
```

This is an important element of *const correctness*, a design idiom in which operations that work on constant objects are consistently marked const, ensuring that programming errors in which a modification is attempted on a const object can be detected at compile time.

Const correctness is an important part of developing robust C++ code, in which errors are detected at compile time, not at runtime. Proper const parameter types and return values go a long way to prevent common programming errors, even without true const correctness in the classic C++ sense. Even so, many C++ programmers do not use const correctness, either because the codebase they are working on did not implement it from the ground up, or because the amount of extra time to design it correctly was too great a price to pay in the results-oriented corporate world. In that sense, full const correctness is like flossing one's teeth. For those who do it, it's unthinkable not to do it. For those who don't, it's just too much hassle, even though they may know deep down that they should do it.

In general, const correctness works well only if all parts of a library implement it consistently. Anyone who's ever tried to retrofit an existing library with const correctness knows this, since anytime you add const in one location, it often requires const to be added in several other locations. Like it or not, the CLI is not designed from the ground up to enable full const correctness in the classic C++ sense. Other CLI languages do not support full C++-style const correctness. Since the .NET Framework isn't implemented with C++ const correctness in mind, attempting to support full C++ const correctness in C++/CLI would be an exercise in futility and force programmers to use const_cast to cast away const when using .NET Framework functionality. Hence, C++/CLI does not support const methods on managed types. At one point early in the development of the C++/CLI language, this support was included, but the results were ugly and nearly unusable, so the effort was dropped. While this knocks out one of the pillars of const correctness, C++/CLI does support const parameter types and return values, and, although they are not alone enough to enforce const correctness, they at least enable many common const correctness errors to be detected at compile time.

Properties, Events, and Operators

Properties represent the "has-a" relationship for a member of a class. They behave as and are used like public fields of a class, except that they have a public interface that is separate from the private implementation, thus enabling data encapsulation. Events encapsulate behavior of a class in response to some stimulus or triggering condition; operators are a classic C++ feature that is extended in C++/CLI. Properties, events, and operators are covered in the next chapter.

Example: A Scrabble Game

Let's look at an extended example combining all the language features covered in detail so far: a simple Scrabble game with Console output (see Listing 6-10). Scrabble is one of my favorite games. I used to play with my family as a kid (back when, for some unknown reason, we thought playing "antitelephonebooth" would be a cool idea). I played so much I thought I was a hotshot Scrabble player, that is, until I subscribed to the *Scrabble Players Newsletter* and found out that I was definitely still at the amateur level. I discovered that there are people who know the *Official Scrabble Player's Dictionary* from front to back by heart and play obscure combinations of letters that only the initiated know are real words. They may not know what they mean, but they sure know their potential for scoring points. Anyway, the game is interesting to us because it involves several arrays, and copious use of string, so, in addition to demonstrating a functioning class, it will provide a review of the last few chapters. We will implement the full game, but implementing the dictionary and the computer player AI are left as exercises for you to try on your own. Also, we will implement this as a console-based game, and players are asked to enter the location of their plays using the hex coordinates. Yes, I know it's geeky. You could also write an interface for this using Windows Forms, another exercise left for you to try as you like.

There are a few things to notice about the implementation. The Scrabble game is one class, and we define some helper classes: Player and Tile. Player and Tile are both reference classes as well. You might think that Tile could be a value class. In fact, it's better as a reference class because in the two-dimensional array of played tiles, the unplayed tiles will be null handles. If we were to create a 2D array of value types, there would be no natural null value for an unoccupied space.

The basic memory scheme is illustrated in Figure 6-1. We use both lists and arrays. We use arrays for the gameboard, since it never changes size. The bag of tiles and the players' racks of tiles are implemented as lists since they may fluctuate in size. You'll see that we copy the list and the arrays into a temporary variable that we use as the play is being formulated. Once the play is final, the changed version is copied back into the original list or array. The former is a deep copy since we're creating a version we can modify. The latter is a shallow copy. The reference is changed to point to the modified object. It's useful to examine this code—see the treatment of the variable workingTiles and workingBoard in the PlayerMove function. Another thing to notice about the arrays is that the array of tiles on the board is an array of handles. You'll see that it starts off as an array of null handles, and as tiles are played, the handles are set to actual objects.

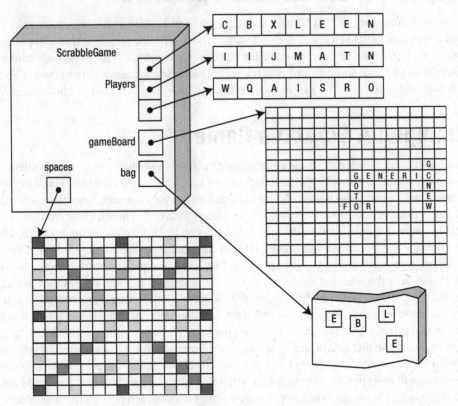

Figure 6-1. *The memory layout of some features in the Scrabble game program*

You'll also notice a few additional features of the Console class that are used: the background color and foreground color. We will restrain ourselves from using the Console::Beep method.

Listing 6-10. *The Scrabble Program*

```cpp
// Scrabble.cpp

using namespace System;
using namespace System::Collections::Generic;

enum class Characters { NEWLINE = 13 };

// Letter represents the different tile letters and the blank, represented
// by _
enum class Letter { _ = 0, A, B, C, D, E, F, G, H, I, J, K, L, M, N, O, P, Q, R, S,
T, U, V, W, X, Y, Z };
```

```cpp
// PlayType represents the direction of play: across, down, or pass.
enum class PlayType { Across, Down, Pass };

// The types of spaces on the board.
// DLS == Double Letter Score
// DWS == Double Word Score
// TLS == Triple Letter Score
// TWS == Triple Word Score
enum class SpaceType { Normal = 0, DLS = 1, DWS = 2, TLS = 3, TWS = 4, Center = 5 };

// A Scrabble Tile contains a letter and a fixed point value
// that depends on the letter. We also include a property for the
// letter that a blank tile represents once it is played.
// Tiles are not the same as board spaces: tiles are placed into
// board spaces as play goes on.
ref struct Tile
{
    property Letter LetterValue;
    property int PointValue;
    property Char BlankValue;

    // This array contains the static point values of each tile
    // in alphabetical order, starting with the blank.
    static array<int>^ point_values =
    {0, 1, 3, 3, 2, 1, 4, 2, 4, 1, 8, 5, 1, 2, 1, 1, 3, 10, 1, 1, 1, 1,
    4, 3, 8, 4, 10};

    // The Tile constructor initializes the tile from its letter
    // and the point value.
    Tile(Letter letter)
    {
        LetterValue = letter;
        PointValue = point_values[ safe_cast<int>( letter )];
    }

    // Used when displaying the tile on the gameboard
    virtual String^ ToString() override
    {
        // Format(LetterValue) won't work because the compiler
        // won't be able to identify the right overload when the
        // type is an enum class.
        return String::Format("{0}", LetterValue);
    }
};
```

```cpp
ref struct Player
{
    int number; // number specifying which player this is

    List<Tile^>^ tiles; // the player's rack of tiles

    // The number of tiles in the player's rack is
    // normally 7, but may be fewer at the end of the game.
    property int TileCount
    {
        int get() { return tiles->Count; }
    }

    property String^ Name; // the name of the player

    property int Score; // the player's cumulative point total

    // the constructor
    Player(String^ s, int n) : number(n)
    {
        Name = s;
        Score = 0;
        Console::WriteLine("Player {0} is {1}.", n, Name);
    }

    // Display the player's rack of tiles.
    void PrintPlayerTiles()
    {
        Console::WriteLine("Tiles in hand: ");
        for (int j = 0; j < TileCount; j++)
        {
            Console::Write("{0} ", tiles[j]->ToString());
        }
        Console::WriteLine();
    }
};

// This class is the main class including all the functionality
// and data for a Scrabble game.
ref class ScrabbleGame
{
    // Literals are constants that can be initialized in the class body.
    literal int TILE_COUNT = 100;  // the number of tiles altogether
    literal int MAX_TILES_IN_HAND = 7;  // the maximum number of tiles in each hand
```

```
// the array of players
array<Player^>^ players;

// spaces is the array of board spaces.
static array<int, 2>^ spaces = gcnew array<int, 2>
{ { 4, 0, 0, 1, 0, 0, 0, 4, 0, 0, 0, 1, 0, 0, 4 },
  { 0, 2, 0, 0, 0, 3, 0, 0, 0, 3, 0, 0, 0, 2, 0 },
  { 0, 0, 2, 0, 0, 0, 1, 0, 1, 0, 0, 0, 2, 0, 0 },
  { 1, 0, 0, 2, 0, 0, 0, 1, 0, 0, 0, 2, 0, 0, 1 },
  { 0, 0, 0, 0, 2, 0, 0, 0, 0, 0, 2, 0, 0, 0, 0 },
  { 0, 3, 0, 0, 0, 3, 0, 0, 0, 3, 0, 0, 0, 3, 0 },
  { 0, 0, 1, 0, 0, 0, 1, 0, 1, 0, 0, 0, 1, 0, 0 },
  { 4, 0, 0, 1, 0, 0, 0, 5, 0, 0, 0, 1, 0, 0, 4 },
  { 0, 0, 1, 0, 0, 0, 1, 0, 1, 0, 0, 0, 1, 0, 0 },
  { 0, 3, 0, 0, 0, 3, 0, 0, 0, 3, 0, 0, 0, 3, 0 },
  { 0, 0, 0, 0, 2, 0, 0, 0, 0, 0, 2, 0, 0, 0, 0 },
  { 1, 0, 0, 2, 0, 0, 0, 1, 0, 0, 0, 2, 0, 0, 1 },
  { 0, 0, 2, 0, 0, 0, 1, 0, 1, 0, 0, 0, 2, 0, 0 },
  { 0, 2, 0, 0, 0, 3, 0, 0, 0, 3, 0, 0, 0, 2, 0 },
  { 4, 0, 0, 1, 0, 0, 0, 4, 0, 0, 0, 1, 0, 0, 4 }};

// spaceTypeColors tell us how to draw the tiles when displaying the
// board at the console.
static initonly array<ConsoleColor>^ spaceTypeColors = { ConsoleColor::Gray,
    ConsoleColor::Cyan, ConsoleColor::Red, ConsoleColor::Blue,
    ConsoleColor::DarkRed, ConsoleColor::Red };

// the gameboard representing all played tiles
array<Tile^, 2>^ gameBoard;

// the bag, containing the tiles that have not yet been drawn
List<Tile^>^ bag;

// an array of the amount of each tile
static initonly array<int>^ tilePopulation = gcnew array<int>
{ 2, 9, 2, 2, 4, 12, 2, 3, 2, 9, 1, 1, 4, 2, 6, 8, 2, 1, 6, 4, 6, 4, 2, 2, 1, 2,
  1 };

int nPlayer; // the number of players in this game
int playerNum; // the current player
int moveNum;  // count of the number of moves
Random^ random; // a random number generator
bool gameOver;  // set to true when a condition results in the end of the game
bool endBonus; // true at the end of the game when a player uses up all of
// his or her tiles
```

```cpp
    // pass_count counts the number of consecutive passes
    // (when players do not make a play).
    // This is used to find out if everyone passes one after the other,
    // in which case the game is over.
    int pass_count;

    // There are 15 spaces in the board. These constants are used in the static
    // constructor to create the board using symmetry.
    literal int BOARD_SIZE = 15;
    literal int BOARD_SIZEM1 = BOARD_SIZE - 1;
    literal int BOARD_MID = 7;
    literal int TILE_TYPES = 27;

public:
    // The instance constructor creates the array of players
    // and the tile bag, which would have to be re-created for
    // each game.
    ScrabbleGame(unsigned int numPlayers) : nPlayer(numPlayers)
    {
        moveNum = 0;
        random = gcnew Random();
        // Create the players.
        players = gcnew array<Player^>(numPlayers);
        for (unsigned int i = 0; i < numPlayers; i++)
        {
            Console::Write("Player {0} enter name: ", i);
            String^ s = Console::ReadLine();
            players[i] = gcnew Player(s, i);
        }
        // Initialize the bag tiles.
        bag = gcnew List<Tile^>(TILE_COUNT);
        for (int i = 0; i < TILE_TYPES; i++)
        {
            for (int j = 0; j < tilePopulation[i]; j++)
            {
                Letter letter = safe_cast<Letter>(i);
                bag->Add(gcnew Tile(letter));
            }
        }
        // The gameboard consists of an array of null pointers initially.
        gameBoard = gcnew array<Tile^, 2>(BOARD_SIZE, BOARD_SIZE);
    }
```

```
// Display the current scores and tiles in the bag or
// in each player's rack.
void PrintScores()
{
    Console::Write("Current stats: ");
    if (bag->Count != 0)
    {
        Console::WriteLine("{0} tiles remaining in tile bag.", bag->Count);
    }
    else
    {
        Console::WriteLine("No tiles remaining in tile bag.");
    }

    for (int i = 0; i < nPlayer; i++)
    {
        Console::WriteLine("{0,-10} -- Score: {1,3} Number of tiles: {2} -- ",
            players[i]->Name, players[i]->Score, players[i]->TileCount);
    }
}

// Display the permanent gameboard (overload).
void PrintBoard()
{
    PrintBoard(gameBoard);
}

// Display the gameboard. This overload takes a board
// as an argument, so it is possible to display the proposed
// play before committing it to the permanent gameboard.
void PrintBoard(array<Tile^, 2>^ board)
{
    Console::WriteLine();
    Console::Write("    ");
    for (int i = 0; i < BOARD_SIZE; i++)
        Console::Write(" {0:X1} ", i);
    Console::WriteLine();
    for (int i = 0; i < BOARD_SIZE; i++)
    {
        Console::Write(" {0:X1} ", i);
        for (int j = 0; j < BOARD_SIZE; j++)
        {
```

```
          if (board[i, j] == nullptr)
          {
             Console::BackgroundColor = spaceTypeColors[spaces[i, j]];
             Console::Write("   ");
             // The foreground and background colors are restored to
             // the colors that existed when the current process began.
             Console::ResetColor();
          }
          else
          {
             Console::BackgroundColor = ConsoleColor::Black;
             Console::ForegroundColor = ConsoleColor::White;
             Letter letter = board[i, j]->LetterValue;
             if (letter == Letter::_)
             {
                Console::Write(" {0:1} ", board[i,j]->BlankValue);
             }
             else
             {
                Console::Write(" {0:1} ", board[i, j]);
             }
             Console::ResetColor();
          }
       }
       Console::WriteLine();
    }
    Console::WriteLine();
}


// Draw a tile from the bag and return it.
// Returns null if the bag is empty.
// The parameter keep is true if the tile is drawn during the game,
// false if the tile is drawn at the beginning of the game
// to see who goes first.
Tile^ DrawTile(bool keep)
{
   if (bag->Count == 0) // Return nullptr if there are no tiles left.
   {
      return nullptr;
   }
   int random_index = safe_cast<int>((random->NextDouble() * bag->Count) );
   Tile^ tile = bag[random_index];
   if (keep)
      bag->RemoveAt(random_index);
   return tile;
}
```

```
// Determine who goes first and draw tiles. Each player draws
// a tile and whoever has the letter closest to the beginning of
// the alphabet goes first. Return the player number of the first
// player.
int PreGame()
{
    Console::WriteLine("Each player draws a tile to see who goes first.\n"
        "The player closest to the beginning of the alphabet goes first.");
    // Each player draws one tile to see who goes first. If both players
    // draw the same tile, everyone redraws.
    array<Tile^>^ drawTiles = gcnew array<Tile^>(nPlayer);
    bool firstPlayerFound = false;
    int firstPlayerIndex = 0;
    do
    {

        for (int i = 0; i < nPlayer; i++)
        {
            drawTiles[i] = DrawTile(false);
            Console::WriteLine("{0} draws {1}.", players[i]->Name,
                drawTiles[i]->LetterValue);
            if (i > 0 && drawTiles[i]->LetterValue <
                drawTiles[firstPlayerIndex]->LetterValue)
            {
                firstPlayerIndex = i;
            }
        }
        firstPlayerFound = true;

        // If someone else has the same tile, throw back and redraw.
        for (int i = 0; i < nPlayer; i++)
        {
            if (i == firstPlayerIndex)
                continue;
            if (drawTiles[i]->LetterValue ==
                drawTiles[firstPlayerIndex]->LetterValue)
            {
                Console::WriteLine("Duplicate tile {0}. Redraw.",
                    drawTiles[i]->LetterValue);
                firstPlayerFound = false;
            }
        }
    } while (! firstPlayerFound );
    Console::WriteLine("{0} goes first.", players[firstPlayerIndex]->Name );
```

```cpp
        // Everyone draws their tiles.
        for (int i = 0; i < nPlayer; i++)
        {
            players[i]->tiles = gcnew List<Tile^>(MAX_TILES_IN_HAND);
            for (int j = 0; j < MAX_TILES_IN_HAND; j++)
            {
                players[i]->tiles->Add( DrawTile(true));
            }
            Console::Write("{0} draws tiles: ", players[i]->Name, i);
            for (int j = 0; j < MAX_TILES_IN_HAND; j++)
            {
                Console::Write("{0} ", players[i]->tiles[j]->ToString());
            }
            Console::WriteLine();
        }
        return firstPlayerIndex;
    }


    // Play plays the game from start to finish
    // return the winning player.
    Player^ Play(int firstPlayer)
    {
        playerNum = firstPlayer;
        gameOver = false;
        do
        {
            gameOver = PlayerMove();
            playerNum = ( playerNum + 1 ) % nPlayer;
            PrintScores();
            Console::WriteLine("Press ENTER to continue...");
            Console::ReadLine();
            Console::Clear();
            moveNum++;
        } while (! gameOver);

        // The game is over.
        AdjustPointTotals();
        Console::WriteLine("Final scores: ");
        PrintScores();
        int winningPlayer = FindWinner();
        if (winningPlayer != -1)
        {
            return players[winningPlayer];
        }
        else return nullptr;
    }
```

```cpp
// At the end of the game, point totals are adjusted according to
// the following scheme: all players lose the point total of any
// unplayed tiles; if a player plays all her tiles, she
// receives the point totals of all unplayed tiles.
void AdjustPointTotals()
{
   int total_point_bonus = 0;
   for (int i=0; i < nPlayer; i++)
   {
      if (players[i]->TileCount > 0)
      {
         Console::WriteLine("{0} remaining tiles and score adjustments: ",
             players[i]->Name);
         int point_deduction = 0;
         for each (Tile^ t in players[i]->tiles)
         {
            Console::Write(" {0} -{1}  ", t->LetterValue, t->PointValue);
            point_deduction += t->PointValue;
         }
         Console::WriteLine();
         players[i]->Score -= point_deduction;
         total_point_bonus += point_deduction;
      }
   }
   if (endBonus)
   {
      Console::WriteLine("{0}'s bonus for using the last tile is {1}.",
          players[playerNum]->Name, total_point_bonus);
      players[playerNum]->Score += total_point_bonus;
   }
}


// Find out which player won.
int FindWinner()
{
   if (! gameOver)
   {
      return -1;
   }
   int leadingPlayer = 0;
   for (int i = 1; i < nPlayer; i++)
   {
      if (players[i]->Score > players[leadingPlayer]->Score)
      {
         leadingPlayer = i;
      }
   }
```

```
        for (int i = 0; i < nPlayer; i++)
        {
            // Check for a tie.
            if (i != leadingPlayer && players[i]->Score ==
                    players[leadingPlayer]->Score)
            {
                return -1;
            }
        }
        return leadingPlayer;
    }


    // Implement a pass move in which a player throws back a certain
    // number of her tiles and draws new ones.
    // Return true if successful.
    bool Pass(List<Tile^>^ workingTiles)
    {
        if (bag->Count != 0)
        {
            int code;
            // Get the desired tiles to replace to
            // the bag from the user.
            Console::WriteLine("Enter tiles to throw back: ");
            do
            {
                code = Console::Read();
                wchar_t character = safe_cast<wchar_t>(code);
                Letter letter = Letter::_;
                if (character == safe_cast<wchar_t>(Characters::NEWLINE))
                {
                    Console::ReadLine();
                    break;
                }
                if (character == '_')
                {
                    letter = Letter::_;
                }
                else if (Char::IsLetter(character))
                {
                    if (Char::IsUpper(character))
                    {
                        letter = safe_cast<Letter>(character - 'A' + 1);
                    }
                    else // character is a lowercase letter.
                    {
                        letter = safe_cast<Letter>(character - 'a' + 1);
                    }
                }
```

```cpp
                // See if the letter is in the player's hand.
                Tile^ tile = gcnew Tile(letter);
                Tile^ tileToRemove = nullptr;
                bool tileFound = false;
                for each (Tile^ t in workingTiles)
                {
                   if (t->LetterValue == tile->LetterValue)
                   {
                      tileToRemove = t;
                      tileFound = true;
                      break;
                   }
                }
                if ( tileFound == true)
                {
                   workingTiles->Remove( tileToRemove );
                   bag->Add(tile);
                }
                else // The letter was not found.
                {
                   Console::WriteLine("You do not have enough {0}s to pass back.",
                      letter);
                   Console::WriteLine("Press any key to continue...");
                   Console::ReadLine();
                   return false;
                }
           } while (code != safe_cast<int>('\n'));
   } // if bag->Count == 0

   Console::Write("Are you sure you want to pass (Y/N)?");
   String^ response = Console::ReadLine();
   if (response->StartsWith( "Y") || response->StartsWith("y"))
   {
       if (bag->Count > 0)
       {
          Console::Write("{0} draws tiles: ", players[playerNum]->Name);
          // Copy the working tiles to the player tiles.
          players[playerNum]->tiles = workingTiles;
          while ( players[playerNum]->tiles->Count < MAX_TILES_IN_HAND)
          {
             Tile^ tile = DrawTile(true);
             if (tile != nullptr)
             {
                players[playerNum]->tiles->Add(tile);
                Console::Write(" {0} ", tile->ToString());
             }
```

```
                else // The bag is empty.
                {
                    Console::WriteLine("\nThe tile bag is empty.");
                    break;
                }
            }
            Console::WriteLine();
        }
    }
    else
    {
        // A false return will indicate that the user has
        // changed his/her mind and may not want to pass.
        return false;
    }
    return true;
}

private:
    PlayType GetPlayType()
    {
        // Input the direction to play.
        Console::WriteLine(
        "Enter Direction to Play (A = across, D = down) or P to pass:");
        String^ playTypeString = Console::ReadLine();

        if (playTypeString == "P")
        {
            return PlayType::Pass;
        }
        if (playTypeString == "A")
        {
            return PlayType::Across;
        }
        else if (playTypeString == "D")
        {
            return PlayType::Down;
        }
        else
        {
            Console::WriteLine("Sorry, I didn't understand that input.");
            throw gcnew Exception();
        }
    }
```

```cpp
// Get the position of the start of the play on the board.
bool GetPlayStartPosition(int% row, int% col)
{
    // Input the row and column of the first letter.
    Console::Write(
    "Enter Location to Play as [row][col]: 00 (top left) to EE (bottom right): ");
    String^ locString = Console::ReadLine();

    // Parse as a hex number.
    int x = Int32::Parse(locString,
        System::Globalization::NumberStyles::HexNumber);
    row = x / 16;
    col = x % 16;
    if (row > 14 || col > 14 || row < 0 || col < 0)
    {
        Console::WriteLine("I did not understand that input.");
        Console::WriteLine("The first digit is the row (0 to E);"
            " the second is the column (0 to E).");
        throw gcnew Exception();
    }

    // Check to see that this is an unoccupied space.
    if (gameBoard[row, col] != nullptr)
    {
        Console::WriteLine("Sorry, that space is occupied by the tile: {0}",
            gameBoard[row, col]);
        return false;
    }
    return true;
}

// Return true if the play is successful.
// Return false if the play is invalid and needs to be restarted.
bool GetTilesForPlay(int row, int col, PlayType playType,
                    List<Tile^>^ workingTiles, array<Tile^, 2>^ workingBoard )
{
    // Get the desired tiles to play from the user.
    Console::WriteLine(
        "Enter letters to play (_<letter> to play a blank as <letter>): ");
    int code;
```

```cpp
do
{
    code = Console::Read();
    wchar_t character = safe_cast<wchar_t>(code);
    Letter letter = Letter::_;
    if (character == safe_cast<wchar_t>(Characters::NEWLINE))
    {
        Console::ReadLine();
        break;
    }
    if (character == '_')
    {
        letter = Letter::_;
        // If a blank is entered, read the next character.
        code = Console::Read();
        character = safe_cast<wchar_t>(code);
    }
    else if (Char::IsLetter(character))
    {
        if (Char::IsUpper(character))
        {
            letter = safe_cast<Letter>(character - 'A' + 1);
        }
        else // character is a lowercase letter.
        {
            letter = safe_cast<Letter>(character - 'a' + 1);
        }
    }

    // See if the letter is in the player's hand.
    Tile^ tile = gcnew Tile(letter);
    if (letter == Letter::_)
    {
        tile->BlankValue = character;
    }
    Tile^ tileToRemove = nullptr;
    bool tileFound = false;
    for each (Tile^ t in workingTiles)
    {
        if (t->LetterValue == tile->LetterValue)
        {
            tileToRemove = t;
            tileFound = true;
        }
    }
```

```
        if ( tileFound )
        {
            workingTiles->Remove( tileToRemove );
            workingBoard[row, col] = tile;
            if (playType == PlayType::Across)
            {
                while (col < BOARD_SIZE && workingBoard[row, col] != nullptr)
                {
                    col++;
                }
                // We've reached the end of the board, so the play is complete.
                if (col == BOARD_SIZE)
                {
                    // Consume any additional input.
                    Console::ReadLine();
                    return true;
                }
            }
            else
            {
                while (row < BOARD_SIZE && workingBoard[row, col] != nullptr)
                {
                    row++;
                }
                if (row == BOARD_SIZE)
                {
                    // Consume any additional input.
                    Console::ReadLine();
                    return true;
                }
            }
        }
        else // The letter was not found.
        {
            Console::WriteLine("You do not have enough {0}s to play.", letter);
            // Consume any additional character input.
            Console::ReadLine();
            return false;
        }

    } while (code != safe_cast<int>('\n'));

    return true;
}
```

```
// Return true if the player accepts the play.
bool ConfirmPlay(int score)
{
    Console::WriteLine("This play is worth {0} points.", score);
    Console::Write("Is this your final play (Y/N)?");
    String^ response = Console::ReadLine();
    if (response->StartsWith( "Y") || response->StartsWith("y"))
    {
        // Reset the pass count.
        pass_count = 0;
        return true;
    }
    return false;
}

// Return the number of tiles drawn.
int ReplacePlayedTiles()
{
    int count = 0;
    Console::Write("{0} draws tiles: ", players[playerNum]->Name);

    while ( players[playerNum]->tiles->Count < MAX_TILES_IN_HAND)
    {
        Tile^ tile = DrawTile(true);
        if (tile != nullptr)
        {
            count++;
            players[playerNum]->tiles->Add(tile);
            Console::Write(" {0} ", tile->ToString());
        }
        else // The bag is empty.
        {
            Console::WriteLine("\nThe tile bag is empty.");
            return count;
        }
    }
    Console::WriteLine();
    return count;
}
// Commit the confirmed play to the permanent gameboard.
void RecordPlay(List<Tile^>^ workingTiles, array<Tile^, 2>^ workingBoard)
{
    // Copy the working tiles to the player tiles.
    players[playerNum]->tiles = workingTiles;
```

```
        // Copy the working board to the board.
        for (int i = 0; i <BOARD_SIZE; i++)
        {
            for (int j = 0; j <BOARD_SIZE; j++)
            {
                gameBoard[i, j] = workingBoard[i, j];
            }
        }
    }


    // Update a player's score.
    // Return the new point total.
    int UpdateScore(int playerNum, int scoreForPlay)
    {
        // Increment the player's score.
        players[playerNum]->Score += scoreForPlay;
        return players[playerNum]->Score;
    }

    array<Tile^, 2>^ GetWorkingBoard()
    {
        array<Tile^, 2>^ workingBoard = gcnew array<Tile^, 2>(BOARD_SIZE, BOARD_SIZE);
        // Copy the board into a working board.
        for (int i = 0; i < BOARD_SIZE; i++)
        {
            for (int j = 0; j < BOARD_SIZE; j++)
            {
                workingBoard[i, j] = gameBoard[i, j];
            }
        }
        return workingBoard;
    }


    List<Tile^>^ GetWorkingTiles()
    {
        List<Tile^>^ workingTiles = gcnew List<Tile^>(MAX_TILES_IN_HAND);
        // Copy each tile into a working hand.
        for each(Tile^ t in players[playerNum]->tiles)
        {
            workingTiles->Add(t);
        }
        return workingTiles;
    }
```

```cpp
public:

    // PlayerMove implements a player making a play.
    // Return true if the game is over.
    bool PlayerMove()
    {
        bool gameOver = false;
        bool moveComplete = false;

        while (! moveComplete)
        {
            try
            {
                List<Tile^>^ workingTiles = GetWorkingTiles();
                array<Tile^, 2>^ workingBoard = GetWorkingBoard();
                PrintBoard();
                Console::WriteLine("{0}'s turn.", players[playerNum]->Name);
                players[playerNum]->PrintPlayerTiles();

                PlayType playType = GetPlayType();

                if ( playType == PlayType::Pass)
                {
                    moveComplete = Pass(workingTiles);
                    if (moveComplete)
                    {
                        // The pass was completed.
                        pass_count++;
                        // If everyone passes and the bag is empty, the game ends.
                        if (pass_count == nPlayer && bag->Count == 0)
                        {
                            gameOver = true;
                        }
                        return gameOver;
                    }
                    else
                    {
                        // The pass was cancelled, restart play.
                        continue;
                    }
                }
                int row, col;
                if (! GetPlayStartPosition(row, col))
                    continue;
                if (! GetTilesForPlay(row, col, playType, workingTiles, workingBoard))
                    continue;
```

```
        // Calculate the score.
        int scoreForPlay = CalculateScore(row, col, playType, workingBoard);
        PrintBoard(workingBoard);
        if (scoreForPlay == -1)
        {
            Console::WriteLine("The move is not a legal move.");
            if (moveNum == 0)
            {
                Console::WriteLine("The first play must use the center square.");
            }
            else
            {
                Console::WriteLine(
                "You must use at least one existing tile on the board.");
            }
            Console::WriteLine();
            continue;
        }

        if (!ConfirmPlay(scoreForPlay))
            continue;

        RecordPlay(workingTiles, workingBoard);

        // If more tiles are in the bag, draw tiles to replace those played.
        if (bag->Count > 0)
        {
            ReplacePlayedTiles();
        }

        // The game ends when a player "goes out" -- she uses up all
        // the tiles in her hand and there are none in the bag.
        // The player is eligible for the end game bonus.
        if (bag->Count == 0 && players[playerNum]->tiles->Count == 0)
        {
            endBonus = true;
            gameOver = true;
        }
        UpdateScore(playerNum, scoreForPlay);
        moveComplete = true;
    }
    catch(Exception^)
    {
        moveComplete = false;
    }
    }
    return gameOver;
}
```

```
// This function calculates the score for a move, if the move is a legal play.
// If the move is not legal, return -1.
int CalculateScore(int row, int col, PlayType direction,
                   array<Tile^, 2>^ newBoard)
{
    int cumScore = 0;
    PlayType crossDirection;

    int wordScore = 0;
    bool letterBonus = false;
    bool wordBonus = false;
    int letterMultiplier = 1;
    int wordMultiplier = 1;
    bool isLegalMove = false;
    int tilesPlayed = 0;

    if (direction == PlayType::Down)
    {
        crossDirection = PlayType::Across;
        // Find the start of the word being made in the main direction.
        while (row >= 0 && newBoard[row, col] != nullptr)
        {
            row--;
        }
        // We overshoot, so now back off by one.
        row++;
    }
    else // PlayType::Across
    {
        crossDirection = PlayType::Down;
        while (col >= 0 && newBoard[row, col] != nullptr)
        {
            col--;
        }
        // We overshoot, so back off by one.
        col++;
    }

    while ( row < BOARD_SIZE && col < BOARD_SIZE && newBoard[row, col] != nullptr)
    {
        if (moveNum == 0 && row == 7 && col == 7)
        {
            isLegalMove = true;
        }
        letterMultiplier = 1;
```

```cpp
// If the old gameboard space here was empty,
// look at the space below the tile.
if (gameBoard[row, col] == nullptr)
{
    tilesPlayed++;
    switch (spaces[row, col])
    {
    case SpaceType::DLS:
        letterBonus = true;
        letterMultiplier = 2;
        break;
    case SpaceType::Center:
    case SpaceType::DWS:
        wordBonus = true;
        wordMultiplier = 2;
        break;
    case SpaceType::TLS:
        letterBonus = true;
        letterMultiplier = 3;
        break;
    case SpaceType::TWS:
        wordBonus = true;
        wordMultiplier = 3;
        break;
    default:
        break;
    }
    // Identify any cross-words by moving backward to the
    // first nonempty space.
    int rowCrossBegin = row;
    int colCrossBegin = col;
    int rowCross = row;
    int colCross = col;
    int crossScore = 0;
    if (crossDirection == PlayType::Down)
    {
        while ( rowCrossBegin >= 0 &&
            newBoard[rowCrossBegin, colCrossBegin] != nullptr)
        {
            rowCrossBegin--;
        }
        rowCrossBegin++; // Increment to beginning of word.
    }
```

```cpp
        else // Cross-direction is across.
        {
            while ( colCrossBegin >= 0 &&
                newBoard[rowCrossBegin, colCrossBegin] != nullptr)
            {
                colCrossBegin--;
            }
            colCrossBegin++; // Increment to the beginning of word.
        }

        // Now scan forward for crosswords.
        int rowCrossEnd = row;
        int colCrossEnd = col;
        if (crossDirection == PlayType::Down)
        {
            while ( rowCrossEnd < BOARD_SIZE &&
                newBoard[rowCrossEnd, colCrossEnd] != nullptr)
            {
                rowCrossEnd++;
            }
            rowCrossEnd--; // Decrement to beginning of word.
        }
        else // Cross-direction is across.
        {
            while ( colCrossEnd < BOARD_SIZE &&
                newBoard[rowCrossEnd, colCrossEnd] != nullptr)
            {
                colCrossEnd++;
            }
            colCrossEnd--; // Decrement to the beginning of word.
        }
        if (rowCrossBegin != rowCrossEnd ||
            colCrossBegin != colCrossEnd)
        {
            // A crossword was found.
            // This counts as using existing tiles,
            // so this is definitely a legal move.
            isLegalMove = true;
            if (crossDirection == PlayType::Down)
            {
                for (rowCross = rowCrossBegin; rowCross <= rowCrossEnd;
                    rowCross++)
                {
                    // You only account for special bonuses if the tile on that
                    // bonus square is one you played.
```

```
                    if (rowCross == row && colCross == col)
                    {
                        crossScore += newBoard[rowCross, colCross]->PointValue
                            * letterMultiplier;
                    }
                    else
                        crossScore += newBoard[rowCross, colCross]->PointValue;
                }
            }
            else
            {
                for (colCross = colCrossBegin; colCross <= colCrossEnd;
                colCross++)
                {
                    if (rowCross == row && colCross == col)
                    {
                        crossScore += newBoard[rowCross, colCross]->PointValue
                            * letterMultiplier;
                    }
                    else
                        crossScore += newBoard[rowCross, colCross]->PointValue;
                }
            }
            crossScore *= wordMultiplier;
            cumScore += crossScore;
        } // end of block for if there is a cross-word

    } // end of block for if the space has a new tile on it
    else
    {
        // The space is occupied by a letter that was already there.
        // All plays other than the first must contain a letter that
        // is already present, so if this is the case, then the play is
        // a legal play.
        isLegalMove = true;
    }

    wordScore += letterMultiplier * newBoard[row, col]->PointValue;

    if (direction == PlayType::Down)
        row++;
    else
        col++;
}
```

```cpp
            wordScore *= wordMultiplier;
            cumScore += wordScore;
            // fifty-point bonus for using all your letters
            if (tilesPlayed == MAX_TILES_IN_HAND)
            {
                cumScore += 50;
            }
            if (isLegalMove)
                return cumScore;
            else
                return -1;
        }
    };

int main()
{

    int nPlayer;
    bool success = false;
    Console::WindowHeight = 50;
    do
    {
        Console::WriteLine(
            "Welcome to Scrabble. Enter the number of players (2 to 4).");
        String^ input = Console::ReadLine();
        try
        {
            nPlayer = Int32::Parse(input);
            if (nPlayer < 2 || nPlayer > 4)
                throw gcnew Exception();
            success = true;
        }
        catch(Exception^ )
        {
            success = false;
        }
    } while (! success);

    ScrabbleGame^ game = gcnew ScrabbleGame(nPlayer);
    int firstPlayer = game->PreGame();
    Player^ winner = game->Play(firstPlayer);
    if (winner != nullptr)
        Console::WriteLine("{0} wins!", winner->Name);
    Console::ReadLine();
    return 0;
}
```

Figure 6-2 shows an example of the Scrabble game in operation. It may be reminiscent of many an old text-based computer game from the pregraphics era.

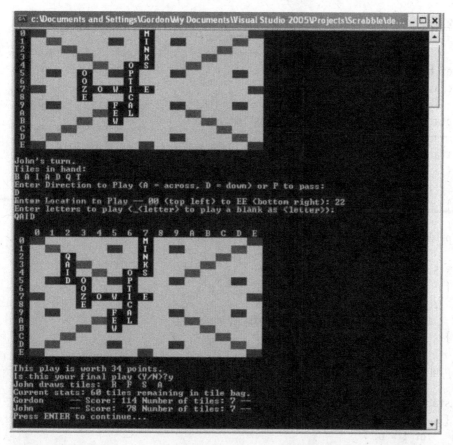

Figure 6-2. *The Scrabble game in progress, with some useful two-letter words and words with Q and no vowels*

As an exercise, try implementing the functionality to save and restore games in progress, by writing the game state out to a text file and reading it back in.

The this Pointer

As you've noticed, we used the this pointer in the previous examples. In a reference type, the this pointer is a handle to the object type. Here's a possible use of the this pointer. The code in Listing 6-11 tracks instances of objects created of that type in a static data structure. Note the use of the static constructor to create the List object. This example uses a destructor (~R) and a finalizer (!R) that work together to orchestrate object cleanup, as explained later in this chapter.

Listing 6-11. *Using the this Pointer*

```cpp
// instance_tracker.cpp

using namespace System;
using namespace System::Collections::Generic;

// ref type
ref class R
{
    static List<R^>^ instanceTrackingList;

    static R()
    {
        instanceTrackingList = gcnew List<R^>;
    }

public:

R(String^ s)
{
    Label = s;
    instanceTrackingList->Add( this );
}

property String^ Label;

static int EnumerateInstances()
{
    int i = 0;
    for each (R^ r in instanceTrackingList)
    {
        i++;
        Console::WriteLine( r->Label );
    }
    return i;
}

~R()    // destructor
{
    // When invoking a function through the this pointer,
    // use the indirection operator (->).
    this->!R();
}
```

```
    !R()    // finalizer
    {
        instanceTrackingList->Remove( this );
    }

    // etc.
};

int main()
{
    R r1("ABC");
    R^ r2 = gcnew R("XYZ");

    int count = R::EnumerateInstances();
    Console::WriteLine("Object count: " + count);

    delete r2;
    count = R::EnumerateInstances();
    Console::WriteLine("Object count: " + count);
}
```

The output of Listing 6-11 is shown here:

```
ABC
XYZ
Object count: 2
ABC
Object count: 1
```

The this pointer in a value type cannot be a handle since a handle points to the managed heap and a value type might not be on the managed heap. Instead, it is an interior pointer. An *interior pointer* is a pointer that points to some address in a managed object. This could be some location within a type or the beginning of the type itself in a value type. The runtime updates the value of the interior pointer (interior_ptr) if the object is moved. Interior pointers are declared like this:

```
interior_ptr<Type> ptr = < pointer expression >
```

where *pointer_expression* evaluates to the address of some part of a managed type. Listing 6-12 demonstrates using the this pointer in a value type. In addition to interior_ptr, this example uses a pinning pointer (pin_ptr), which causes a potentially movable object to be fixed in position. Pinning pointers are declared like this:

```
pin_ptr<Type> pin_ptr = < pointer expression >
```

The pinning pointer is necessary to convert an interior pointer into an integral value to display, since the compiler will only allow pointers to managed types (including interior pointers) to be converted to integers if they are first pinned by creating a `pin_ptr`. Interior pointers can be converted to pinning pointers of the same type.

Listing 6-12. *Using this in a Value Type*

```cpp
// valuetype_this.cpp

using namespace System;

value class V
{
   int i, j;

   public:

   void PrintStartingAddress()
   {
      interior_ptr<V> ptr_to_this = this;
      pin_ptr<V> pinned_this = ptr_to_this;
      Console::WriteLine("Starting address of object is 0x{0:x}",
               reinterpret_cast<int>(pinned_this));
   }
};

int main()
{
   V v;
   v.PrintStartingAddress();
}
```

Access Levels for Classes

As you saw in Chapter 3, in C++/CLI it is possible to apply type visibility modifiers such as public or private to a class as a whole, not just to members of the class. This affects the visibility of the types from outside the assembly in which they are defined. The rules are the same as those for functions discussed in Chapter 5. For example, you can use the modifier internal to make a type visible in its own assembly but not outside of it.

In addition to the usual three levels of access control (public, private, and protected), additional levels of access control are available that provide the ability to specify separate levels of access for client code outside and inside the assembly. For example, the new access control specifier internal is used to indicate that the given element is available only to other code in the same assembly. In other words, the code is private outside the assembly, but public inside the assembly. In addition to internal, you can use protected public to refer to members that are public inside the assembly and protected outside; and private protected to refer to members that are protected inside the assembly and private outside. The order of the accessibility modifiers is not significant, so protected public means the same as public protected, and private protected means the same as protected private. The key to remembering the meaning of these pairs is to remember that the more restrictive permissions always apply outside the assembly. Table 6-2 summarizes the accessibility modifiers.

Table 6-2. *Accessibility Modifiers and Their Effect in Whether an Entity Is Visible*

Modifiers Used	Within Same Assembly	Outside Assembly
public	Yes	Yes
private	No	No
protected	To derived classes	To derived classes
internal	Yes	No
protected public	Yes	To derived classes
private protected	To derived classes	No

Native and Managed Classes

In this chapter, you've looked at reference classes and value classes, the two broad categories of managed types. If you deal with native code, you may be wondering how native classes fit into the picture. Native and managed types may coexist, even in the same class. It is possible for a native type to be contained in a managed type, and vice versa. The details are often somewhat cumbersome, so I reserve them for Chapter 12, but a sneak preview will give you a hint of what's possible and also help give the background for some of what I say about finalizers later in this chapter.

But first, a little background and context. When would you need to write code like this? If you are extending a native application with managed types, you'll probably need to use the native types in your managed types. If in addition the native types need to refer to managed types, you need to use the gcroot template to refer to them.

Using a Native Object in a Managed Type

When including native types in managed types, you must reference the native types via a pointer to the object on the native heap. You cannot actually make the native type part of the layout of the class, but everything in the class layout must be a managed type since the whole object will be managed by the common language runtime. Thus, the code in Listing 6-13 is legal.

Listing 6-13. *Using a Native Type in a Managed Type*

```
// Forestry.cpp
using namespace System;
using namespace System::Runtime::InteropServices;

// a native class
class PlantData
{
    private:
```

```cpp
    wchar_t* family;
    wchar_t* genus;
    wchar_t* species;

public:

    PlantData(const wchar_t* botanical_name)
    {
        // Let's assume this method
        // populates its
        // fields with data from the database.
    }

};

// The following managed class contains a pointer to a native class.

ref class TreeSpecies
{
    PlantData* treedata;

public:
    TreeSpecies(String^ genus, String^ species)
    {
        String^ botanical_name = gcnew String(genus + " " + species);

        // Use the Marshal class to create a pointer.
        // The managed class corresponding to a
        // pointer is IntPtr.
        IntPtr ip = Marshal::StringToHGlobalAnsi(botanical_name);

        // Cast that to the appropriate pointer type.
        const wchar_t* str = static_cast<const wchar_t*>(ip.ToPointer());
        treedata = new PlantData(str);
        Marshal::FreeHGlobal( ip );

    }

    ~TreeSpecies() { this->!TreeSpecies(); }
    !TreeSpecies() { if (treedata) delete treedata; }
};
```

Don't worry too much about the details of the conversions from String to wchar_t*—this is typical of the kind of type conversions you need to do when mixing managed and native code. We're simply using the Marshal class defined in the .NET Framework to create, ultimately, a pointer to a character array. The term *marshal* is a synonym for convert, although usually it suggests converting parameters from native to managed and vice versa in the context of a function call from managed to native code. However, it has come to mean converting between native and managed objects in a general sense. More information on marshaling will be discussed in Chapter 12.

We include the native type PlantData as a pointer, but it would be illegal to include the native type by value. Including a pointer to the native heap creates code that cannot be verified to be safe, since the runtime has no way of knowing whether you are accessing a valid native pointer. Thus, you cannot have a native pointer or a native class in a class when compiling with /clr:safe. You can, however, use pointers when compiling with /clr:pure, because a pointer itself doesn't result in the generation of native code. The intermediate language is actually capable of representing pointers even if they are not verifiable. This is exactly what happens in C# when in an unsafe block.

Finally, we include a destructor and finalizer in the type. The delete is called from the finalizer, not the destructor, and we call the finalizer from the destructor. You'll see more about this later this chapter, but in this case it's necessary to make sure that the native pointer is freed even if the destructor is never called. A more robust way to do this by writing a template class to embed the native pointer will be discussed in Chapter 12, after managed templates and some other background have been covered.

Yes, it is also possible to include a managed type in a native class. To do it, you use the gcroot template in the native type, with the managed type as a template parameter (see Listing 6-14). A *root* is a handle that tracks a garbage-collected object. When roots exist, the object is still alive. The idea behind the name gcroot is that the pointer designates the *root* of a garbage-collected object on the managed heap. The gcroot template does not call the destructor on the managed object when it goes out of scope, but there is a variant, auto_gcroot, that does. Both templates are defined in the msclr namespace and require the inclusion of the appropriate header file. Listing 6-14 illustrates the basic syntax.

Listing 6-14. *Using a Managed Type in a Native Type*

```cpp
// gcroot_and_auto_gcroot.cpp

#include <msclr/gcroot.h>
#include <msclr/auto_gcroot.h>
using namespace System;
using namespace msclr;

// managed class R
ref class R
{
    public:
        void f()
        {
            Console::WriteLine("managed member function");
        }
```

```
    ~R()
    {
        Console::WriteLine("destructor");
    }

};

// native class N
class N
{
    gcroot<R^> r_gcroot;
    auto_gcroot<R^> r_auto_gcroot;

    public:
    N()
    {
        r_gcroot = gcnew R();
        r_gcroot->f();
        r_auto_gcroot = gcnew R();
        r_auto_gcroot->f();
    }

};

int main()
{
    N n;
    // When n goes out of scope, the destructor for the auto_gcroot object
    // will be executed, but not the gcroot object.
}
```

The output of Listing 6-14 is as follows:

```
managed member function
managed member function
destructor
```

You see only one call to the destructor—the destructor for the auto_gcroot object. Chapter 12 will present more examples of interoperability between managed and native types and functions.

Class Destruction and Cleanup

Typically, C++ classes that use limited resources, such as operating system device contexts, database connections, files, and so on, are implemented using an idiom called RAII (Resource Acquisition is Initialization). RAII specifies that acquiring resources is to be done in a constructor. Having adopted such a pattern, the class design will have to deal with properly freeing these resources in a prompt and predictable manner to ensure an application's best behavior and performance. Native C++ programs use the destructor for this, and they can be assured that whenever a block or stack frame is completed, temporary objects created on the stack will be released, their destructors called, and any limited resources freed. Such assurances of prompt freeing of resources are, at first glance, not available in the managed environment, when the object isn't really cleaned up until the garbage collector runs.

The CLI provides the Dispose method (and the interface IDisposable, which defines this one method) to solve this problem. The Dispose method is never called directly from C++/CLI code, as for example, you might in C# code. If you're a C# programmer, you'll want to pay close attention to the information in this section since it differs markedly from the C# behavior. In C#, you might call Dispose directly, or you might use the using statement to create a scope for your object, and have the Dispose method called automatically at the end of that scope.

Instead, C++/CLI provides a more familiar (to classic C++ programmers) way to use the RAII model. You implement a destructor much as you would in classic C++. Implementing a destructor causes the object to implicitly implement IDisposable. The destructor, in fact, becomes the Dispose method and hence implements the interface.

In C++/CLI, if you define a destructor as usual, you can be assured that your object's destructor will be called when the object goes out of scope as a result of the stack going out of scope or the destruction of the enclosing object, or an explicit call to delete on a handle to the object. delete is used to call the destructor for a handle object, so use delete if you need to call the destructor, but aren't using stack semantics. (There is no such thing as gcdelete; the delete operator is able to serve for both native pointers and managed handles, since the appropriate form may be determined from the entity being deleted.) The destructor is not called when the garbage collector cleans up the object, so if you do not call delete for your handle, the destructor won't get called at all.

Finalizers

C++/CLI allows you to also define a function that gets called when the garbage collector actually frees your object. This special function is called the *finalizer*. If you don't deal with unmanaged resources (e.g., native classes, native file handles, window handles, device contexts, and the like), you don't need finalizers, and you can skim this section. Just use destructors for your usual cleanup operations. If you do use these resources, you need to read and understand this section closely.

The runtime is allowed to call the finalizer at any time after the object is no longer being used. There is no guaranteed order in which objects' finalizers are called. The practical result of this is that an object's members (if they are also managed objects) may have already been finalized by the time the finalizer runs on your object. Thus, you should use the destructor for explicit cleanup of managed objects, or just allow the garbage collector to handle it.

The finalizer is indicated by a function preceded by an exclamation mark (!), as in this example:

```
!R() { Console::WriteLine("R finalizer"); }
```

Try an experiment with the code in Listing 6-15 to see when the destructor and finalizer get called.

Listing 6-15. *Using a Destructor and Finalizer*

```cpp
// finalizer.cpp
using namespace System;

ref class R
{
    int ID;

    public:

    R(int id) : ID(id)  { Console::WriteLine("R constructor {0}", ID); }
    ~R() { Console::WriteLine("R destructor {0}", ID); }
    !R() { Console::WriteLine("R finalizer {0}", ID); }
};

void MakeObjects()
{
    R^ r;
    R r1(0);
    for (int i = 1; i < 7; i++)
    {
        r = gcnew R(i);
    }
}

int main()
{
    MakeObjects();
    // Normally, you should avoid calling GC::Collect and forcing garbage
    // collection rather than letting the garbage collection thread determine
    // the best time to collect; I do it here to illustrate a point.
    GC::Collect();
}
```

Here is the output of Listing 6-15:

```
R constructor 0
R constructor 1
R constructor 2
R constructor 3
R constructor 4
R constructor 5
R constructor 6
R destructor 0
R finalizer 5
R finalizer 6
```

```
R finalizer 4
R finalizer 3
R finalizer 2
R finalizer 1
```

You'll notice that the destructor only got called once, and the finalizer got called six times. The destructor was for the object created in MakeObjects with stack semantics when the object went out of scope. The destructor is not called for a handle type that is not explicitly deleted. The finalizer was called when the garbage collection ran (which in this case was forced by calling GC::Collect). If you have a finalizer that does something important, you'll want your destructor to call your finalizer to make sure that the cleanup operations occur promptly rather than waiting until a garbage collection cycle occurs. A destructor call suppresses the finalizer. Now try removing the call to GC::Collect and rerunning the program. The finalizer is still called six times even though the process may have shut down. Finalizers will be run when the process ends.

Finalizers are not to be used routinely; in fact, if you can avoid them, you should. A possible use is for the last-ditch cleanup of unmanaged resources in cases where you can't be sure whether the destructor is called. Examples of unmanaged resources are native file handles, device contexts, and so on. However, the .NET Framework provides wrapper classes for most of these unmanaged resources, for example, the HWnd class and the SafeHandle family of classes. When using the wrapper classes, the wrapper classes will take care of their own cleanup. Finalizers are particularly difficult to write correctly, because when they execute, their members may be disposed, in the process of finalization, or already finalized themselves. Also, to be truly robust, they need to correctly handle various rare circumstances, such as being called more than once. When the runtime invokes a finalizer, other threads are locked out automatically, so there is no need to acquire a lock within the finalizer itself.

If a finalizer is implemented, you should have a destructor, and you should recommend that users of your class call that destructor, because it is very inefficient to rely on finalization to perform the cleanup operations.

The basic pattern is shown in Listing 6-16.

Listing 6-16. *Pattern for Using a Destructor and Finalizer*

```cpp
// destructor_and_finalizer.cpp

ref class ManagedResource
{
   public:
      void Free() { /* free resource */ }
};

class NativeResource
{
   public:
      void Free() { /* free resource */ }
};
```

```
ref class R
{
    ManagedResource^ resource1;
    NativeResource* nativeResource;

    public:
      ~R()
      {
          // You may clean up managed resources that you want to free up promptly
          // here. If you don't, they WILL eventually get cleaned up by the garbage
          // collector.
          // If the destructor is NOT called, the GC will eventually clean
          // them up.
          resource1->Free();
          this->!R();
      }
      !R()
      {
          // Clean up unmanaged resources that the
          // garbage collector doesn't know how to clean up.
          // That code shouldn't be in the destructor because
          // the destructor might not get called.
          nativeResource->Free();
      }
};
```

You might guess from what I've just said about the destructor suppressing the finalizer that the finalizer doesn't get called directly for objects created with stack semantics. When objects with stack semantics are destroyed at the end of a function scope, the destructor is called, but not the finalizer.

Code that frees the resources should be written in the finalizer, and the destructor should call the finalizer. That way, you know your cleanup will be called regardless of whether the destructor is called or not. If it is called, the cleanup executes because the destructor calls the finalizer, and the finalizer cleans up. If it is not called, the finalizer eventually is called by the garbage collector or application shutdown process, that is, when the application domain (the CLR term for the entire space that all the application's names exist in) shuts down.

In Listing 6-17, one file is opened using a native file handle, an unmanaged resource. Another file is opened using the StreamWriter class.

Listing 6-17. *Handling Managed and Unmanaged Resources*

```
// file_converter.cpp
#include <stdio.h>
#include <string.h>
#include <stdlib.h>
#include <vcclr.h> // for PtrToStringChars
```

```cpp
using namespace System;
using namespace System::IO;


// a native class

class FileNative
{
    // a CRT file pointer
    FILE* fp;

    public:

    void Open(const char* filename)
    {
        int err = fopen_s(&fp, filename, "r");
        if (err)
        {
            printf("Error opening file %s. Error code %d.\n", filename, err);
        }
    }

    int Read(char* line)
    {
        int val = fread(line, 1, 1, fp);
        if (feof(fp))
        {
            return 0;
        }
        return val;
    }

    void Close()
    {
        if (fp)
            fclose(fp);
    }
};

// a managed class that contains a managed resource (StreamWriter)
// and a native resource (fileNative, a native class containing a native file)
ref class FileConverter
{
    FileNative* fileNative;
    StreamWriter^ sw;

    public:
```

```
FileConverter(String^ source_file)
{
    fileNative = new FileNative();
    pin_ptr<const wchar_t> wfilename = PtrToStringChars(source_file);
    size_t convertedChars = 0;
    size_t  sizeInBytes = ((source_file->Length + 1) * 2);
    errno_t err = 0;
    char    *filename = (char *)malloc(sizeInBytes);

    err = wcstombs_s(&convertedChars,
                filename, sizeInBytes,
                wfilename, sizeInBytes);
    if (err != 0)
    printf_s("wcstombs_s  failed!\n");

    fileNative->Open(filename);
}

void Convert(String^ dest_file)
{
    String^ text;
    char ptr[1024];
    int len;
    try
    {
        sw = gcnew StreamWriter(dest_file);
    }
    catch(Exception^ e)
    {
        Console::WriteLine("Error occurred. {0}", e->Message);
    }
    while ((len = fileNative->Read(ptr)) != 0)
    {
        // This version of the string constructor takes
        // a char* pointer, an offset, and a number of characters
        // to create the String from a portion of a character array.
        text = gcnew String(ptr, 0, len);
        Console::Write(text);
        sw->Write(text);
    }
}
```

```
// A way to close the files promptly without waiting
// for the cleanup to occur.
void Close()
{
    if (sw != nullptr)
        sw->Close();
    fileNative->Close();
}


// Destructor: close the managed filestream, and call finalizer.
~FileConverter()
{
    if (sw != nullptr)
        sw->Close();
    this->!FileConverter();
}

// Finalizer: close the native file handle.
!FileConverter()
{
    fileNative->Close();
}

};


int main(array<String^> ^ args)
{
    if (args->Length < 2)
    {
        Console::WriteLine("Usage: file_converter <sourcefile> <destfile>");
        return -1;
    }

    // Try both true and false values.
    bool stack_semantics = true;

    if (stack_semantics)
    {
        // Converter is created with stack semantics, so the destructor
        //  (and finalizer) get called when main exits.
        FileConverter converter(args[0]);
        converter.Convert(args[1]);
    }
```

```
    else
    {
        // Converter used with heap semantics. Destructor is not called,
        // so the file must be closed by calling the Close method. It will not
        // work to close the file from the finalizer, since the StreamWriter
        // object may be in an invalid state.
        FileConverter^ converter = gcnew FileConverter(args[0]);
        converter->Convert(args[1]);
        converter->Close(); // or: delete converter;
    }
}
```

Pitfalls of Finalizers

You should be aware that in a finalizer, your object could be partially destroyed already. Any managed objects that are also on the heap may already be destroyed, because the garbage collector may have cleaned them up already. The finalizer code should not assume that any managed objects are still valid. Let's say you wanted to avoid having to call Close when using heap semantics, as in Listing 6-17, and you decide to move the closing of the stream to the finalizer, as in Listing 6-18.

Listing 6-18. *Closing a Stream in a Finalizer*

```
!FileConverter()
{
    if (sw != nullptr)
        sw->Close();          // problem here
    fileNative->Close();
}
```

The problem is that the underlying stream object may be released already by the garbage collection process and an exception will be thrown. This will likely crash the process. In general, objects of reference type may be in an invalid state in the finalizer. Objects of value type are safe to use, as are unmanaged objects that have not been cleaned up yet.

I've noticed that many people who are trying to learn C++/CLI destruction and finalization, who don't yet fully understand the details of how destruction and finalization work, find themselves unable to remember whether the destructor should call the finalizer, or vice versa. The key to remembering this pattern is to remember that finalizer code is very limited. You cannot access managed objects in your finalizer. There is no such restriction in the destructor. So, it will not be possible for the finalizer to call the destructor if the destructor works with freeing the managed resources, because that would put the destructor code under the same restrictions as the finalizer code, which would probably prevent some cleanup from being possible.

Let's look at one more example, Listing 6-19, that should make clear the dangers of finalizers.

Listing 6-19. *A Dangerous Finalizer*

```cpp
// finalizer_pitfalls.cpp
#using "System.dll"
#using "System.Data.dll"

using namespace System;
using namespace System::Data::SqlClient;

ref class DataConnection
{
    SqlConnection^ conn;

public:

    DataConnection()
    {
        conn = gcnew SqlConnection(
            "Server=(local);Uid=sa;Pwd=****;Initial Catalog=master");
        conn->Open();
    }

    // ... more code ...

    ~DataConnection()
    {
        this->!DataConnection();
    }

    !DataConnection()
    {
        try {
            Console::WriteLine("Closing connection...");
            conn->Close();
        }
        catch(Exception^ e)
        {
            Console::WriteLine("Error occurred! " + e->Message);
        }
    }

};
```

```
void UseData()
{
   DataConnection connection1;
   DataConnection^ connection2 = gcnew DataConnection();
   // Use the connection.

}

int main()
{
   UseData();
   // Force a garbage collection, to illustrate a point.
   GC::Collect();
}
```

Here, we create two connection objects, this time using a `SqlConnection`. One connection is declared in the function UseData with stack semantics; the other is created with heap semantics. When the UseData function exits, the destructor gets called for connection1, but not for connection2, which becomes an orphaned object. Then, when a garbage collection occurs (in this case artificially forced by the call to GC::Collect, but in principle this could happen at some point in real-world code), an exception is generated. In this case the error reported is

```
Error occurred! Internal .Net Framework Data Provider error 1.
```

More often, you won't have caught the exception, and the process will simply crash. The question is, What went wrong? These errors can be extremely hard to diagnose until you realize what is happening. The problem here is that you cannot rely on managed objects to remain in existence when called from the finalizer. On the other hand, it is safe to reference these objects from the destructor because when the destructor runs, the object and all its members are still fully intact. In this case, you should move the data connection close operation into the destructor, and be sure to call delete or use stack semantics to force the destructor call and the closure of the connection.

The bottom line is that you can't ignore calling delete for classes that hold onto resources. If this seems disappointing, just remember that the managed environment may be very good at cleaning up memory, but it is not designed to provide the same automatic cleanup for other resources, which are best handled by matching every gcnew *for a class with a destructor* with a corresponding delete, or, better, using stack semantics.

Summary

In this chapter, you looked at C++/CLI reference and value classes (and structs) and how they differ from native classes. You looked at class initialization and literal and initonly members. You saw how to implement an example of a complete class—the Scrabble game. You also learned how to use the this pointer in reference and value types and the way to control access to types in an assembly. You saw how to hold a pointer to a native type in a managed class, and vice versa, and finally, you learned about object cleanup, including destructors and finalizers.

In the next chapter, you'll look closely at members of .NET classes, in particular, properties, operators, and events.

CHAPTER 7

Features of a .NET Class

You've been using properties throughout the text, and you looked at an example of an event in Chapter 2. This chapter will go into a bit more detail on properties and events, and will also discuss some features of operators unique to C++/CLI, including static operators and how conversion operators work in C++/CLI versus classic C++. You'll also learn about casts and conversions.

Properties

As you saw in Chapter 2, in terms of object-oriented programming, properties capture the "has-a" relationship for an object. Properties seem a lot like fields to the consumer of a class. They represent values that can be retrieved and/or written to. You can use them inside the class as well as outside the class (if they are public). There is a special syntax for using them that makes them look like fields, but operations on these "fields" invoke the accessor (get and set) methods that you've defined. Properties fully encapsulate the underlying data, whether it's a single field or something more complex, meaning that you are free to change the underlying field's representation without affecting the users of the class. Say we want to declare some typical properties we might find in a periodic table of the elements. Listing 7-1 shows how.

Listing 7-1. *Declaring Properties*

```cpp
// declaring_properties.cpp
using namespace System;

value class ElementType
{
    public:
        property unsigned int AtomicNumber;
        property double AtomicWeight;
        property String^ Name;
        property String^ Symbol;
};
```

```
int main()
{
    ElementType oxygen;
    oxygen.AtomicNumber = 8;
    oxygen.AtomicWeight = 15.9994;
    oxygen.Name = "Oxygen";
    oxygen.Symbol = "O";

    Console::WriteLine("Element: {0} Symbol: {1}", oxygen.Name, oxygen.Symbol);
    Console::WriteLine("Atomic Number: {0} Atomic Weight: {1}",
                       oxygen.AtomicNumber, oxygen.AtomicWeight);
}
```

The output of Listing 7-1 is as follows:

```
Element: Oxygen Symbol: O
Atomic Number: 8 Atomic Weight: 15.9994
```

As you can see, the property is invoked by using its name in a member access expression. You do not call get and set explicitly; they are called for you whenever code specifies a construct that either retrieves the value (for example, using the property in an expression or as a function parameter) or sets the value (when the property is used as an lvalue).

Expressions involving properties may not be chained. That is to say, a property cannot be an lvalue and an rvalue at the same time. So, code like this does not work:

```
a = oxygen.AtomicNumber = 8; // error
```

In this example, we use the shorthand syntax for declaring properties that map directly onto a field and have trivial get and set methods. A field is created automatically for such a property, as well as the default get and set methods. Such a field is not intended to be accessed in any way other than through the property. If you use this syntax, you can change it later to the full form of the syntax (for example, to provide an alternative implementation of the property's underlying data, or add some custom code to the get and set methods) without changing the property's interface to outside users of the type. In Listing 7-2, we change the AtomicWeight property from a simple double value to a computed value based on the isotopic abundances and number of isotopes. Once the value is computed, the stored result is used. The set method just sets the value as usual, and would perhaps be used if looking up the information from a periodic table.

Listing 7-2. *Computing a Property Value*

```
// periodic_table.cpp
using namespace System;
using namespace System::Collections::Generic;
```

```
value class Isotope
{
    public:
        property double Mass;
        property unsigned int AtomicNumber;
};

value class ElementType
{
    List<Isotope>^ isotopes;
    List<double>^ isotope_abundance;
    double atomicWeight;

    public:
        property unsigned int AtomicNumber;
        property String^ Name;
        property String^ Symbol;

        property double AtomicWeight
        {
            double get()
            {
                // Check to see if atomic weight has been calculated yet.
                if (atomicWeight == 0.0)
                {
                    if (isotopes->Count == 0)
                        return 0.0;
                    for (int i = 0; i < isotopes->Count; i++)
                    {
                        atomicWeight += isotopes[i].Mass * isotope_abundance[i];
                    }
                }
                return atomicWeight;
            }
            void set(double value)
            {
                // used if you look up atomic weight instead of calculating it
                atomicWeight = value;
            }
        }

        // other properties same as before
};
```

You can see how creating a trivial property isn't like exposing a field directly to users of a class. If you expose a field directly, you run into problems later if the implementation of the field changes. With a trivial property, you can always later define the get and set methods yourself and change the backing store for the property to suit your needs, while preserving the interface the property presents to other consumers. When defining get and set explicitly, the set method must return void and the get method must return the type of the property. The parameter list for get must be void and the parameter list for set must be the type of the property.

Properties need not map onto a field's value. For example, you could eliminate the atomicWeight field from the class and simply compute the value whenever get is called. The set method would then have to be eliminated. This is fine, though, since if only a get method is defined, the property can be retrieved but not set.

As these methods get more complicated, you'll want to move them out of the class declaration. When defining property get and set methods out of the body of the class, use the class name and property name as qualifiers, as in Listing 7-3.

Listing 7-3. *Defining Property Accessors Outside of a Class*

```
value class ElementType
{
   public:

   property double AtomicWeight
   {
      double get();
   }
};

double ElementType::AtomicWeight::get()
{
   // same implementation as before
}
```

In fact, this notation is how the property accessor is referred to when you need to refer to the method name, such as when you assign a delegate to a get or set method; you use the name of the property in the qualified name, as shown in Listing 7-4.

Listing 7-4. *Using a Delegate with a Property Accessor*

```
// property_accessor_delegate.cpp
using namespace System;

delegate double ValueAccessor();

value class ElementType
{
   public:
      property double AtomicWeight;
};
```

```
int main()
{
   ElementType oxygen;
   oxygen.AtomicWeight = 15.9994;
   ValueAccessor^ get_method = gcnew ValueAccessor(oxygen,
            &ElementType::AtomicWeight::get);

   Console::WriteLine("{0}", get_method->Invoke());
}
```

Say we'd like to also have some static properties in our Element class. In fact, we'd like to make a periodic table class with a static array property. There is nothing special about a static property; all the rules for static methods and fields apply. Static properties are intended to be used for properties of a type, not properties of a particular instance. Listing 7-5 is a first attempt at this.

Listing 7-5. *Trying to Define a Static Property*

```
// property_static.cpp
value class ElementType
{
   public:

      // Periodic Table of the Elements
      static property array<ElementType>^ PeriodicTable;

      static ElementType()
      {
         PeriodicTable = gcnew array<ElementType>(120);
         // Initialize each element and its properties.
      }
};
```

That's great, but if we later want to change the implementation from an array to a List or Hashtable, we might need to rewrite the code that uses the property. A better way to implement collection-like properties is to use *vector properties*, also called *indexed properties*.

Using Indexed Properties

A special type of property is allowed in C++/CLI that enables properties to act like arrays. You can also use indexed properties to provide array indexing on objects, the equivalent of defining the array indirection operator (operator[]) for your type.

To make a property support the indexing syntax, use the square brackets in the property declaration. Inside the square brackets, put the type you will use as the index. You can index on any type. Listing 7-6 shows a simple indexed property named ordinal. Note the type of the index appears inside square brackets, and the index is used as the first parameter of both the get and set methods.

Listing 7-6. *Using an Indexed Property*

```cpp
// properties_indexed1.cpp
using namespace System;

ref class Numbers
{
    array<String^>^ ordinals;

    public:

    Numbers()
    {
        ordinals = gcnew array<String^> { "zero", "one", "two", "three" };
    }

    property String^ ordinal[unsigned int]
    {
        String^ get(unsigned int index)
        {
            return ordinals[index];
        }
        void set(unsigned int index, String^ value)
        {
            ordinals[index] = value;
        }
    }
};

int main()
{
    Numbers^ nums = gcnew Numbers();

    // Access the property values using the indexer
    // with an unsigned int as the index.
    Console::WriteLine( nums->ordinal[0] );
}
```

Here is the output of Listing 7-6:

```
zero
```

You can also define a default indexed property by naming the property default, which enables the index to be used directly on the instance of the object (see Listing 7-7). Whether you are accessing a default indexed property using a handle or a variable declared with stack semantics, you can use the array indirection operator directly.

Listing 7-7. *Using a Default Property*

```cpp
// properties_indexed2.cpp
using namespace System;

ref class Numbers
{
    array<String^>^ ordinals;

    public:

        Numbers()
        {
            ordinals = gcnew array<String^> { "zero", "one", "two", "three" };
        }

        property String^ default[unsigned int]
        {
            String^ get(unsigned int index)
            {
                return ordinals[index];
            }
            void set(unsigned int index, String^ value)
            {
                ordinals[index] = value;
            }
        }
};

int main()
{
    Numbers nums;

    // Access property using array indexing operators on the
    // instance directly.
    Console::WriteLine( nums[0] );

    // If using a handle, you can still use array syntax.
    Numbers^ nums2 = gcnew Numbers();
    Console::WriteLine( nums2[1] );

    // You can also use the name "default" and access like a
    // named property.

    Console::WriteLine( nums.default[2] );
    Console::WriteLine( nums2->default[3] );
}
```

The output of Listing 7-7 is as follows:

```
zero
one
two
three
```

Listing 7-8 shows a class with an indexed property whose backing store is a collection class. The indexed property on the class PeriodicTable invokes the default indexed property on a .NET Framework collection class, Hashtable (here accessed through the interface IDictionary). The ElementType class now overrides the ToString method on Object to allow custom output. Chapter 8 discusses the override keyword.

Listing 7-8. *Backing a Property with a Collection*

```
// periodic_table.cpp
using namespace System;
using namespace System::Collections;

value class ElementType
{
  public:
    property unsigned int AtomicNumber;
    property double AtomicWeight;
    property String^ Name;
    property String^ Symbol;

    // You cannot use initializer list syntax to initialize properties.
    ElementType(String^ name, String^ symbol,
                double a, double n)
    {
        AtomicNumber = n;
        AtomicWeight = a;
        Name = name;
        Symbol = symbol;
    }

    // Override the ToString method (you'll learn more about the override
    // keyword in the next chapter).
    virtual String^ ToString() override
    {
        return String::Format(
          "Element {0} Symbol {1} Atomic Number {2} Atomic Weight {3}",
            Name, Symbol, AtomicNumber, AtomicWeight);
    }
};
```

```
ref class PeriodicTable
{
    private:

        Hashtable^ table;

    public:

        PeriodicTable()
        {
            table = gcnew Hashtable();

            ElementType element("Hydrogen", "H", 1.0079, 1);

            // Add to the Hashtable using the key and value.
            table->Add(element.Name, element);

            // Add the other elements...
        }

        property ElementType default[String^]
        {
            ElementType get(String^ key)
            {
                return safe_cast<ElementType>( table[key] );
            }
        }
};

int main()
{
    PeriodicTable^ table = gcnew PeriodicTable();

    // Get the element using the indexed property and print it.
    Console::WriteLine( table["Hydrogen"] );
}
```

The output of Listing 7-8 is shown here:

```
Element Hydrogen Symbol H Atomic Number 1 Atomic Weight 1.0079
```

Now suppose we want to implement a table of the isotopes, as envisioned in Chapter 2. Isotopes are different versions of the same element, so there is a many-to-one relationship between isotopes and elements. Isotopes are distinguished by a number, the isotope number, which is equal to the number of protons plus the number of neutrons. The number of protons determines the type of element, and the different isotopes of an element just vary by the number of neutrons. In Listing 7-9, a hashtable is used to store the various isotopes. The key is based on the element type and the isotope number, which uniquely identifies the isotope. For example, for carbon-14, the key is "C14". Since you can have more than one index variable, separated by commas, in an indexed property, we could look up an isotope by the name of the element and the isotope number, as the ElementIsotope property in Listing 7-9 shows. The key is computed by appending the element symbol and the isotope number, which are the arguments of the indexed property.

Listing 7-9. *Using Multiple Indexes*

```cpp
// isotope_table.cpp
using namespace System;
using namespace System::Collections::Generic;

value class Isotope
{
   public:
     property unsigned int IsotopeNumber;
     property unsigned int AtomicNumber;
};

ref class IsotopeTable
{
    private:

        Dictionary<String^, Isotope>^ isotopeTable;

    public:

        IsotopeTable()
        {
            isotopeTable = gcnew Dictionary<String^, Isotope>();

            // Add the elements and their isotopes...
            // Additional code for the elements is assumed.
            for each (ElementType element in PeriodicTable::Elements)
            {

                // Add each isotope to the isotopes table.
                for each (Isotope isotope in element.Isotopes)
                {
                    isotopeTable->Add(element.Name + isotope.IsotopeNumber, isotope);
                }
            }
        }
```

```
    // Pass in the element symbol and isotope number, e.g., "C" and 14 for
    // carbon-14.
    property Isotope ElementIsotope[String^, int ]
    {
        Isotope get(String^ key, int isotopeNumber)
        {
            key = key + isotopeNumber.ToString();
            return isotopeTable[key];
        }
    }
};
```

For many of these examples, we omit the set accessor to make the property read-only. You can do the opposite for a write-only property (see Listing 7-10). You can also use access control to set individual access to the set and get methods. Recalling the Atom class from Chapter 2, and the derived class RadioactiveAtom, it makes sense to use the access control specifier protected to limit setting the AtomicNumber property to the class and its derived classes. That way the radioactive atom can change the atomic number to process a decay event, but consumers of the atom class can't otherwise change the atomic number.

Listing 7-10. *Defining a Write-Only Property*

```
ref class Atom
{
    unsigned int atomic_number;

    public:
        property unsigned int IsotopeNumber;
        property unsigned int AtomicNumber
        {
            // Anyone can get the atomic number.
            public: unsigned int get()
            {
                return atomic_number;
            }
            // Only derived classes (such as RadioactiveAtom)
            // can change the atomic number.
            protected: void set(unsigned int n)
            {
                atomic_number = n;
            }
        }
};

ref class RadioactiveAtom : Atom
{
    // other stuff
```

```
public:

    void AlphaDecay()
    {
        AtomicNumber -= 2;
        IsotopeNumber -= 4;
    }
};
```

AlphaDecay is a function representing a decay of the atom, releasing two protons and two neutrons in the form of an alpha particle. This changes the atomic number and isotope number, which are updated. As you recall, the decay events in a radioactive atom were modeled using delegates and events. The delegate or event was used to call the designated decay method. The next section covers delegates and events in more detail.

Delegates and Events

Delegates can be viewed as the function pointers of the managed world. As a C++ programmer, you probably often use typedef to hide some of the complexity of the syntax for declaring and using function pointers. A delegate is an object that designates a function to call on a specific object (if the function is an instance method) or class (if the function is a static method), or a global function. The delegate is not the function itself; it simply represents the address of a function to call, along with a specific object whose method is to be called, if applicable.

Delegates are strongly typed, in that the parameter types and return type are part of the type of a delegate. A delegate variable may only be assigned to a function that matches the delegate signature. Delegates may not be used to designate a family of overloaded functions. They may only be used to designate specific function prototypes with specific arguments.

You saw in Chapter 2 how to declare and use a simple delegate. Delegates are actually instances of the .NET Framework class System::MulticastDelegate. The name "multicast" implies that many functions may be called when a delegate is invoked. This is, in fact, the case. The delegate keeps an internal list of functions in an invocation list, and all the functions on that list are invoked every time the Invoke method is called. You use the += operator to add functions to the invocation list, and the -= operator to remove them. You can also use the () operator to call the Invoke method implicitly, as in Listing 7-11.

Listing 7-11. *Using a Delegate*

```
// delegate_operators.cpp

using namespace System;

delegate void MyDelegate();

ref class R
{
    public:
```

```
    void f() { Console::WriteLine("R::f"); }
    void g() { Console::WriteLine("R::g"); }
};

int main()
{
    MyDelegate^ d;
    R^ r = gcnew R();

    d += gcnew MyDelegate(r, &R::f);
    d += gcnew MyDelegate(r, &R::g);

    d->Invoke();

    d -= gcnew MyDelegate(r, &R::g);

    // Use operator() instead of calling Invoke.
    d();
}
```

The output of Listing 7-11 is as follows:

```
R::f
R::g
R::f
```

Don't worry that when you use the -= operator, you are passing a newly created delegate to the -= operator. This seems counterintuitive, since you're actually deleting something, not creating it anew. The -= operator compares the invocation list of the right-side delegate to the invocation list of the delegate from which you are removing it, and removes the matching function (or functions) from the list.

Let's say the functions we're invoking have return values.

```
delegate String^ MyDelegate();
```

You'll find that the line

```
d += gcnew MyDelegate(r, &R::f);
```

triggers a compiler warning:

```
warning C4358: '+=': return type of combined delegates is not 'void';
  returned value is undefined
```

The issue is that if there are multiple functions called, each of which returns a different value, how do we know which function's return value gets returned from the delegate? And what happens to the return values for the others? In the CLR, the actual return value is the return value of the last delegate called. However, it would not be wise to rely on which function is the last one called, as this is implementation dependent. The Invoke function is too simplistic to deal with this situation. What we need to do is get the invocation list and walk through it, calling each target function and examining the return value separately, as in Listing 7-12. In order to avoid the warning, we can use the Combine and Remove methods instead of the operators.

Listing 7-12. *Walking Through an Invocation List*

```
// delegate_invocation_list.cpp
using namespace System;

delegate String^ MyDelegate();

ref class R
{
   public:

   String^ f() { return "R::f"; }
   String^ g() { return "R::g"; }
   String^ h() { return "R::h"; }
};

int main()
{
   MyDelegate^ d;
   R^ r = gcnew R();

   d = gcnew MyDelegate(r, &R::f);
   // Cast the return value to this particular delegate type.
   // Note: the C-style cast evaluates to a safe_cast.
   d = (MyDelegate^) d->Combine(d, gcnew MyDelegate(r, &R::g));
   d = (MyDelegate^) d->Combine(d, gcnew MyDelegate(r, &R::h));

   String^ s = d->Invoke();
   Console::WriteLine("Return value was {0}", s);

   d = (MyDelegate^) d->Remove(d, gcnew MyDelegate(r, &R::g));

   s = d->Invoke();
   Console::WriteLine("Return value was {0}", s);

   for each (MyDelegate^ del in d->GetInvocationList())
   {
      s = del->Invoke();
      Console::WriteLine("Return value was {0}", s);
   }

}
```

Here is the output for Listing 7-12:

```
Return value was R::h
Return value was R::h
Return value was R::f
Return value was R::h
```

The output shows us that, in reality, the last function added is the one whose value is returned. But since this is implementation-defined, we should heed the warning and always use a manual walk of the invocation list with these delegates.

Using `GetInvocationList` is also useful if exceptions might be thrown by the functions called through the delegate. If one delegate function throws an exception, other target functions may never execute. Walking through the invocation list manually enables you to wrap each invocation in a try/catch block, giving you more control over the functions that are invoked. Listing 7-13 demonstrates this technique.

Listing 7-13. *Manually Walking Through an Invocation List*

```cpp
// delegate_with_exceptions.cpp
using namespace System;

delegate String^ MyDelegate();

ref class R
{
    public:

    String^ f() { throw gcnew Exception(); return "R::f"; }
    String^ g() { return "R::g"; }
    String^ h() { return "R::h"; }
};

int main()
{
    MyDelegate^ d;
    R^ r = gcnew R();

    d = gcnew MyDelegate(r, &R::f);
    d = safe_cast<MyDelegate^>(d->Combine(d, gcnew MyDelegate(r, &R::g)));
    d = safe_cast<MyDelegate^>(d->Combine(d, gcnew MyDelegate(r, &R::h)));

    for each (MyDelegate^ del in d->GetInvocationList())
    {
```

```
        try
        {
            String^ s = del->Invoke();
            Console::WriteLine("Return value was {0}", s);
        }
        catch(Exception^)
        {
            // Handle the exception.
        }
    }

}
```

The output of Listing 7-13 is shown here:

```
Return value was R::g
Return value was R::h
```

Without the try/catch, g and h would never have been called.

Asynchronous Delegates

If the function you are calling via a delegate takes a long time to execute, you may want your code to perform other work while the called function is executing asynchronously on another thread. The .NET Framework provides support for calling delegates asynchronously, using a worker thread to call the function indicated by the delegate and allowing the initiating thread to continue with other work. Instead of using the Invoke method, use the BeginInvoke method to initiate the function call, and later in your code, call EndInvoke to retrieve the result. A variety of design patterns may be used. If you simply have a few other tasks to complete, you can perform those tasks and then simply wait for the result by calling EndInvoke. When EndInvoke is called before the worker thread has completed its work, execution on the main thread will block waiting for the function to complete. You can also poll the secondary thread, enabling you to continue working and keep checking the secondary thread until it's done. Another design pattern allows you to set up a callback function that is called when the function called by the delegate completes.

The BeginInvoke has a signature that is determined by the delegate declaration. BeginInvoke has the same parameters as the usual Invoke function, plus two additional parameters: the first is an AsyncCallback class and the second is the delegate. EndInvoke has only one parameter of type IAsyncResult. So, for example if you have a delegate like this one:

```
delegate void MyDelegate(R^ r);
```

the invoke methods have the following signatures:

```
AsyncResult^ BeginInvoke(R^, AsyncCallback^, MyDelegate^ );
void EndInvoke(IAsyncResult^);
```

The classes AsyncCallback and AsyncResult and the associated interface IAsyncResult provide the methods needed to implement these designs, such as providing a way to check on whether the function has completed. The BeginInvoke function returns an object of type AsyncResult. Listing 7-14 shows an example.

Listing 7-14. *Checking Function Completion*

```cpp
// async_delegates.cpp

using namespace System;
using namespace System::Threading;

ref class R
{
public:
   property String^ Value;

   R(String^ s) { Value = s; }
};

delegate void QueryFunc(String^, R^);

ref class Document
{

   IAsyncResult^ result;
   R^ m_r;

   public:

      Document(String^ s) { m_r = gcnew R(s); }

   // Query the database.
   void Query(String^ queryString, R^ r)
   {
       // Execute a long query.
       r->Value = "New Value";
   }

   void InitiateQuery(String^ queryString)
   {
       QueryFunc^ qf = gcnew QueryFunc(this, &Document::Query);
       Console::WriteLine(m_r->Value);
       result = qf->BeginInvoke(queryString, m_r,
                       gcnew AsyncCallback(this, &Document::ProcessResult),
                       qf);
   }
```

```cpp
    bool IsQueryCompleted()
    {
        return result->IsCompleted;
    }

    // This function gets called when the asynchronous call
    // completes.
    void ProcessResult(IAsyncResult^ result)
    {
        // Retrieve the delegate.
        QueryFunc^ caller = (QueryFunc^) result->AsyncState;

        // Get the data back (fill in DataSet parameter).
        caller->EndInvoke(result);
        Console::WriteLine(m_r->Value);
    }

    void UseData()
    {
        // Do something...
    }

};

int main()
{
    Document doc("Old Value");
    doc.InitiateQuery("SELECT * FROM Plants WHERE Plant.Genus = 'Lycopersicon'");
    // Do other work while the query executes.

    // Poll for completion.
    while (! doc.IsQueryCompleted() )
    {
        Thread::Sleep(100);
    }

    // Do work with the data.

    doc.UseData();

}
```

Here is the output of Listing 7-14:

```
Old Value
New Value
```

Events

Event-driven programming is common in applications that use graphical user interfaces, including Windows and web applications. User actions such as clicking a button cause events to be raised within the program, and code can be written to respond to those events. Events can also be raised by other programs or by the operating system. Within C++/CLI there are a number of abstractions that help implement event-driven programming. C++/CLI events are defined as members of a managed type. Events in C++/CLI must be defined as members of a managed type. The idea of defining an event in a class is to associate a method that is to be called (or multiple methods that are to be called) when those events are raised. On a practical level, events are fired by calling a specific method, although those who are interested in handling the event often do not see the code that raises the event. At that point any event handlers that have been attached to that event are called to respond to the event.

If you're going to write event-driven GUI applications, events are a mainstay since every time a mouse moves or the user hits the keyboard, an event occurs—even if your application does not handle it. If you use Microsoft Foundation Classes (MFC), you know about the message map. Events in C++/CLI are a language feature that builds into the language the idea of a mapping between events and functions that handle those events. The context-sensitive keyword event is used to declare an event in a managed type. Like properties, there is a simple form and a more complex form of the declaration. You saw the simple form in Chapter 2. As a reminder, the simple form of the declaration looks like this:

```
event EventHandler^ anEvent;
```

Like the more complex form of the property declaration, the more complex form of the event declaration lets you define your own methods for adding and removing event handlers, and raising events (see Listing 7-15). The arguments to add and remove must match the event's declared type.

Listing 7-15. *Customizing Methods for an Event Handler*

```
event EventHandler^ Start
{
    void add(EventHandler^ handler)
    { /* code to add an eventhandler to the invocation list */  }
    void remove(EventHandler^ handler)
    { /* code to remove an eventhandler from the invocation list */ }
    void raise(Object^ sender, EventArgs^ args)
    { /* code to fire the event */ }
}
```

Let's look at Listing 7-16. In this code, we create a managed class called Events that declares two events, Start and Exit. The type EventHandler, defined in the .NET Framework System namespace, is used. There are many types derived from EventHandler that could also be used. In fact, any delegate type could be used. Both events may be fired by calling a method on the class, RaiseStartEvent or RaiseExitEvent, which in turn invoke the event by simply using the name of the event as if it were a function call with the appropriate arguments. The appropriate arguments are determined by the delegate type that is used as the type of the event, in this case System::EventHandler, which takes an Object and the System::EventArgs parameter.

Listing 7-16. *Declaring an Event and Event Handlers*

```cpp
// events.cpp
using namespace System;
using namespace System::Threading;

ref class Events
{
    public:
        event EventHandler^ Start;

        event EventHandler^ Exit;

        // Function calls to raise the events from outside the class.
        void RaiseStartEvent()
        {
            Start(this, gcnew EventArgs());
        }

        void RaiseExitEvent()
        {
            Exit(this, gcnew EventArgs());
        }

        // event handler for Start event
        void OnStart(Object^ sender, EventArgs^ args)
        {
            Console::WriteLine("Starting");
        }

        // event handler for Exit event
        void OnExit(Object^ sender, EventArgs^ args)
        {
            Console::WriteLine("Exiting");
        }
};

void f(Events^ e)
{
    // Raise event for starting this function.
    e->RaiseStartEvent();

    Console::WriteLine("Doing something.");

    // Raise event for exiting this function.
    e->RaiseExitEvent();
}
```

```
int main()
{

    Events^ events = gcnew Events();

    // Add the event handlers for Start and Exit.
    events->Start += gcnew EventHandler(events, &Events::OnStart);
    events->Exit += gcnew EventHandler(events, &Events::OnExit);

    f(events);

    // Remove the event handlers.
    events->Start -= gcnew EventHandler(events, &Events::OnStart);
    events->Exit -= gcnew EventHandler(events, &Events::OnExit);
}
```

This code works because, as for a trivial property, methods are automatically generated by the compiler for adding and removing event handlers and raising events. In addition, an underlying delegate is created. You can certainly go far with events simply using "trivial" events, since often the add, remove, and raise methods are just what you need. However, if your application requires special handling for adding or removing event handlers, or raising events, you can go beyond these default methods and define your own. Listing 7-17 rewrites this to define custom add, remove, and raise methods. In this case, we use the custom methods to track what's going on by writing to the console.

If you do write your own add and remove accessors, you should take care to ensure thread safety. The default add and remove accessors lock on the containing object (the this pointer), meaning that any other thread attempting to access these methods on the same object will be locked out. You can use the lock template provided in the msclr namespace (#include msclr\lock.h to access it) to accomplish this. Locking the add and remove accessors will prevent corruption of the list that keeps track of the functions to be called when an event is fired. Locking the raise method is not a good idea since the code you call from your event handler might lead to an invocation of the event, which will lead to a deadlock.

Listing 7-17. *Customizing add, remove, and raise*

```
// events_custom.cpp
#include <msclr\lock.h>
using namespace System;
using namespace msclr;

ref class Events
{
    public:

        // underlying delegates to use for the events
        EventHandler^ _start, ^ _exit;
```

```
event EventHandler^ Start
{
    // Use the += operator to add a function to the
    // (multicast) delegate.
    void add(EventHandler^ handler)
    {
        lock lockEvent(this);
        Console::WriteLine(" Adding Start event handler. ");
        _start += handler;
    }
    void remove(EventHandler^ handler)
    {
        lock lockEvent(this);
        Console::WriteLine(" Removing Start event handler. ");
        _start -= handler;
    }

protected:

    // If the underlying delegate is non-null, invoke the
    // event with the given event arguments.
    void raise(Object^ sender, EventArgs^ args)
    {
        Console::WriteLine(" Firing Start event. ");
        if (_start)
            _start->Invoke(sender, args);
    }
}

event EventHandler^ Exit
{
    void add(EventHandler^ handler)
    {
        lock lockEvent(this);
        Console::WriteLine(" Adding Exit event handler. ");
        _exit += handler;
    }
    void remove(EventHandler^ handler)
    {
        lock lockEvent(this);
        Console::WriteLine(" Removing Exit event handler. ");
        _exit -= handler;
    }
```

```cpp
        void raise(Object^ sender, EventArgs^ args)
        {
            Console::WriteLine(" Firing Exit event. ");
            if (_exit)
                _exit->Invoke(sender, args);
        }
    }


    // Function calls to raise the events from outside the class.
    void RaiseStartEvent()
    {
        Start(this, gcnew EventArgs());
    }

    void RaiseExitEvent()
    {
        Exit(this, gcnew EventArgs());
    }

    // event handler for Start event
    void OnStart(Object^ sender, EventArgs^ args)
    {
        Console::WriteLine("Starting");
    }

    // event handler for Exit event
    void OnExit(Object^ sender, EventArgs^ args)
    {
        Console::WriteLine("Exiting");
    }
};


void f(Events^ e)
{
    // Raise event for starting this function.
    e->RaiseStartEvent();

    Console::WriteLine("Doing something.");

    // Raise event for exiting this function.
    e->RaiseExitEvent();
}

int main()
{
```

```
    Events^ events = gcnew Events();

    // Add the event handlers for Start and Exit.
    events->Start += gcnew EventHandler(events, &Events::OnStart);
    events->Exit += gcnew EventHandler(events, &Events::OnExit);

    f(events);

    // Remove the event handlers.
    events->Start -= gcnew EventHandler(events, &Events::OnStart);
    events->Exit -= gcnew EventHandler(events, &Events::OnExit);
}
```

The output of Listing 7-17 is as follows:

```
Adding Start event handler.
 Adding Exit event handler.
 Firing Start event.
Starting
Doing something.
 Firing Exit event.
Exiting
 Removing Start event handler.
 Removing Exit event handler.
```

The lock object will release its lock when it goes out of scope at the end of the method in which it is used.

We have used the EventHandler and EventArgs classes provided by the framework, although in fact any delegate may be used as the event type instead with this pattern. Listing 7-18 is an example of using a delegate unrelated to the System::EventHandler class. You can see that much of the earlier example applies, but the parameters to the event are determined by parameters of the delegate type, EventProcessor. Differences are indicated in boldface.

Listing 7-18. *Using a Delegate Unrelated to System::EventHandler*

```
// events_custom2.cpp
#include <msclr\lock.h>
using namespace System;
using namespace msclr;

delegate void EventProcessor(String^ eventString);

ref class Events
{
    public:
```

```cpp
// underlying delegates to use for the events
EventProcessor^ _start, ^ _exit;

event EventProcessor^ Start
{
    void add(EventProcessor^ handler)
    {
        lock lockEvents(this);
        Console::WriteLine(" Adding Start event handler. ");
        _start += handler;
    }
    void remove(EventProcessor^ handler)
    {
        lock lockEvents(this);
        Console::WriteLine(" Removing Start event handler. ");
        _start -= handler;
    }

    protected:

    void raise(String^ eventString)
    {
        Console::WriteLine(" Firing Start event. ");
        if (_start)
            _start->Invoke(eventString);
    }
}

event EventProcessor^ Exit
{
    void add(EventProcessor^ handler)
    {
        lock lockEvents(this);
        Console::WriteLine(" Adding Exit event handler. ");
        _exit += handler;
    }
    void remove(EventProcessor^ handler)
    {
        lock lockEvents(this);
        Console::WriteLine(" Removing Exit event handler. ");
        _exit -= handler;
    }
```

```cpp
        void raise(String^ eventString)
        {
            Console::WriteLine(" Firing Exit event. ");
            if (_exit)
                _exit->Invoke(eventString);
        }
    }

    // function calls to raise the events from outside the class
    void RaiseStartEvent(String^ eventString)
    {
        Start(eventString);
    }

    void RaiseExitEvent(String^ eventString)
    {
        Exit(eventString);
    }

    // event handler for Start event
    void OnStart(String^ eventString)
    {
        Console::WriteLine("Starting: " + eventString);
    }

    // event handler for Exit event
    void OnExit(String^ eventString)
    {
        Console::WriteLine("Exiting: " + eventString);
    }
};

void f(Events^ e)
{
    // Raise event for starting this function.
    e->RaiseStartEvent("Start event occurred!");

    Console::WriteLine("Doing something.");

    // Raise event for exiting this function.
    e->RaiseExitEvent("Exit event occurred.");
}
```

```
int main()
{

    Events^ events = gcnew Events();

    // Add the event handlers for Start and Exit.
    events->Start += gcnew EventProcessor(events, &Events::OnStart);
    events->Exit += gcnew EventProcessor(events, &Events::OnExit);

    f(events);

    // Remove the event handlers.
    events->Start -= gcnew EventProcessor(events, &Events::OnStart);
    events->Exit -= gcnew EventProcessor(events, &Events::OnExit);
}
```

The output of Listing 7-18 is shown here:

```
Adding Start event handler.
 Adding Exit event handler.
 Firing Start event.
Starting: Start event occurred!
Doing something.
 Firing Exit event.
Exiting: Exit event occurred.
 Removing Start event handler.
 Removing Exit event handler.
```

The expressions for creating the delegates (the gcnew expressions in the main method) remain the same, but the arguments for the custom delegate are used throughout instead of the System::EventHandler arguments. However, the EventHandler class is quite general and, since it includes an EventArgs parameter that is flexible enough for most uses, it is common to use these classes provided by the framework.

Event Receivers and Senders

Events are often fired by a different object than the one that receives or handles the event. A handle to the object involved in generating the event can be passed in. The design of the EventHandler class reflects this, including the sender parameter.

Listing 7-19 is a simplification of the code in the previous listing, but it illustrates the more common case of separate sender and receiver classes.

Listing 7-19. *Using Separate Sender and Receiver Classes*

```cpp
// sender_receiver.cpp
using namespace System;

// This class generates an event.
ref class EventSender
{

  public:

  event EventHandler^ MyEvent;

  void Fire(EventArgs^ args)
  {
    // Raise event for starting this function.
    MyEvent(this, args);

  }
};


// This class will handle the event.
ref class EventReceiver
{
  public:

    // event handler for Start event
    void OnMyEvent(Object^ sender, EventArgs^ args)
    {
      Console::WriteLine("My Event");
    }

    void SetUpToReceive(EventSender^ sender)
    {
      // Add the event handler.
      sender->MyEvent += gcnew EventHandler(this, &EventReceiver::OnMyEvent);
    }

};


int main()
{
    EventReceiver^ receiver = gcnew EventReceiver();
    EventSender^ sender = gcnew EventSender();
```

```
    // Configure the receiver to listen to events
    // from the specified sender.
    receiver->SetUpToReceive(sender);

    EventArgs^ args = gcnew EventArgs();
    sender->Fire(args);
}
```

Here is the output of Listing 7-19:

My Event

Using the EventArgs Class

The System::EventArgs class is itself not capable of passing custom event arguments. To define events that do contain additional data, you need to define a class derived from EventArgs that contains the required data. Listing 7-20 demonstrates how to use a class derived from EventArgs to send data about an event that can be used in the event handler to customize the response. You'll want to create a new event handler delegate type to match the custom EventArgs type.

Listing 7-20. *Providing Custom Event Data*

```
// eventargs.cpp
using namespace System;

ref class MyEventArgs : EventArgs
{
  public:
    property String^ Info;

    MyEventArgs(String^ info)
    {
      Info = info;
    }
};

delegate void MyEventHandler(Object^ sender, MyEventArgs^ args);

// This class generates an event.
ref class EventSender
{

  public:

    event MyEventHandler^ MyEvent;
```

```
    void Fire(MyEventArgs^ args)
    {
        // Raise event for starting this function.
        MyEvent(this, args);

    }
};


// This class will handle the event.
ref class EventReceiver
{
    public:

        // event handler for Start event
        void OnMyEvent(Object^ sender, MyEventArgs^ args)
        {
            Console::WriteLine("My Event with info: " + args->Info );
        }

        void SetUpToReceive(EventSender^ sender)
        {
            // Add the event handler.
            sender->MyEvent += gcnew MyEventHandler(this, &EventReceiver::OnMyEvent);
        }

};


int main()
{
    EventReceiver^ receiver = gcnew EventReceiver();
    EventSender^ sender = gcnew EventSender();

    // Configure the receiver to listen to events
    // from the specified sender.
    receiver->SetUpToReceive(sender);

    MyEventArgs^ myargs = gcnew MyEventArgs("abc");
    sender->Fire(myargs);
}
```

The output of Listing 7-20 is as follows:

```
My Event with info: abc
```

Reserved Names

Whenever properties or events are declared in a class, certain methods get created that implement the properties and events. Thus, certain names become reserved in a class that has these properties or events. In a class with a property named P, the names get_P and set_P are reserved, and in a class with an event named E, add_E, remove_E, and raise_E are reserved. Also, get_Item and set_Item are reserved since these are emitted to support default indexed properties.

Operator Overloading

The purpose of operator overloading is to implement types that behave like built-in types. The basic rules for operator precedence and evaluation remain the same regardless of whether the operators are used with primitive types (int, double, etc.) or user-defined types, so if you wanted to define a new operator with its own precedence rules—such as an exponentiation operator—you couldn't do it. Unfortunately, C++/CLI adds to the long list of highly sophisticated languages that suffer from the omission of the exponentiation operator, so until some enlightened language designer chooses to change that, we have to concede to the FORTRAN fans that theirs is, after all, the language designed better for the expression of mathematical formulas. I'm sorry, but the pow function is as poor an alternative as the add function would be for the + operator. I can only conclude that it's obvious that there is a cultural gap between computer language designers and computational scientists. OK, I'll get off my soap box now. However, despite these limitations, operator overloading is useful for many situations.

Static Operators

C++/CLI allows you to define static operators on a class. This avoids the need for some operators to be global, such as addition between a class type and a primitive type. Usually, these functions require access to the internals of a class, so the concept of friend functions and friend classes is often used in C++ to allow external operator functions to access the internals of a type. To illustrate the problem, in C++ implement a class that allows addition as an integer. Perhaps it's a class called Complex (see Listing 7-21). To support the + operator with complex numbers and ordinary doubles, you have to implement several global functions.

Listing 7-21. *Defining a Class to Represent Complex Numbers*

```
// complex.h
using namespace System;

class Complex
{
    double re;
    double im;

    public:

        Complex() : re(0.0), im(0.0) { }
```

```cpp
Complex(double real, double imag) : re(real), im(imag) { }

// Allow a complex number to be created from a double.
Complex(double real) : re(real), im(0.0) { }

Complex(const Complex& c)
{
    this->re = c.re; this->im = c.im;
}

// assignment operator
Complex& operator=(const Complex& c)
{
    this->re = c.re; this->im = c.im;
    return *this;
}

// equality operator for comparing two complex numbers
bool operator==(const Complex& c)
{
    return (this->re == c.re && this->im == c.im);
}


// unary minus
Complex operator-()
{
    return Complex(-re, im);
}

// Add a complex number to a complex number.
Complex operator+(const Complex& rhs)
{
    return Complex(this->re + rhs.re, this->im + rhs.im);
}
// Add a complex number to a complex number.
Complex operator+(double d)
{
    return Complex(this->re + d, this->im);
}
// Add a double and a complex number.
// This must be a global friend operator.
friend Complex operator+(double d, Complex c)
{
    return Complex(c.re + d, c.im);
}
```

```
    // ditto for ambition, distraction, uglification, and derision...

};
```

Notice the operator + declared as a friend, which is a global function, not actually a member of the class. The friend operator is necessary if you want addition to be commutative (necessary for any sensible system of operators). Consider the following expressions:

```
double d;
Complex c1, c2;
c2 = c1 + d; // Complex::operator+(double d) member function called
c2 = d + c1;  // global friend operator+(double d, const Complex& c) called
```

It's not possible for an instance method to be called on a class when the class is on the right side of the expression.

In C++/CLI, the operators that in classic C++ you would define as global friend functions, you define as static operators in the class. This is considered a superior design in that you do not need to make any special exceptions to the encapsulation of the private data for a class in order to support commutative operators that work with primitive types.

In Listing 7-22, the addition operators between Complex and double are declared as static operators in the class. These operators would have been global friend functions in a native C++ class.

In addition, the operator for adding two complex numbers could also be defined as static, as in Listing 7-22, rather than as a member operator as it would be in classic C++.

Listing 7-22. *Defining a Static Operator*

```
// complex.h
using namespace System;

value class Complex
{
    double re;
    double im;

    public:

    Complex(double real, double imag) : re(real), im(imag)
    { }

    // unary minus
    Complex operator-()
    {
        return Complex(-re, im);
    }
```

```
    // Addition of two complex numbers.
    // Could also be defined as a member operator.
    static Complex operator+(Complex c1, Complex c2)
    {
        return Complex(c1.re + c2.re, c1.im + c2.im);
    }
    // This cannot be a member operator, since a double is on the left.
    static Complex operator+(double d, Complex c)
    {
        return Complex(c.re + d, c.im);
    }
    // If Complex is the first argument, this could also be
    // a member operator.
    static Complex operator+(Complex c, double d)
    {
        return Complex(c.re + d, c.im);
    }

    // etc.

};
```

Conversion Operators and Casts

As you know, in classic C++ you can define type conversion operators to enable automatic conversions between your type and another type. You can do this in managed types as well as in C++/CLI. The additional option you have in C++/CLI is to specify whether the conversion requires an explicit cast, or not. You do this with the explicit keyword. While the explicit keyword is also used in classic C++, in classic C++ it is used only on constructors, to prevent the constructor from being used to define an implicit conversion. In C++/CLI, the situation is different. Constructors for managed types are never used for implicit conversions, whether or not the explicit keyword is used on them, so using the keyword would be redundant. However, the keyword is used on conversion operators. Without the keyword, the conversion operator is assumed to be implicit, as it is in classic C++. With the keyword, the conversion operator is only invoked with an explicit cast (see Listing 7-23).

Listing 7-23. *Using explicit with a Conversion Operator*

```
// explicit_conversion.cpp

using namespace System;

value class BigIntExplicit
{
    __int64 m_i;
```

```
    public:

    explicit BigIntExplicit(int i) : m_i(i)
    { }

    explicit operator int()
    { return m_i; }

    explicit static operator BigIntExplicit(int i)
    { return BigIntExplicit(i); }

    void takeBigIntExplicit(BigIntExplicit b) {}
};


value class BigIntImplicit
{
    __int64 m_i;

    public:

    BigIntImplicit(int i) : m_i(i)
    { }

    operator int()
    { return m_i; }

    static operator BigIntImplicit(int i)
    { return BigIntImplicit(i); }

    void takeBigIntImplicit(BigIntImplicit b) {}
};


int main()
{
    BigIntExplicit b_exp(400);
    BigIntImplicit b_imp(500);

    int i = safe_cast<int>( b_exp );  // OK: requires explicit cast

    int j = b_imp;     // OK: implicit

    // int cannot implicitly be converted to BigInt1 and BigInt2
    // with the constructor; instead, you define the static conversion operator.
    // This is different from standard C++, which uses the constructor
    // for such implicit conversions.
    b_exp.takeBigIntExplicit(safe_cast<BigIntExplicit>(i));
    b_imp.takeBigIntImplicit(j);
}
```

In Listing 7-23, observe several things:

The explicit keyword on operator int used in BigIntExplicit disallows implicit conversions from BigIntExplicit to int. This is useful if you want to prevent unexpected conversions from taking place without an explicit cast.

The explicit keyword on the constructor for BigIntExplicit has no effect. We need the static operator BigInt that takes an int to convert. Again we have the choice of making the operator explicit or implicit.

We use the preferred safe_cast casting mechanism. C-style casts (i.e., using the target type name in parentheses) are supported in C++/CLI, and if used, evaluate to another type of cast. All of the preceding conversion functions will work with C-style casts and static_cast as well. In the next sections, I'll explain casting in C++/CLI and review the various casting mechanisms in classic C++, which are also available in C++/CLI. The next chapter will revisit dynamic_cast in the context of inheritance.

C-Style Casts

C-style casts are casts that use the parentheses syntax used in C. The use of C-style casts is not recommended since it can be difficult to tell what type of cast will actually be performed. However, there are definite rules that determine the type of cast actually performed. Basically, the compiler attempts various types of casts ranging from the safest to the least safe. If possible, the validity of the cast will be determined at compile time. If the types involved in the conversion differ only by whether or not they are constant, the cast is interpreted as a const_cast. If the two types are in the same inheritance chain or are both interface handles, the safe_cast is used. Next, the compiler will attempt to interpret the cast as a static_cast. This will succeed if the types have a defined conversion (for example, a conversion operator). Also, if a safe_cast or static_cast will work if combined with a const_cast, the compiler will do so. Finally, if the compiler cannot determine whether a static_cast is valid, a runtime check will be performed. If the runtime check fails, an InvalidCastException will be generated.

static_cast

static_cast is used in the usual way. It is commonly used to convert a pointer to a base class to a pointer to a derived class. When used in this context, there is no runtime check to verify that the object really is of the derived class. This means that it's possibly unsafe, but often faster. If the object is not of the derived class, your code has a potentially serious error that will not be checked at runtime.

One potential problem with static_cast is that the code that is generated can't always be verified to be safe. Compiler checking for unsafe code can be enabled by using a particular compiler option (/clr:safe), so depending on the specific cast, static_cast may or may not be allowed when using the /clr:safe compiler option. Verifiably safe code has many uses, for example, running in restrictive environments such as a web browser. Chapter 12 will discuss how to write verifiably safe code. You'll probably want to use constructs, like safe_cast, that can be verified to be safe whenever possible, even if you don't specifically intend to use /clr:safe.

dynamic_cast

Dynamic casts are used when converting a type from a base class pointer into a derived class pointer. A runtime check will be performed at the time of the conversion. If the conversion fails, the value returned is nullptr but no exception is thrown. The behavior on failure is basically the only difference between dynamic_cast and safe_cast. This difference means that dynamic_cast is not as slow as safe_cast, since throwing an exception is a particularly expensive and time-consuming operation.

const_cast

This construct is used when you need to convert a const pointer, handle, or reference to a non-const pointer, handle, or reference. Its use is considered more dangerous than static_cast since it introduces the possibility of writing to read-only memory.

reinterpret_cast

This construct breaks type safety since it is an unchecked cast. It cannot be used in verifiable code (safe code), and should be used sparingly, if at all. Using reinterpret_cast is equivalent to asserting that you know for certain that the object can be converted to the given type, even though it is not evident from the types involved.

safe_cast

This construct, which is new with C++/CLI, performs a verifiably safe cast for managed types or interfaces. The cast is checked at runtime. safe_cast may be used wherever static_cast is used, and is recommended. safe_cast may also be used to cast an interface pointer to an unrelated interface (a cast that static_cast cannot perform). The compiler will detect whether a cast is safe without a runtime type check and only insert it if necessary for type safety, so there is no performance loss unless the runtime check is required.

See Table 7-1 for a summary of the types of casts available in C++/CLI programs.

Table 7-1. *Types of Casts Available in C++/CLI Programs*

Type of Cast	Example	When Used	Notes
C-style cast	R^ r; (Object^) r;	Anywhere	Evaluates to another type of cast.
const_cast	const int i; const_cast<int>(i);	When casting away const or casting to a constant	Can only remove or add const (or volatile).
static_cast	int i; static_cast<double>(i)	Conversions between compile-time compatible types	No runtime check; use for types in which the validity of the cast is checkable at compile time.
dynamic_cast	Base^ b; dynamic_cast<Derived^>(b)	Conversions with runtime check in inheritance hierarchies	Evaluates to nullptr on failed cast.

Table 7-1. *Types of Casts Available in C++/CLI Programs (Continued)*

Type of Cast	Example	When Used	Notes
reinterpret_cast	int address; reinterpret_cast<void*> (address)	Force conversion between incompatible types	Considered dangerous.
safe_cast	Base^ b; safe_cast<Derived^>(b)	Conversion with runtime check when necessary	Throws InvalidCastException on failed cast.

Summary

In this chapter, you learned about several special elements that can be declared in classes to model commonly used concepts: properties, to model the "has-a" relationship; delegates and events, to model actions and responses; and operators, to model mathematical and other functionality. The text looked specifically at conversion operators and the expanded use of the explicit keyword. You also saw various types of conversions and casts.

Next, you'll learn all about inheritance.

CHAPTER 8

∎∎∎

Inheritance

The inheritance model for C++/CLI classes is not the same as that in C++. Multiple inheritance (of managed class types) is not supported. Instead, C++/CLI reference types may only inherit from one base class, but may implement multiple interfaces. This is the only supported inheritance model in the CLI, so languages such as C# and VB .NET support the same model as C++/CLI. Other features of the model include the ability to specify whether a function with the same name as a base class's virtual function is intended to be an override to that function, or whether it is a new function with the same name.

The philosophy behind this inheritance model is based on several ideas. One idea is that multiple inheritance of class types leads to a lot of ambiguous calls when method names in different bases collide. In large inheritance hierarchies with virtual base classes, the rules for disambiguation of method calls are quite complicated and not easily comprehended. Another issue is the difficulty of handling situations where the same base class appears more than once in the inheritance chain. In such a case, the base class could be a virtual base class, which means that only one instance of the base class should be in the most derived object, or a nonvirtual base class, in which separate instances of the base object exist for every occurrence in the inheritance tree. Initialization is also a troublesome issue—virtual base classes must be initialized by the most derived object (to avoid ambiguity as to which class in the hierarchy is supposed to do this). It's very complicated, and as a language feature, most people find it difficult to learn all the rules.

Multiple inheritance has its merits. The iostreams library is designed as a diamond-shaped inheritance hierarchy with a virtual base class, ios, at its root, and I can see how this design makes sense. The classes istream and ostream each inherit from ios, and iostream inherits from both istream and ostream. The virtual base class ios gives both input streams (istream) and output streams (ostream) some common functionality, such as status flags, and the iostream combines the input and output streams into a stream that can handle both. This is a case where multiple inheritance works well. However, some people have also seen some very convoluted inheritance hierarchies that required a fine-toothed comb to untangle. Maybe the blame for these should be placed at the feet of the library designers who created these hierarchies, not on the language designers.

I'll return to this discussion in the next chapter, which covers interfaces. Since the CLI inheritance model does allow multiple inheritance of interfaces, it is quite expressive, and most people say that it is flexible enough to handle most of the issues that true, full multiple inheritance supports. Of course, there will no doubt be some multiple inheritance fans who will point out design patterns that seem to absolutely require C++ multiple inheritance. Technically, you can still create and use a native, multiple-inheritance-based C++ class hierarchy in your C++/CLI programs (as long you're not using safe mode) if your design requires it. You just can't have it be a managed type.

Another difference between inheritance in C++/CLI and classic C++ is the absence of private or protected inheritance. Inheritance is always public, but the public keyword is optional. Private inheritance was sometimes used in classic C++ to inherit an implementation: it is intended to model the "has-a" relationship, which can also be modeled by containing the type as a field.

It is sometimes said that value types cannot participate in inheritance. This is not strictly true; value types can implement interfaces, but not inherit from other value classes or reference types. Value types do inherit from System::ValueType, although they have to be boxed in order to realize this inheritance relationship. Unboxed value types have no virtual function table with which to participate in polymorphism.

Name Collisions in Inheritance Hierarchies

C++/CLI provides some additional ways to control whether functions in a derived class override a base class function, or whether they simply provide a new function that hides the base class function. The question is, Why? The answer has to do with real-world problems associated with updating the base class to a new version. Library vendors often add new functions, including virtual functions, to their base classes to support new features. Consumers of these libraries generally have their own classes that use the library's base classes. It's possible that method name conflicts arise between the library consumer's derived classes and the library vendor's base classes.

To make this a little more concrete, let's say we're creating an adventure game in which we have a player up against numerous monsters. Our game is extensible, so we ship our game library, and developers create their own monster types by inheriting from the Monster type in our library. We also have other objects in the game other than monsters, such as weapons, armor, and the like (all represented by an Item class) and tiles on the game map. So, our hierarchy looks like Listing 8-1.

Listing 8-1. *The Monster Hierarchy*

```
// game_library.cpp
public ref class GameObject
{
};

public ref class Monster : GameObject
{
};

public ref class MapTile : GameObject
{
};

public ref class Item : GameObject
{
};
```

To explore versioning issues, suppose a client of this game library has a Scroll class (see Listing 8-2) representing magic spells written out on a scroll. This class supports a Read method that invokes a spell:

Listing 8-2. *A Class for Magic Spells*

```
// client_game.cpp
#using "game_library.dll"
ref class Scroll : Item
{
    public:
        void Read() { /* read the scroll and invoke the spell */ }
};
```

Let's say that we are shipping a new version of our library, and we add functionality to read and write GameObject instances from a file. So we add Read and Write methods, as in Listing 8-3.

Listing 8-3. *New Functionality for Game Objects*

```
public ref class GameObject
{
    public:
        void Initialize();
        virtual void Read() { /* read data from file */ }
        virtual void Write() { /* write data to file */ }
};
```

They're virtual so that derived classes can read and write their own information, if needed. The question is, What happens when the user upgrades to the new version? In C++, what might happen is that the virtual Read method for reading the scroll would silently override the Read method to read from a file. Then, at runtime, when we try to read data (as in Listing 8-4), the Read function in the Scroll class gets called and the game character casts a spell—not what was intended at all!

Listing 8-4. *Reading with an Unintended Method*

```
void GameObject::Initialize()
{
    if (reading_from_file)
    {
        Read();  // Oops! Scroll method called.
    }

    // ...
}
```

Ideally, the compiler should catch any conflicts and allow these conflicts to be dealt with appropriately by the consumers of the new library. If name conflicts occur, users could rename your derived class functions or take some other action to eliminate the conflict. In some cases, when a vendor's base class implements the functionality you were implementing in a derived class, you might just decide to eliminate your version of this functionality. In any event, you would want to make a conscious decision as to what to do.

The problem was solved initially by the designers of the CLI. C++/CLI follows the same pattern. The designers of the CLI decided to eliminate accidental overriding by making overriding explicit in every case. You must use either the override keyword or the new keyword to specify whether a derived class's function is meant to *replace* the base class function or *hide it*. If not, you get a compiler error. This design means that when you upgrade to a newer version of a base class, you'll know at compile time whether your application's derived class has a conflict before it causes problems.

Using the new Keyword on Virtual Functions

If we want to specify that the derived class function is a new function, not intended to override the base function, we append new to the function signature as in Listing 8-5.

Listing 8-5. *Using new to Override Overriding*

```cpp
// new_method.cpp
using namespace System;

// the game library's classes
ref class GameObject
{
   public:
      void Initialize(bool fromFile)
      {
         if (fromFile)
         {
            Read();
         }
         else
         {
            // other code
         }
      }
      virtual void Read()
      {
         Console::WriteLine("GameObject::Read");
      }
};
```

```
ref class Item : GameObject
{
    // ...
};

// the user's class
ref class Scroll : Item
{
   public:
      virtual void Read() new
      {
          // Read the scroll in the game environment.
          Console::WriteLine("Scroll::Read");
      }
};

int main()
{
   Scroll^ scroll = gcnew Scroll();
   Item^ item = scroll;
   item->Initialize(true);
   scroll->Read();
}
```

The output of Listing 8-5 is as follows:

```
GameObject::Read
Scroll::Read
```

You might wonder about the new keyword being used here in a different context. Isn't that a problem? It's not a problem because the compiler is sensitive to the context in which the new keyword is used.

Using the override Keyword on Virtual Methods

The contextual keyword override is used to indicate an intentional override of a virtual function. Because new and override are required when overriding a virtual function, you are always forced to make a conscious decision about whether your newly created function is intended to override the virtual function or be a new function altogether.

Some methods are intended to be overridden frequently. The ToString method on Object is commonly overridden to provide type-specific output. In Chapter 7 (Listing 7-8), you saw a class that overrides the ToString method:

```
class ElementType
{
   public:

      virtual String^ ToString() override
      {
          return String::Format(
            "Element {0} Symbol {1} Atomic Number {2} Atomic Weight {3}",
              Name, Symbol, AtomicNumber, AtomicWeight);
      }

      // ...
};
```

Other methods are less frequently overridden, such as the Equals method on Object.

Continuing with the role-playing game example, suppose we need to modify the Read method since we are storing the spell information in the file, so that needs some additional parsing in the Read method. We use override to implement the Read virtual function for the Scroll class differently from the GameObject class, as shown in Listing 8-6.

Listing 8-6. *Using override to Implement a Virtual Function*

```
// override.cpp
using namespace System;

// the game library's classes
ref class GameObject
{
   public:
      void Initialize(bool fromFile)
      {
          if (fromFile)
          {
              Read();
          }
          else
          {
              // other code .
          }
      }
      virtual void Read()
      {
          // general reading from a file for the GameObject
          Console::WriteLine("GameObject::Read");
      }
};
```

```
ref class Item : GameObject
{
    // ...
};

// the user's class
ref class Scroll : Item
{
    public:
        virtual void Read() override
        {
            // special reading from a file pertaining to scroll class
            Console::WriteLine("Scroll::Read");
        }
};

int main()
{
    Scroll^ scroll = gcnew Scroll();
    Item^ item = scroll;
    item->Initialize(true);
    scroll->Read();
}
```

Here is the output of Listing 8-6:

```
Scroll::Read
Scroll::Read
```

What if you want both? Is it possible to have the same method in the class twice, one that overrides and the other that is new? You cannot declare two Read methods with the same argument list, but you can achieve the effect of overriding any virtual calls to GameObject's Read method by explicitly specifying the function you are overriding using the syntax shown in Listing 8-7.

Listing 8-7. *Explicitly Specifying a Function to Override*

```
// explicit_override.cpp
using namespace System;

// the game library's classes
ref class GameObject
{
    public:
        void Initialize(bool fromFile)
        {
```

```
                if (fromFile)
                {
                    Read();
                }
                else
                {
                    // other code
                }
            }
            virtual void Read()
            {
                Console::WriteLine("GameObject::Read");
            }
    };

    ref class Item : GameObject
    {
        // ...
    };

    // the user's class
    ref class Scroll : Item
    {
        public:
            virtual void GameObjectRead() = GameObject::Read
            {
                // Read a file with additional parsing.
                Console::WriteLine("Scroll::GameObjectRead");
            }
            virtual void Read() new
            {
                // Read the scroll.
                Console::WriteLine("Scroll::Read");
            }

    };

    int main()
    {
        Scroll^ scroll = gcnew Scroll();
        Item^ item = scroll;
        item->Initialize(true);
        scroll->Read();
    }
```

The output of Listing 8-7 is shown here:

```
Scroll::GameObjectRead
Scroll::Read
```

By specifying the function you are overriding, you can use a different name for the override, saving the Read name for your Scroll class's functionality.

Abstract Classes

In classic C++, an abstract class is any class that contains one or more pure virtual methods. C++\CLI has the same concept, but instead of being implicit, you explicitly declare such a class with the abstract keyword.

As in classic C++, abstract classes in C++/CLI cannot be instantiated; they are usually used as base classes. Individual methods may be declared abstract in two ways—in the old way using the pure specifier (that funny = 0 appended after the function prototype), or using the abstract contextual keyword on the function; that is,

```
virtual void f() = 0;
```

is the equivalent of

```
virtual void f() abstract;
```

If you do declare any function in a class abstract using either syntax just described, it makes the class abstract, but it does not require that the class be declared as such. However, you can also declare a class or structure abstract even if it doesn't have any abstract methods. Derived classes of abstract classes may themselves be abstract, but the first nonabstract class in the hierarchy will have to provide an implementation or have inherited an implementation for all the abstract methods inherited from abstract base classes (and, as you will see in the next chapter, any abstract methods from interfaces, too). Listing 8-8 shows an example.

Listing 8-8. *Declaring Abstract Classes*

```
// abstract_classes.cpp

// Notice that the abstract keyword follows the class name.
ref class GameObject abstract
{
    int ID;

    public:

        // an abstract method with no implementation
        // provided
        virtual void ReadFromFile() abstract;
```

```
        // a nonabstract virtual method with an implementation
        virtual void UpdateID(int id)
        {
            ID = id;
        }
};

ref class Monster : GameObject
{

    public:
        // overrides the base class abstract function
        virtual void ReadFromFile() override
        {
            // code to read in data for the type
        }
};
```

As you can see in Listing 8-8, the abstract modifier appears after the class name. If this seems odd, just realize that it allows abstract to be a contextual keyword rather than a normal keyword, thus preventing problems if you have an identifier called abstract in your code.

Handles may be created with the abstract class type, and they may be used to reference instances of nonabstract derived classes. This lets you define methods that take the abstract base class as a handle type that will work with instances of any of the derived classes.

A value type may be declared abstract. Since a value type is also *sealed* (as discussed in the next section), such a class would be abstract and sealed. It would not be possible to create an instance of such a type, and although you could call static methods on it, you would have to provide an implementation of these methods.

There are many ways in which abstract classes are different from interfaces. Abstract classes can inherit from nonabstract classes. Instance functions (including properties) and instance fields may be defined, not just declared, in abstract classes. None of that is possible in an interface class. This difference has big implications for the choice between abstract classes and interfaces when designing a library, especially a library that you intend to update with a new version. Abstract classes are more easily changed in subsequent versions. If you add a method to an interface, all the classes that implement that interface must implement the new method. If you add a method to an abstract class, you can provide an implementation in the class. You just add a nonabstract method to the abstract class.

Sealed Classes

The sealed modifier may be applied to methods, classes, or structs. Methods marked sealed may not be overridden by derived classes. Classes and structs marked sealed cannot be inherited from. The syntax for a sealed class is as in Listing 8-9.

Listing 8-9. *Sealed Class Syntax*

```
// sealed.cpp

ref class C sealed
{
};

ref class B : C // Error: cannot inherit from a sealed class.
{
};
```

Value classes are implicitly sealed; the use of sealed in the class declaration is not an error, although it is not necessary.

Like abstract, the sealed modifier may also be used on an individual function. A sealed type indicates that all the functions in the class are sealed, but when used on an individual function, sealed indicates that only that function cannot be overridden.

Derived classes can use new on a sealed base class function; however, they may not use override. If you use new on a sealed base class function, you are creating a totally unrelated method.

The abstract or sealed modifiers apply to individual overloads of overloaded functions. Thus, one of a series of function overloads may be sealed, but this does not prevent the other overloads from being overridden in derived classes.

Abstract and Sealed

You can use both abstract and sealed. Applied to a type, this makes the type rather like a namespace or "static class." You cannot create any instances of such a type, but you can define static fields and methods on the type, as in Listing 8-10.

Listing 8-10. *An Abstract Sealed Class*

```
// abstract_sealed.cpp
using namespace System;

ref class A abstract sealed
{
    static int i = 1;
    static int j = 2;
    public:
        static A() { Console::WriteLine("A::A()"); }
        static void f() { Console::WriteLine("A::f " + i); }
        static void g() { Console::WriteLine("A::g " + j); }
};
```

```
int main()
{
    A::f();
    A::g();
}
```

The output of Listing 8-10 is as follows:

```
A::A()
A::f 1
A::g 2
```

The modifiers abstract and sealed may be reversed in order.

Virtual Properties

Properties participate in inheritance-like methods, but it's worth discussing some particulars. Property getter and setter methods may be virtual. The virtual keyword may be applied to the property, and thereby to both the get and the set methods, or to the individual get and set methods.

A property that overrides a base class virtual property cannot be written out as a trivial property, because there would be no way to make it any different from the base class property. You can successfully override a base class trivial property with a fully specified property, as in Listing 8-11. The get and set methods must be fully specified, and the override modifier must be applied to them individually.

Listing 8-11. *Overriding a Trivial Property*

```
// virtual_properties.cpp
using namespace System;

ref class Base
{
    public:

    virtual property int Prop;
};

ref class Derived : Base
{
    int prop;

    public:
```

```
    virtual property int Prop
    {
        int get() override { return prop; }
        void set(int value) override { prop = value; }
    }

};
```

The virtual keyword may also be applied to the individual get and set methods rather than to the property, as in Listing 8-12. This might be useful if you are only overriding one of the accessors, or if you need to make one nonvirtual and one virtual.

Listing 8-12. *Using Virtual Accessors*

```
// virtual_properties2.cpp

using namespace System;
using namespace System::Collections::Generic;

value class Isotope
{
    public:
        property unsigned int IsotopeNumber;
        property unsigned int AtomicNumber;
        property double Mass;
};

ref class Element
{
        double atomicWeight;

    public:
        property unsigned int AtomicNumber;
        property String^ Name;
        property String^ Symbol;

        property double AtomicWeight
        {
            virtual double get() { return atomicWeight; }
            void set(double a) { atomicWeight = a; }
        }

        Element(String^ name, String^ symbol,
                double a, double n)
```

```
        {
            AtomicNumber = n;
            AtomicWeight = a;
            Name = name;
            Symbol = symbol;
        }
};

ref class HydrogenWithIsotopes : Element
{


    double atomicWeight;

    public:


        property List<Isotope>^ Isotopes;
        property List<double>^ IsotopeAbundance;

        property double AtomicWeight
        {
            virtual double get() override
            {
                // Check to see if atomic weight has been calculated yet.
                if (atomicWeight == 0.0)
                {
                    double total = 0.0;
                    if (Isotopes->Count == 0)
                        return 0.0;
                    for (int i = 0; i < Isotopes->Count; i++)
                    {
                        total += Isotopes[i].Mass * IsotopeAbundance[i];
                    }
                    atomicWeight = total /* / Isotopes->Count */ ;
                }
                return atomicWeight;
            }
        }


    public:
```

```
HydrogenWithIsotopes() : Element("Hydrogen", "H", 0.0, 1)
{
    Isotopes = gcnew List<Isotope>();
    IsotopeAbundance = gcnew List<double>();

    Isotope isotope1;   // Hydrogen 1
    isotope1.IsotopeNumber = 1;
    isotope1.AtomicNumber = 1;
    isotope1.Mass = 1.0078250320710; // from about.com
    Isotopes->Add(isotope1);
    IsotopeAbundance->Add(.99985);

    Isotope isotope2; // Hydrogen 2 : Deuterium
    isotope2.IsotopeNumber = 2;
    isotope2.AtomicNumber = 1;
    isotope2.Mass = 2.01410177784;
    Isotopes->Add(isotope2);
    IsotopeAbundance->Add(.000115);

    Isotope isotope3;   // Hydrogen 3 : Tritium
    isotope3.IsotopeNumber = 3;
    isotope3.AtomicNumber = 1;
    isotope3.Mass = 3.016049277725 ;
    Isotopes->Add(isotope3);
    IsotopeAbundance->Add(0); // too small

}
};

int main()
{
    Element e("Hydrogen", "H", 1.00794, 1);
    Console::WriteLine("AtomicWeight is listed as {0}", e.AtomicWeight );
    HydrogenWithIsotopes h;
    Console::WriteLine("AtomicWeight is computed as {0}", h.AtomicWeight );
}
```

Here is the output of Listing 8-12:

```
AtomicWeight is listed as 1.00794
AtomicWeight is computed as 1.00790548002064
```

Special Member Functions and Inheritance

Special member functions such as constructors, destructors, and finalizers are not inherited. In this section, you will see the implications of this in inheritance hierarchies.

Constructors

As in classic C++, constructors are not inherited. Each derived class must define appropriate constructors. The base class constructor may be called from the derived class constructor for reference classes in the usual way by using the initializer list, as in Listing 8-13.

Listing 8-13. *Calling a Base Class Constructor*

```cpp
// constructor_inheritance.cpp
using namespace System;

ref class MyBase
{
    int data;
  public:
    MyBase() { Console::WriteLine("MyBase::MyBase()"); }
    MyBase(int data_in) : data(data_in)
    { Console::WriteLine("MyBase::MyBase(int)"); }
};

ref class Derived : MyBase
{
    public:
     // Invoke the base class constructor.
     Derived(int data) : MyBase(data)
     { Console::WriteLine("Derived::Derived(int)"); }

};

int main()
{
    // Derived d; // illegal: ctor w/o args not inherited
    MyBase b;
    Derived d(100);
}
```

The output of Listing 8-13 is shown here:

```
MyBase::MyBase()
MyBase::MyBase(int)
Derived::Derived(int)
```

Even though the code looks very similar to what you would do with native classes in classic C++, there is an important difference. The order in which initializer code is called is not the same as in classic C++. Listing 8-14 demonstrates this. In this example, there is a classic C++ inheritance hierarchy in a native type, and the same hierarchy with a reference type. In both cases, a field is initialized by the derived class constructor. The code is parallel in every way, and yet the behavior is different.

Listing 8-14. *Order of Initialization*

```cpp
// constructor_order.cpp
using namespace System;

class NativeClass
{
   public:

   NativeClass()
   {
      Console::WriteLine("NativeClass: Field constructor.");
   }
};

ref class ManagedClass
{
   public:

   ManagedClass()
   {
      Console::WriteLine("ManagedClass: Field constructor.");
   }
};

class NativeBase
{
   public:
   NativeBase()
   {
      Console::WriteLine("NativeBase: Base class constructor.");
   }
};

class NativeDerived : NativeBase
{
   NativeClass field;

   public:
   NativeDerived() : field()
   {
      Console::WriteLine("Native: Derived class constructor.");
   }
};
```

```
ref class ManagedBase
{
   public:
     ManagedBase()
     {
        Console::WriteLine("ManagedBase: Base class constructor.");
     }
};

ref class ManagedDerived : ManagedBase
{
   ManagedClass field;

   public:
     ManagedDerived() : field()
     {
        Console::WriteLine("ManagedDerived: Derived class constructor.");
     }
};

int main()
{
   NativeDerived nd;
   ManagedDerived md;
}
```

The different behavior is revealed when the code in Listing 8-14 is executed. The constructors are called in a different order in the two cases:

```
NativeBase: Base class constructor.
NativeClass: Field constructor.
Native: Derived class constructor.
ManagedClass: Field constructor.
ManagedBase: Base class constructor.
ManagedDerived: Derived class constructor.
```

In the native type hierarchy, the base class constructor is called before the field initializer is called. In the reference type hierarchy, the initializer for the field is called first, before the base class constructor.

As long as your initializers have no dependency on base class's fields, you don't have to worry about this difference. If your initializers do depend on base class fields, the initialization code should be moved from the initializer list into the body of the constructor.

Virtual Functions in the Constructor

In classic C++, virtual functions behave differently in the constructor than they do elsewhere. This is because it was seen as undesirable to call virtual functions on derived classes whose constructors had not yet been called. Instead, the most derived function that is already constructed is called, which is usually the version of the virtual function in the class whose constructor is being executed, but could be a function closer to the root of the tree if the function isn't implemented at that level in the inheritance tree. In C++/CLI, virtual functions act as they always do: the most derived method is called. Given that, can you predict the output of Listing 8-15?

Listing 8-15. *Using Virtual Functions in a Constructor*

```cpp
// native_managed_virtual.cpp

class NativeBase
{
   public:

   NativeBase()
   {
      f_virt();
   }

   virtual void f_virt()
   {
      System::Console::WriteLine("NativeBase::f_virt");
   }
};

class NativeDerived : public NativeBase
{
   public:

   NativeDerived()
   {
      f_virt();
   }

   virtual void f_virt()
   {
      System::Console::WriteLine("NativeDerived::f_virt");
   }
};

ref class ManagedBase
{
   public:

   ManagedBase()
   {
      f_virt();
   }
```

```
    virtual void f_virt()
    {
        System::Console::WriteLine("ManagedBase::f_virt");
    }
};

ref class ManagedDerived : ManagedBase
{
    public:

    ManagedDerived()
    {
        f_virt();
    }

    virtual void f_virt() override
    {
        System::Console::WriteLine("ManagedDerived::f_virt");
    }
};

int main()
{
    NativeDerived nd;
    ManagedDerived rd;
}
```

The output of Listing 8-15 is as follows:

```
NativeBase::f_virt
NativeDerived::f_virt
ManagedDerived::f_virt
ManagedDerived::f_virt
```

Surprised? For CLI types, virtual function dispatch is always deep, meaning that the most derived override is always called. In classic C++, it is shallow in the constructor, but deep everywhere else. In fact, you've arrived at the explanation of the difference in constructor initialization order as well. Because the most derived virtual function gets called, functions can execute on objects that have not been fully constructed. Having the fields get initialized first at least means that fields will be valid objects when derived class virtual functions get called, although you still need to take care in calling virtual functions in constructors, and also when implementing virtual functions that are called by base class constructors, to remember that objects are in a partially constructed state.

To override this behavior, specify the fully scoped base class function, like this:

```
ManagedBase()
{
    ManagedBase::f_virt();
}
```

Destructors and Inheritance

There is a difference in the way destructors behave in managed types in an inheritance hierarchy. You may recall that for native class hierarchies, it is usually recommended that destructors be virtual. In classic C++, using virtual destructors meant that all destructors in the inheritance hierarchy would be called. Using nonvirtual destructors prevents this from happening. In C++/CLI, destructors, whether declared virtual or not, are called up the inheritance hierarchy. This behavior change reflects a general trend in the language to make life easier by making almost universally recommended customs mandatory. Listing 8-16 demonstrates this behavior.

Listing 8-16. *Calling Destructors*

```
// destructors_and_inheritance.cpp
using namespace System;

ref class Base
{
    public:
      Base() {}
      ~Base() { Console::WriteLine("~Base"); }
};

ref class Derived : Base
{
    public:
      Derived() { }
      ~Derived() { Console::WriteLine("~Derived"); }
};

// The destructor will be called at the end of main.
int main()
{
    Derived d;
}
```

The output of Listing 8-16 is

```
~Derived
~Base
```

---

since the base class destructor was implicitly invoked. The most derived destructor always executes first, just as it does in C++.

Finalizers and Inheritance

Finalizers are not inherited and cannot be virtual. Like destructors, base class finalizers are called when the finalizer for a derived class is called, as in Listing 8-17.

Listing 8-17. *Calling Finalizers*

```cpp
// finalizers_and_inheritance.cpp
using namespace System;

ref class Base
{
  public:
    Base() { }
    ~Base() { Console::WriteLine("~Base"); this->!Base(); }
    !Base() { Console::WriteLine("!Base"); }
};

ref class Derived : Base
{
  public:
    Derived() { }
    ~Derived() { Console::WriteLine("~Derived"); this->!Derived(); }
    !Derived() { Console::WriteLine("!Derived"); }
};

void F()
{
    // Use stack semantics to create the object.
    Derived d;
}

void G()
{
    // Use the GC heap to create the object.
    Derived^ dh = gcnew Derived();

    // If you want to call the destructor for this object,
    // call it explicitly here, or delete the handle.
}

int main()
{
    // Since the destructor gets called, the finalizers
    // also get called when F goes out of scope.
    F();
    G();
    Console::WriteLine("Collecting after G()");
```

```
    // Force a collection of dh: finalizer only, not
    // the destructor.
    GC::Collect();
}
```

Here is the output of Listing 8-17:

```
~Derived
!Derived
~Base
!Base
Collecting after G()
!Derived
!Base
```

The output of Listing 8-17 shows that the finalizer for the derived class is called first, followed by any base classes. If there is more than one base class, the finalizers are called in order from the most derived class up to the root base class.

Casting in Inheritance Hierarchies

As you know, in classic C++ casting up the conversion hierarchy doesn't require an explicit cast. The same is true in C++/CLI. For example:

```
Derived^ d = gcnew Derived();
Base^ b = d;
```

Casting down the inheritance hierarchy requires the use of safe_cast or dynamic_cast.

```
Base^ b = gcnew Derived();
Derived^ d = safe_cast<Derived^>(b);
d = dynamic_cast<Derived^>(b);
```

Both will work, but the behavior is different in the case that the cast fails. dynamic_cast will return nullptr when the cast fails, requiring a null handle check after the cast statement. safe_cast will throw an InvalidCastException instead. Listing 8-18 shows the proper usage:

Listing 8-18. *Properly Checking Casts*

```
Derived^ d;
// using safe_cast
try
{
    d = safe_cast<Derived^>(b);
}
```

```
catch (InvalidCastException^ e)
{
    // handle error
}

// using dynamic cast
d = dynamic_cast<Derived^>(b);
if (d == nullptr)
{
    // handle error
}
```

safe_cast illustrates that the .NET platform error-handling mechanism is exception handling. You will need to use exception handling if you use the .NET Framework. Chapter 10 will cover this.

Summary

In this chapter, you've learned about several aspects of inheritance in managed type hierarchies. You've examined the use of new and override for virtual functions, the use of abstract and sealed modifiers for methods and types, and the specifics of virtual properties and events. You've also looked at some of the special members of a class, constructors, destructors, and finalizers, and examined how they behave in an inheritance hierarchy. You also looked at casts in class hierarchies.

In the next chapter, you'll explore interfaces.

CHAPTER 9

Interfaces

Interfaces may contain method declarations (including properties and events) and static methods, but no instance method definitions and no instance data members. As you already know, interfaces partially take the place of multiple inheritance in C++/CLI. However, the words "inherit from" are not used; rather, the word used is "implements," since the class that implements an interface must provide the method bodies for all the instance methods declared in the interface, even if it is an abstract class.

Note Although the CLI itself does allow an abstract class implementing an interface to leave unimplemented methods, this is not allowed in C++/CLI.

You're probably used to using pointers or references to base classes in classic C++ to write polymorphic functions. You can do this with handles to interfaces, too. Frequently, you write code that uses interface handles if you want that code to be usable on a wide variety of possibly unrelated objects (for example, a method that takes an interface handle as a parameter). As long as all those object types implement the interface, you can use the function and never need to know the actual underlying object type. And because each class that implements an interface defines its own implementation of the interface methods, the behavior of different classes implementing the same interface can be quite diverse.

Interfaces vs. Abstract Classes

Abstract classes and interfaces are somewhat similar in functionality but have different uses in CLI programming. A class may implement many interfaces, but it can only be derived from one class. In a well-designed class library, the relationship between a derived class and an abstract base class is usually referred to as an "is-a" relationship. The interface relationship is slightly different—a class that implements an interface has a relationship with the interface that might be described as "as-a." Accessing an object of type R through a specific interface I is equivalent to treating the object of type R "as an" I. You could also say that implementing an interface is like fulfilling a contract. Interfaces generally encapsulate some aspect of the behavior of an object, not the identity of an object as an abstract base class does. A quick glance at the .NET Framework interface shows that many have the "-ible" or "-able" suffix: IEnumerable,

IComparable, IDisposable. Often, but not always, interfaces relate to specific activities that an object is capable of participating in.

In practical terms, abstract classes are easier to change in later versions of a library. If you ship a library with an interface and later release a new version of the library with an additional method, you force everyone who uses that interface to add the method to their classes. With an abstract class, you have a choice to provide a virtual implementation of the method, so as long as that implementation is acceptable for any derived classes, users of the abstract class don't need to make any changes. With interfaces, there is no choice: any classes implementing the modified interface will have to add the implementation. Depending on the situation, this might or might not be desirable.

Declaring Interfaces

Listing 9-1 shows how an interface is declared and used in C++/CLI. The contextual keyword interface is used with class. All members of an interface are automatically public, so no access specifier is necessary in the interface declaration. Any other access control specifier is an error. The interface is used rather like a base class, except that more than one interface may be specified in the interface list. Methods that implement interface methods must be virtual.

Listing 9-1. *Declaring and Implementing an Interface*

```
// interface.cpp

interface class IInterface
{
    void f();
    int g();
};

ref class R : IInterface
{
    public:
        // The virtual keyword is required to implement the interface method.
        virtual void f() { }

        virtual int g() { return 1; }
};
```

If multiple interfaces are to be implemented, they are separated by commas on the base list, as shown in Listing 9-2.

Listing 9-2. *Implementing Multiple Interfaces*

```
// interfaces_multiple.cpp

interface class IA { void f(); };
```

```
interface class IB { void g(); };

// Implement multiple interfaces:
ref class R : IA, IB
{
   public:
      virtual void f() {}
      virtual void g() {}
};
```

The base list after the colon following the class name lists all the interfaces to be implemented and the base class (if specified) in no particular order. An implicit base class, Object, for reference types, or System::ValueType, for value types, may be listed explicitly, as in Listing 9-3.

Listing 9-3. *Explicitly Specifying Implicit Base Classes*

```
// interface_list.cpp

using namespace System;

interface class IA {};
interface class IB {};

ref class Base : IA    // OK
{ };

ref class Derived : Base, IA  // OK : Base class first.
{ };

ref class A : Object, IA   // OK: Object may be explicitly stated.
{ };

value class V : ValueType, IA  // OK: Value class inherits from ValueType.
{ };

ref class B : IB, Base  // OK. Base class need not appear first (as in C#).
{ };
```

Interfaces Implementing Other Interfaces

An interface declaration may itself call for the implementation of other interfaces. When this construct is used, it means that the class implementing the interface must implement all the methods declared in the interface body, as well as any methods declared in interfaces added to the base class list. Listing 9-4 illustrates this pattern.

Listing 9-4. *Interface Inheritance*

```cpp
// interfaces_implementing_interfaces.cpp

interface class IA { void f(); };

interface class IB : IA { void g(); };

ref class R : IB
{
    public:
        virtual void f() {}
        virtual void g() {}
};
```

When interfaces inherit from other interfaces, the new and override specifiers are not used on the method declarations. These specifiers are only applicable to class inheritance. In fact, an interesting case is the one of a class that inherits a method from a base class and also implements a method with the same name from an interface. In that case, new would indicate that the method is different from the base class method (see Listing 9-5).

Listing 9-5. *Using new to Implement an Interface Method*

```cpp
// base_and_interface.cpp

using namespace System;

ref class B
{
    public:

        virtual void f() { Console::WriteLine("B::f"); }
        virtual void g() { Console::WriteLine("B::g"); }
};

interface class I
{
    void f();
    void g();
};

ref class C : B, I
{
    public:
```

```
    // f implements I::f but doesn't override B::f
    virtual void f() new
    {
        Console::WriteLine("C::f");
    }
    // g overrides B::g AND implements I::g
    virtual void g() override
    {
        Console::WriteLine("C::g");
    }
};

int main()
{
    B^ b = gcnew B();
    C^ c = gcnew C();
    I^ i = c;

    // behavior with the new specifier
    b->f(); // calls B::f
    c->f(); // calls C::f
    i->f(); // calls C::f since C::f implements I::f

    B^ bc = c;  // b pointing to instance of C
    bc->f(); // calls B::f since C::f is unrelated

    // behavior with the override specifier
    b->g();  // calls B::g
    c->g();  // calls C::g
    i->g();  // calls C::g since C::g implements I::g

    bc->g(); // calls C::g since C::g overrides B::g
}
```

The output of Listing 9-5 is as follows:

```
B::f
C::f
C::f
B::f
B::g
C::g
C::g
C::g
```

Interface Name Collisions

Interfaces with Properties and Events

Interfaces may have properties and events, but not fields. An implementing class must implement a trivial property's get and set methods, or an event. This could occur by redeclaring the trivial property or event in the implementing class, as in Listing 9-6.

Listing 9-6. *Implementing Properties and Events*

```cpp
// interface_properties_events.cpp
using namespace System;

interface class I
{
   property int P1;
   event EventHandler^ E;

   property int P2
   {
      int get();
      void set(int v);
   }
};

ref class R : I
{
   int value;

public:

   virtual property int P1;
   virtual event EventHandler^ E;

   virtual property int P2
   {
      int get() { return value; }
      void set(int v) { value = v; }
   }

};
```

Interface Name Collisions

Name conflicts can occur between interface methods and class methods or between methods in multiple interfaces being implemented by the same class. In the case of a class that has a method conflict with an interface, you use the explicit implementation syntax you saw in the previous chapter to specify which method implements the interface method (see Listing 9-7).

Listing 9-7. *Disambiguating Name Collisions*

```cpp
// class_interface_method_ambiguity.cpp
using namespace System;

interface class IA
{
  void f();
};

ref class A : IA
{
  public:

    // Note that new is not used here.
    void f()
    {
      Console::WriteLine("A::f");
    }
    // explicit implementation syntax
    virtual void fIA() = IA::f
    {
      Console::WriteLine("A::fIA implementing IA::f");
    }
};

int main()
{
  A^ a = gcnew A();
  IA^ ia = a;
  ia->f();
  a->f();
}
```

Here is the output of Listing 9-7:

```
A::fIA implementing IA::f
A::f
```

As you can see, the method that gets called is determined by whether the method is accessed through the interface or through the object. Now let's turn to the case of a class implementing two interfaces with the same name.

Inheritance in C++/CLI (and in other CLI languages such as C# and VB .NET) is different from interface inheritance in some other languages, such as Java. The big difference between the interface inheritance model in Java and the CLI is that CLI interfaces are independent of each other, whereas in Java, interfaces can interfere with each other when name collisions arise, such as when two or more interfaces implemented by the same type have methods with the same name. In the Java inheritance model, this is an ambiguity that must be resolved to a single method. In the CLI inheritance model, both methods may be available on the type, and you may access them both depending on what interface pointer you might be using. This rule is like the rule used for interfaces in COM.

What this really means is that when you're creating a class that implements two interfaces that have methods with similar names, you don't have to care about what potential name conflicts might arise. In Java, it can be difficult to create one method that is a viable implementation of both interfaces. In CLI-based languages, both methods can coexist, and the interface handle that is used determines which method is called.

Explicit interface implementation is the language construct that allows you to support interfaces that have name conflicts. You create one method definition for each interface that has the method, and you mark it in such a way that the compiler knows that it's the version of the method to be used when accessed through a given interface handle type. If it's not being accessed through an interface handle, but rather through a handle with the type of the object, the calling code must resolve the ambiguity by specifying the interface in the call.

Consider the code in Listing 9-8.

Listing 9-8. *Disambiguating by Specifying an Interface*

```cpp
// interface_name_collision.cpp
using namespace System;

interface class I1 { void f(); };

interface class I2 { void f(); };

ref class R : I1, I2
{
   public:

   virtual void f()
   { Console::WriteLine("R::f"); }
};

int main()
{
   R^ r = gcnew R();
   r->f();  // R::f() implements both I1's f and I2's f
}
```

The name conflict in Listing 9-8 is not an error, and the output is as you would expect:

R::f

In Listing 9-8, the function f in the class R implements both I1's and I2's version of f. This might be desirable if the function that has the conflict has the same meaning in both interfaces, but if the interfaces have different notions of what f means and does, you need to explicitly implement the functions inherited from each interface separately. The language provides support for doing this, as in Listing 9-9.

Listing 9-9. *Implementing Inherited Functions Separately*

```
// explicit_interface_implementation.cpp
using namespace System;

interface class I1 { void f(); };

interface class I2 { void f(); };

ref class R : I1, I2
{
  public:

    virtual void f1() = I1::f
    {
      Console::WriteLine("R::f1 == I1::f");
    }

    virtual void f2() = I2::f
    {
      Console::WriteLine("R::f2 == I2::f");
    }
};

int main()
{

  R^ r = gcnew R();

  I1^ i1 = r;
  I2^ i2 = r;

  r->f1();        // OK -- call through the object.
  r->f2();        // OK -- call through the object.

  // r->f();      // Error: f is not a member of R.

  i1->f();        // OK -- call f1.
  i2->f();        // OK -- call f2.

  // r->I1::f();    // Compiler error: "direct call will fail at runtime".
  // r->I1::f1();   // Error: f1 is not a member of I1.
}
```

The final two calls are not supported. The output of Listing 9-9 is as follows:

```
R::f1 == I1::f
R::f2 == I2::f
R::f1 == I1::f
R::f2 == I2::f
```

Interfaces and Access Control

You can also force a method to be available *only* through an interface, and *not* as a method on the object instance. Using explicit implementation syntax, you set up a private method that explicitly implements the interface method. Attempting to call the method outside the class through the class handle or object will produce a compile error. The method may be called through the interface without error (see Listing 9-10).

Listing 9-10. *Using a Private Method to Implement an Interface*

```cpp
// interface_private.cpp

interface class IInterface
{

    void f();
    int g();
};

ref class R : IInterface
{
    // The virtual keyword is required to implement the interface.
    virtual void f() sealed = IInterface::f
    { }

public:
    virtual int g() { return 1; }
};

int main()
{
    R^ r = gcnew R();
    IInterface^ ir = r;
    ir->f();  // f may be called through the interface.

    // r->f();  // Error: f is private.
    r->g();      // OK
}
```

Interfaces and Static Members

In addition to virtual methods, interfaces may have static methods and static fields. Code like that in Listing 9-11 is legal. Static methods on interfaces are nonvirtual, like all static methods, so if your implementing class also defines a method with the same name, it is a different method. Which method gets called depends on how the method is accessed.

Listing 9-11. *Interfaces with Static Fields and Methods*

```cpp
// interfaces_static.cpp
using namespace System;

interface class IA
{
    static int i = 6;
    static const int j = 100;

    static void f()  { Console::WriteLine("IA::f " + i); }
};

ref class A : IA
{
public:

    static void f() { Console::WriteLine("A::f " + IA::j); }
};

int main()
{
    A^ a = gcnew A();
    IA^ ia = a;
    ia->f();       // Call IA::f through interface handle.
    a->f();        // Call A::f through object handle.
    IA::f();       // Call IA::f.
    A::f();        // Call A::f.
    a->IA::f();    // Call IA::f
}
```

Here is the output of Listing 9-11:

```
IA::f 6
A::f 100
IA::f 6
A::f 100
IA::f 6
```

Literals in Interfaces

Interfaces may have literal fields, but not nonstatic constant fields. Recall from Chapter 6 that static constant fields do not appear constant to assemblies that import the constants via #using, whereas literal fields do appear constant in that case (see Listing 9-12).

Listing 9-12. *Using Literals in Interfaces*

```
// interfaces_constants.cpp

interface class I
{
    static const int i = 100;     // OK : static members OK
    literal int j = 50;           // OK : literals OK
    // const int k;               // error : nonstatic field
};
```

Commonly Used .NET Framework Interfaces

The .NET Framework uses a large number of interfaces. Anyone programming with the .NET Framework should know the most common ones. I'll introduce you to a few of them.

IComparable

You implement IComparable whenever you want your type to support sorting algorithms that expect to call a comparison method between objects of the same type. IComparable is about the simplest interface you could imagine, since it only has one method, CompareTo. CompareTo takes an Object as a parameter, so you should check the type of the object to make sure that the comparison makes sense. IComparable also has a generic form. The generic form uses a typed argument instead of an untyped argument, so there's no need to check the type of the object passed in. The generic forms of these common .NET Framework interfaces were introduced in .NET 2.0 and are preferred over the nongeneric forms. Listing 9-13 is an example using the generic form of IComparable.

Listing 9-13. *Using Generic IComparable*

```
// message_comparable_generic.cpp

using namespace System;

enum class SortByEnum
{
    SortByDate,
    SortByFrom,
    SortBySubject
};
```

```cpp
ref class Message : IComparable<Message^>
{
    public:

    static property SortByEnum SortCriterion;

    property DateTime DateReceived;
    property String^ From;
    property String^ Subject;
    property String^ Body;

    Message(DateTime dt, String^ from, String^ subject, String^ body)
    {
        DateReceived = dt;
        From = from;
        Subject = subject;
        Body = body;
    }

    virtual int CompareTo(Message^ msg)
    {

        switch ( SortCriterion )
        {
            case SortByEnum::SortByDate:
                return this->DateReceived.CompareTo(msg->DateReceived);
            case SortByEnum::SortByFrom:
                return this->From->CompareTo(msg->From);
            case SortByEnum::SortBySubject:
                return this->Subject->CompareTo(msg->Subject);
            default:
                throw gcnew InvalidOperationException();
        }

    }

    // other methods...

};

// Print the message headers in sorted order.
void PrintHeaders(array<Message^>^ messages, SortByEnum sortOrder)
{
    Message::SortCriterion = sortOrder;
    Array::Sort(messages);
```

```
    for (int i = 0; i < messages->Length; i++)
    {
        Console::WriteLine("Received: {0} From: <{1}> Subject: {2}",
            messages[i]->DateReceived, messages[i]->From,
            messages[i]->Subject );
    }
    Console::WriteLine();
}


int main()
{
    // Create some messages.
    array<Message^>^ message_array =
    {
        gcnew Message( DateTime(2006, 1, 12), "Nancy Carlisle", "Dog Jokes", ""),
        gcnew Message( DateTime(2006, 1, 15), "George Jones", "Bark mulch order", ""),
        gcnew Message( DateTime(2006, 1, 2), "George Jones", "Bark mulch offer", ""),
        gcnew Message( DateTime(2005, 12, 31), "Jeni Hogenson",
                       "Wedding Anniversary", "")
    };

    PrintHeaders(message_array, SortByEnum::SortByDate);
    PrintHeaders(message_array, SortByEnum::SortByFrom);
    PrintHeaders(message_array, SortByEnum::SortBySubject);

}
```

IEnumerable and IEnumerator

Instances of a class that implements IEnumerable can be iterated over with the for each statement. The code we'd like to be able to write might look like this (we'll develop the Card class
representing a playing card in Listing 9-15 later in this chapter):

```
    for each (Card c in deck)
    {
        Console::WriteLine("{0} of {1}", c.Rank, c.Suit.ToString());
    }
```

To use for each with your own data structures, you must implement IEnumerable. IEnumerable
declares a single method: GetEnumerator. The GetEnumerator method returns an IEnumerator
handle. The actual type returned is an enumerator, which is an object you define that implements the IEnumerator interface. The IEnumerator interface looks like the code in Listing 9-14.

Listing 9-14. *IEnumerator*

```
interface class IEnumerator
{
    property Object^ Current;
    bool MoveNext();
    void Reset();
};
```

Listing 9-15 is an example of a data structure that implements IEnumerable and therefore supports iteration using the for each statement. There are several things to notice about this code. First, there are two different versions of some methods implemented. We need to implement GetEnumerator from IEnumerable, but we've used explicit interface implementation to make that method private and implemented a different public GetEnumerator. The for each statement will use the nonvirtual method, which results in some modest efficiency gains. We've done the same thing with the CardEnumerator::Current property; the explicit interface implementation must be on the accessor method, not the property.

Second, CardEnumerator is a nested class. I haven't specifically said anything so far about nested classes, but they work in C++/CLI in the same way that they work in classic C++. The nesting makes the implementation more tidy, since otherwise we would need a forward declaration or some out-of-line definitions, since Cards and CardEnumerator both reference each other.

Third, we create a snapshot of the collection before iterating over it. This is an often neglected but very important part of implementing IEnumerable. Enumerating a collection when the collection changes invalidates the enumeration. There are a couple of ways of dealing with this. One is to create a snapshot of the collection at the time enumeration starts. This could be slow depending on how it is done. A faster way would be to add a Boolean field, changed, and set it to true in the methods that change the collection, such as the Shuffle method. Then, the MoveNext and Current properties check this field, and if it is set, they throw an InvalidOperationException. When you see how to implement a generic linked list in Chapter 11, you'll encounter the latter method. The two methods produce somewhat different runtime behavior. With the snapshot method, we can call methods that modify the collection, and they will affect the original collection, but not the copy we are interating over. With the other method, an InvalidOperationException is generated whenever the collection is modified.

Listing 9-15. *Enumerating Playing Cards*

```
// cards_enumerable.cpp

using namespace System;
using namespace System::Text;
using namespace System::Collections;

enum class SuitEnum { Diamonds, Clubs, Hearts, Spades };
```

```cpp
// represents a playing card
value struct Card
{
    SuitEnum Suit;
    unsigned int Rank;
    literal int CHAR_HEART = 3; // ANSI heart character
    literal int CHAR_DIAMOND = 4; // ANSI diamond
    literal int CHAR_CLUB = 5; // ANSI club
    literal int CHAR_SPADE = 6;  // ANSI spade

    // Render the two-character card using ANSI card values.
    virtual String^ ToString() override
    {
        StringBuilder^ s = gcnew StringBuilder();
        if (Rank <= 0 || Rank > 13)
            throw gcnew InvalidOperationException();
        else if (Rank < 11)
        {
            s->Append(Rank);
        }
        else
        {
            switch (Rank)
            {
            case 11: // Jack
                s->Append("J");
                break;
            case 12:  // Queen
                s->Append("Q");
                break;
            case 13:  // King
                s->Append("K");
                break;
            default:
                throw gcnew InvalidOperationException();
            }
        }
        switch (Suit)
        {
        case SuitEnum::Clubs:
            s->Append(CHAR_CLUB, 1);
            break;
        case SuitEnum::Hearts:
            s->Append(CHAR_HEART, 1);
            break;
```

```
        case SuitEnum::Diamonds:
            s->Append(CHAR_DIAMOND, 1);
            break;
        case SuitEnum::Spades:
            s->Append(CHAR_SPADE, 1);
            break;
        default:
            throw gcnew InvalidOperationException();
        }
        return s->ToString();
    }
};


// Cards: represents a collection of cards
ref class Cards : IEnumerable
{
    array<Card>^ card_array;

    literal int K = 13; // King's ordinal position
    literal int CARDS_IN_DECK = 52; // cards in the deck
public:
    Cards()
    {
        // Create a standard deck.
        card_array = gcnew array<Card>(CARDS_IN_DECK + 1);
        for (int i = 1; i <= K; i++)
        {
            card_array[i].Suit = SuitEnum::Diamonds;
            card_array[i].Rank = i;
            card_array[i + K].Suit = SuitEnum::Clubs;
            card_array[i + K].Rank = i;
            card_array[i + 2*K].Suit = SuitEnum::Hearts;
            card_array[i + 2*K].Rank = i;
            card_array[i + 3*K].Suit = SuitEnum::Spades;
            card_array[i + 3*K].Rank = i;
        }
    }


    Cards(const Cards% c)
    {
        card_array = gcnew array<Card>(c.card_array->Length);
        for (int i = 0; i < c.card_array->Length; i++)
        {
            card_array[i] = c.card_array[i];
        }
    }
```

```cpp
    // Default indexed property. Allows use of
    // Cards[i] syntax to get a card by index.
    property Card default[int]
    {
       Card get(int index)
       {
          return card_array[index];
       }
       void set(int index, Card card)
       {
          card_array[index] = card;
       }
    }


    // the number of cards in this collection
    property int Count
    {
       int get()
       {
          return card_array->Length;
       }
    }


    // Shuffle the cards in this collection.
    void Shuffle()
    {
       // Swap 5000 cards.
       Random^ random = gcnew Random();
       for (int i = 0; i < 5000; i++)
       {
          int card1 = (int)Math::Ceiling(random->NextDouble() * CARDS_IN_DECK);
          int card2 = (int)Math::Ceiling(random->NextDouble() * CARDS_IN_DECK);
          Card temp = this[card1];
          this[card1] =  this[card2];
          this[card2] = temp;
       }
    }

private:
    // IEnumerable::GetEnumerator method
    // Compiler requires a private virtual method to be marked sealed.
    virtual System::Collections::IEnumerator^ GetEnumeratorNonGeneric() sealed
       = System::Collections::IEnumerable::GetEnumerator
    {
       return GetEnumerator();
    }
```

```cpp
public:
   // Nonvirtual GetEnumerator method for efficiency; the virtual
   // methods call the nonvirtual method. For each uses the
   // nonvirtual method.
   IEnumerator^ GetEnumerator()
   {
      return (IEnumerator^) gcnew CardEnumerator(this);
   }

   // nested enumerator class
   ref class CardEnumerator : IEnumerator
   {
      int current;
      Cards^ cards;

   public:
      CardEnumerator(Cards^ cards_in)
      {
         // Snapshot the collection by calling the copy constructor.
         cards = gcnew Cards(*cards_in);
         // The enumerator should always start *before* the first element, so
         // in a zero-based collection that is -1, but here it is 0.
         current = 0;
      }

   private:
      // implements the IEnumerator Current property
      virtual property Object^ _Current
      {
         // Use explicit interface implementation syntax on the get
         // method, not the property. The compiler requires a private
         // virtual method to be marked "sealed".
         Object^ get() sealed = System::Collections::IEnumerator::Current::get
         {
            return Current;
         }
      }

   public:

      // nonvirtual Current property for maximum efficiency
      property Card Current
      {
         Card get()
         {
```

```
            if (current <= 0 || current >= cards->Count )
                throw gcnew InvalidOperationException();
            return cards[current];
        }
    }

    // Implement the IEnumerator::MoveNext method.
    virtual bool MoveNext()
    {
        current++;
        if (current <= 0 || current > cards->Count)
            throw gcnew InvalidOperationException();
        else
            return current < cards->Count;
    }

    // Implement the IEnumerator::Reset method.
    virtual void Reset()
    {
        current = 0;
    }
};

};

void PrintAll(Cards^ deck)
{
    for each (Card c in deck)
    {
        Console::Write("{0} ", c, c.Rank, c.Suit);
        // has no effect on iteration since collection is snapshot
        // but deck will remain shuffled when next used
        deck->Shuffle();
    }
    Console::WriteLine();
}

int main()
{
    Cards^ deck = gcnew Cards();
    PrintAll(deck);
    PrintAll(deck);
}
```

The output of Listing 9-15 will be something like this:

1♦ 2♦ 3♦ 4♦ 5♦ 6♦ 7♦ 8♦ 9♦ 10♦ J♦ Q♦ K♦ 1♣ 2♣ 3♣ 4♣ 5♣ 6♣ 7♣ 8♣ 9♣ 10♣ J♣ Q♣ K♣
1♥ 2♥ 3♥ 4♥ 5♥ 6♥ 7♥ 8♥ 9♥ 10♥ J♥ Q♥ K♥ 1♠ 2♠ 3♠ 4♠ 5♠ 6♠ 7♠ 8♠ 9♠ 10♠ J♠ Q♠ K♠

1♠ 3♦ 4♣ 9♥ 5♦ Q♦ 2♥ 4♠ J♠ Q♣ K♠ 9♣ 7♣ J♣ 1♥ K♣ J♦ 10♠ 3♣ 8♣ 1♣ 10♥ 3♥ 6♦ 3♠ 6♠
8♠ 5♣ 2♠ 9♠ 5♠ 8♦ 4♦ Q♠ 4♥ 7♥ 2♠ 8♥ 6♥ 10♣ J♥ 9♦ K♦ 2♦ 5♥ K♥ 7♥ 1♦ 7♠ 10♦ 6♣ Q♥

Like IComparable, the IEnumerable interface has a generic as well as a nongeneric form. The generic form inherits from the nongeneric form, so if your class implements the generic form, you have to implement both IEnumerable and IEnumerable<T>. This will give you two versions of GetEnumerator: one generic, one not.

Of course, there are many other interfaces defined in the .NET Framework. Many of them are intended to be implemented by your classes in order to take advantage of some functionality in the framework.

Interfaces and Dynamically Loaded Types

A common use of interfaces is to allow runtime extensibility, perhaps to allow your users to add their own objects into the system at runtime. You would provide a public interface to your users. Your code would then be written with interface handles internally, so that your users' methods are called whenever their type is loaded. To make this work, you need to dynamically load the users' assembly, then call some method in that assembly that creates the objects and returns an interface handle with the user's object as the underlying type.

You'll use the .NET Framework Assembly class to dynamically load the assembly, and you'll use the .NET Framework *reflection* functionality to get at the types in the dynamically loaded assembly. Reflection is like a souped-up version of runtime type information (RTTI) in classic C++. It's much more sophisticated than RTTI, mainly because of all the metadata that is tracked by the CLR for .NET Framework types. In fact, reflection is a key reason why writing modern applications is easier with the CLR. Because modern applications often need to be much more extensible than the monolithic applications of the past, you need to interact with types and objects at runtime that you may never have envisioned at compile time. Let's return to our example of an extensible online role-playing game.

We want our users to be able to implement their own creatures or monsters within the game. We publish an interface and distribute it in an assembly in our extension kit. Our interface might look something like Listing 9-16. Our assembly would also include any classes that are used in the interface, such as the AnimationSequence2D class, the Attack class, and AttackTypeEnum referred to Listing 9-16.

Listing 9-16. *An Interface to Extend the Monster Game*

```cpp
// extension_monster.cpp

namespace MonsterExtensions
{

    // public classes AnimationSequence2D, Attack and AttackTypeEnum assumed

    public interface class IMonster
    {
        property String^ Name;
        property int Strength;
        property AnimationSequence2D^ Frames;
        Attack^ GenerateAttack(AttackTypeEnum attacktype);
        void DefendAttack(Attack^ attack);
        // etc.
    };
}
```

Our users implement the interface methods for generating an attack and defending against attacks, and implement all the necessary initialization code to set values for the interface properties, as in Listing 9-17.

Listing 9-17. *Implementing the Monster Game Interface*

```cpp
// mymonster.cpp
#using "extension_monster.dll"

using namespace System;
using namespace MonsterExtensions;

public ref class MyMonster : IMonster
{
    public:

        virtual property String^ Name;
        virtual property int Strength;
        virtual property AnimationSequence2D^ Frames;


        virtual Attack^ GenerateAttack(AttackTypeEnum attacktype)
        {
            // Generate an attack.
            return gcnew Attack(/* attack details go here */);
        }
```

```
    virtual void DefendAttack(Attack^ attack)
    {
        // code to process the attack
    }
};
```

We would provide a way to load the users' assemblies using the .NET Framework Assembly class. We will query users for their assembly name and the class name that implements IMonster (see Listing 9-18).

Listing 9-18. *Loading Users' Assemblies*

```
#using "IMonster.dll"
#using "extension_monster.dll"

using namespace System;
using namespace MonsterExtensions;
using namespace System::Reflection;

IMonster^ GetExtensionMonsterInterface(String^ userMonsterAssemblyFileName,
    String^ userMonsterClassName)
{
    Assembly^ userMonsterAssembly =
            Assembly::LoadFrom( userMonsterAssemblyFileName );
    IMonster^ userMonster = (IMonster^) userMonsterAssembly->CreateInstance(
        userMonsterClassName );
    return userMonster;
}
```

From then on, we would use the user-supplied class through the IMonster interface. You'll learn more about reflection in the next chapter.

Summary

In this chapter, you learned about the design philosophy of interfaces in C++/CLI as well as explicit interface implementation and special considerations when using properties on an interface. You were also introduced to some of the commonly used interfaces in the .NET Framework, such as IComparable, which enables you to use collection classes to sort instances of your types, and IEnumerable, which enables you to use the for each statement on your types. You also considered the question of when abstract types are to be used and when interfaces are best used, and considered the use of interfaces as stand-ins for dynamically loaded types.

You'll get a chance to look at exceptions and attributes, and more closely at reflection, next.

CHAPTER 10

Exceptions, Attributes, and Reflection

In this chapter, you'll begin by looking at aspects of exception handling in C++/CLI that are not present in classic C++. Then you'll look at attributes, which supply metadata for a type and, although not part of standard C++, may be familiar if you've used previous versions of Visual C++. You'll learn how to use the existing .NET Framework attributes, examine some of the common ones, and look at how to define and use your own attributes. Finally, you'll get a brief overview of the reflection features of the .NET Framework, which provide a way to discover information on a type at runtime and use that information to interact dynamically with a type.

Exceptions

Exceptions are supported in classic C++, but not universally used. In .NET Framework programming, exceptions are ubiquitous, and you cannot code without them. This chapter assumes you are aware of the basic concepts of exception handling, throwing exceptions, and the try/catch statement. All of these features of classic C++ are valid in C++/CLI code.

A key difference between exception handling in C++/CLI and in classic C++ is that exceptions are always thrown and caught by reference (via a handle), not by value. In classic C++, exceptions could be thrown by value, which would result in a call to the copy constructor for the exception object. In C++/CLI, exceptions are always on the managed heap, never the stack. Therefore, you must use a handle when throwing a C++/CLI exception, as in Listing 10-1.

Listing 10-1. *Throwing an Exception*

```
try
{
    bool error;
    // other code

    if (error)
    {
        throw gcnew Exception();
    }
}
```

```
catch( Exception^ exception)
{
    // code to handle the exception
}
```

The Exception Hierarchy

All .NET exceptions inherit from a single root class, System::Exception. Table 10-1 shows some of the common exceptions thrown by the runtime in C++/CLI code.

Table 10-1. *Some Common .NET Framework Exceptions*

Exception	Condition
System::AccessViolationException	Thrown when an attempt to read or write protected memory occurs.
System::ArgumentException	Thrown when an argument to a method is not valid.
System::ArithmeticException	Thrown when an error occurs in an arithmetic expression or numeric casting operation. This is a base class for DivideByZeroException, NotFiniteNumberException, and OverflowException.
System::DivideByZeroException	Thrown when division by zero occurs.
System::IndexOutOfRangeException	Thrown when an array access out of bounds occurs.
System::InvalidCastException	Thrown when a cast fails.
System::NullReferenceException	Thrown when a null handle is dereferenced or used to access a nonexistent object.
System::OutOfMemory	Thrown when memory allocation with gcnew fails.
System::TypeInitializationException	Thrown when an exception occurs in a static constructor but isn't caught.

What's in an Exception?

A .NET Framework exception contains useful information that captures information about what triggered the exception and how to address the problem. For example, the exception source is stored as a string in the Source property; a text representation of the call stack is included in the form of the StackTrace property; and there's a Message property, which contains a message suitable for display to a user. It's use is demonstrated in Listing 10-2.

Listing 10-2. *Using the Properties of the Exception Class*

```cpp
// exception_properties.cpp

using namespace System;

int main()
{
    try
    {
        bool error = true;
        // other code

        if (error)
        {
            throw gcnew Exception("XYZ");
        }
    }
    catch( Exception^ exception)
    {
        Console::WriteLine("Exception Source property {0}", exception->Source);
        Console::WriteLine("Exception StackTrace property {0}",
            exception->StackTrace);
        Console::WriteLine("Exception Message property {0}", exception->Message);
    }
}
```

The output of Listing 10-2 is as follows:

```
Exception Source property exception_properties
Exception StackTrace property    at main()
Exception Message property XYZ
```

When an unhandled exception occurs in a console application, the Message and
StackTrace data are printed to the standard error stream, like this:

```
Unhandled Exception: System.Exception: XYZ
   at main()
```

There's also a property of the Exception class called InnerException, which may reference
an exception that gives rise to the exception we're looking at. In this way, a cascading series of
exceptions may be nested one within the other. This could be useful if an exception occurs
deep down in low-level code, but there are several layers of libraries between the problem and
the code that knows how to handle such situations. As a designer of one of the intermediate
libraries, you could choose to wrap that lower exception as an inner exception and throw a
higher exception of a type that is more intelligible to your clients. By passing the inner exception,

the inner exception information can be used by the error-handling code to respond more appropriately to the real cause of the error.

Creating Exception Classes

You will often want to create your own exception classes specific to particular error conditions; however, you should avoid doing this and use one of the standard Exception classes, if possible. Writing your own exception class lets you filter on and write exception handlers specific to that error. To do this, you may derive from System::Exception. You would normally override the Message property in the Exception base class to deliver a more relevant error message (see Listing 10-3).

Listing 10-3. *Creating a Custom Exception*

```
// exceptions_custom.cpp
using namespace System;

ref class MyException : Exception
{
   public:

     virtual property String^ Message
     {
         String^ get() override
         {
            return "You must supply a command-line argument.";
         }
     }
};

int main(array<String^>^ args)
{
     try
     {
         if (args->Length < 1)
         {
            throw gcnew MyException();
         }
         throw gcnew Exception();
     }
     // The first catch blocks are the specific exceptions that
     // you are looking for.
     catch (MyException^ e)
     {
         Console::WriteLine("MyException occurred! " + e->Message);
     }
```

```
    // You may also catch other exceptions with multiple try blocks,
    // although it's better.
    catch (Exception^ exception)
    {
        Console::WriteLine("Unknown exception!");
    }
}
```

The output of Listing 10-3 (with no command-line arguments) is shown here:

```
MyException occurred! You must supply a command-line argument.
```

Using the Finally Block

C++/CLI recognizes the finally contextual keyword, which is a feature of other languages that support exception handling such as Java and C#. The finally keyword precedes a block of code known as a *finally block*. Finally blocks appear after catch blocks and execute whether or not an exception is caught.

Use a finally block (see Listing 10-4) to put any cleanup code that you don't want to duplicate in both the try block and the catch blocks. The syntax is like that in other languages.

Listing 10-4. *Using a Finally Block*

```
try
    {
    // ...
    }
    catch( Exception^ )
    {
    }
    finally
    {
        Console::WriteLine("finally block!");
    }
```

In the case of multiple finally blocks, they are executed "from the inside out" as demonstrated in Listing 10-5.

Listing 10-5. *Using Multiple Finally Blocks*

```
// multiple_finally_blocks.cpp

using namespace System;
```

```cpp
int main()
{
    try
    {
        Console::WriteLine("Outer try");

        try
        {
            Console::WriteLine("Inner try");
            throw gcnew Exception("XYZ");

        }
        catch( Exception^ exception)
        {
            Console::WriteLine("Inner catch");
        }
        finally
        {
            Console::WriteLine("Inner finally");
        }
    }
    catch(Exception^ exception)
    {
        Console::WriteLine("Outer catch");
    }
    finally
    {
        Console::WriteLine("Outer finally");
    }
}
```

Here is the output of Listing 10-5:

```
Outer try
Inner try
Inner catch
Inner finally
Outer finally
```

The first finally block to execute is the one paired with the last try block to execute. The finally block is a separate scope from the try block, so, for example, any variables declared in the try block aren't available in the finally block. Also, if you created any stack objects, their destructors would be called at the end of the try block and before the finally block executes.

Don't try to use jump statements (e.g., continue, break, or goto) to move into or out of a finally block; it is not allowed. Also, you cannot use the return statement from inside a finally block. If allowed, these constructs would corrupt the stack and return value semantics.

Dealing with Exceptions in Constructors

A difficult problem in any language is what to do with objects that fail to be constructed properly. When an exception is thrown in a constructor, the result is a partially constructed object. This is not a largely theoretical concern; it's almost always possible for an exception to be thrown in a constructor. For example, OutOfMemoryException could be thrown during any memory allocation. The finalizer will run on such partially constructed objects. In C++, destructors do not run on partially constructed objects. The finalizer is called by the runtime to clean up before the runtime reclaims the memory. As usual, the execution of the finalizer is nondeterministic, so it won't necessarily happen right away, but will happen eventually. This is another reason to write finalizers carefully, without assuming any objects are valid. In Listing 10-6, an exception is thrown in the construction of a member of A in A's constructor. The finalizer is called to clean up; the destructor is not called.

Listing 10-6. *Throwing an Exception in a Constructor*

```
// exceptions_ctor.cpp

using namespace System;

// the type of the member
ref class Class1
{
    public:

    Class1()
    {
        // Assume a fatal problem has occurred here.
        throw gcnew Exception();
    }
};

ref class A
{

    Class1^ c1;
    Class1^ c2;

    public:

    A()
    {
        // c1 has a problem; it throws an exception.
        c1 = gcnew Class1();
```

```
        // c2 never gets created.
        c2 = gcnew Class1();
    }

    void F() { Console::WriteLine("Testing F"); }

    ~A() // Never gets called, even if A is created with stack semantics
    {
        Console::WriteLine("A::~A()");
    }

    !A()  // Gets called for partially constructed object
    {
        Console::WriteLine("A::!A()");
        // Don't try to use C2 here without checking for null first.
    }

};

int main()
{
    A a;
    a.F();  // never reached
}
```

This example shows what happens in the simple case of a class without a base class other than Object. In the case where some base classes have already been initialized, the finalizers for any base classes will also execute.

Throwing Nonexception Types

C++/CLI allows you to throw objects that are not in the exception class hierarchy. If you've done a lot of programming in C# or Visual Basic .NET, this may be somewhat of a surprise, since in those languages, you are limited to throwing exception objects that derive, directly or indirectly, from System::Exception. In C++/CLI, you're not limited in this way. However, if you are calling C++/CLI code from C# or VB .NET code, and an exception object of an unusual type is thrown, it will be wrapped in an exception from the point of view of the C# or VB .NET code.

The basic idea is simple, as Listing 10-7 shows.

Listing 10-7. *Throwing an Object That's Not an Exception*

```
// throw_string.cpp

using namespace System;

public ref class R
{
```

```
public:
   static void TrySomething()
   {
      throw gcnew String("Error that throws string!");
   }
};

int main()
{
   try
   {
      R::TrySomething();
   }
   catch(String^ s)
   {
      Console::WriteLine(s);
   }
}
```

The subtlety arises when you run this C++/CLI code from another language. If the code in Listing 10-7 is compiled to a DLL assembly and reference in C#, and you call the R::TrySomething method, a RuntimeWrappedException object is created.

Note that cross-language work is best done in the Visual Studio IDE, so you can be sure that the right references, assembly signing, and manifests are all done properly. Create two projects in the same solution (see Listing 10-8). Set the C# project as the startup project, and configure the C++/CLI project as a DLL. Reference the C++/CLI project from the C# project, and build.

Listing 10-8. *Wrapping a Nonexception Object*

```
// runtimewrappedexception.cs
using System;
using System.Collections.Generic;
using System.Text;
using System.Runtime.CompilerServices;

class Program
{
   static void Main(string[] args)
   {
      try
      {
         R.TrySomething();
      }
```

```
      catch (RuntimeWrappedException e)
      {
          String s = (String)e.WrappedException;
          Console.WriteLine(e.Message);
          Console.WriteLine(s);
      }
   }
}
```

The output of Listing 10-8 is as follows:

```
An object that does not derive from System.Exception has been wrapped in a
RuntimeWrappedException.
Error that throws string!
```

I do not recommend throwing nonexception objects. Throwing exception objects that all derive from the root of the same exception hierarchy has the advantage in that a catch filter that takes the Exception class will capture all exceptions. If you throw objects that don't fit this scheme, they will pass through those filters. There may be times when that behavior is desired, but most of the time you are introducing the possibility that your nonstandard exception will be erroneously missed, which would have undesired consequences. (The paradox is that a non-Exception exception is an exception to the rule that all exceptions derive from Exception. You can see how confusing it could be.)

Unsupported Features

Exception specifications are a C++ feature that allow a programmer to declare what exceptions a particular function can throw. This is intended as a heads-up to users of a function that they should be prepared to deal with these exceptions. Exception specifications are not supported in Visual C++ even in native code, and C++/CLI does not support this feature either. In general, this feature is impractical because it is not usually feasible to list the complete set of exceptions that a given block of code might generate, most particularly exceptions that propagate from any function called that doesn't have exception specifications. Furthermore, some common exceptions, such as OutOfMemoryException, could be generated almost anywhere. Should these be included in all exception specifications? Another problem is performance, since this feature adds to the already intensive runtime overhead associated with exception handling. For all these reasons, the designers of the CLI chose not to implement this feature.

Exception-Handling Best Practices

Exception handling is controversial. All aspects of exception handling, it seems, are up for debate. Regardless of what your position is, one thing remains certain: if your framework uses exceptions, you, too, must use exceptions. For CLI types, there is no option *not* to use exception handling. However, you must use it sensibly and with restraint. Exceptions should not be used in normal flow control, because they do incur a significant performance penalty when thrown and caught. Exceptions should be used for truly exceptional conditions, errors that would not be expected from normal, correct program functioning.

Here are some best practices for handling exceptions:

Avoid unnecessary proliferation of exception types. If an appropriate .NET Framework standard exception exists, then it should be used. For example, if you are reporting invalid arguments to a function, you should throw ArgumentException, not an exception of your own making. It is appropriate to define your own exception when it is important to filter on that exception and respond uniquely to it.

Throw and catch specific exceptions, not the System::Exception class at the root hierarchy. Also, catch blocks should be ordered so that you catch the most specific exceptions first, followed by more general exceptions. If you do both of these things, you can write code that knows how to handle the specific exceptions and be sure that it is called when those specific errors occur.

Catch only those exceptions that you can reasonably handle. Any exceptions that your code at this particular level in the application doesn't know how to handle should be allowed to propagate up the chain, rather than "recovering" from an exception and attempting to continue when complete recovery isn't possible. This poor practice is known as *swallowing errors*. It's usually better to bring down an application with an unhandled exception than to continue in an unknown state.

Put cleanup code in the finally block, rather than in the catch block. The catch block is for handling and recovering from the error, not cleaning up.

When rethrowing exceptions in a catch block, use the throw statement without providing the exception object. This is interpreted correctly by the runtime as continuing the propagation of the same exception, rather than starting a new exception. The complete call stack is then preserved in the exception's StackTrace property.

Much more could be said about exception-handling best practices, and since exception handling is common to many languages, guidance in one language often applies to all languages. I've only scratched the surface here. There are many resources available to help use exceptions properly. See, for example, *Framework Design Guidelines: Conventions, Idioms, and Patterns for Reusable .NET Libraries* by Krzysztof Cwalina and Brad Abrams (Addison-Wesley, 2005).

Exceptions and Errors from Native Code

When dealing with an application that includes native code and managed code, you will be dealing with potentially many different types of error codes and exceptions. In addition to C++/CLI exceptions, you will have C++ exceptions, COM and Win32 error codes, and possibly structured exceptions, which are a Microsoft-specific extension to C. You also have to deal with all the error codes and exceptions in libraries that you're using. Exceptions from native code are wrapped in managed exceptions. Also, error codes from COM (HRESULTs) are wrapped in exceptions when they propagate to managed code. While I cannot go into all the details behind dealing with these diverse situations in this introductory text, you'll learn some of the basics in Chapter 12.

Attributes

Literally, *metadata* means "data about data." *Attributes* represent metadata for the program element to which it is applied. Attributes may be applied to many program elements, including assemblies, classes, constructors, delegates, enumerated types, events, fields, interfaces, methods, portable executable file modules, parameters, properties, return values, structures, or even other attributes.

In the context of this discussion, metadata means data that is not directly part of whatever it is applied to. In this sense, attributes allow information to be associated with program entities without affecting the internal structure of the entity. For example, an attribute naming the author of a type is not really part of the internal structure of a type. Attributes for program elements may be queried at runtime, so programs may make use of the metadata to manipulate objects. The program element to which an attribute is applied is referred to as the *attribute target.*

How Attributes Work

Attributes are classes defined either in the .NET Framework BCL or another library. You can define your own attributes as well by creating a class that derives from another attribute. The attribute class contains the data to be associated with a program element. Attributes are then applied to program elements using a syntax involving square brackets, called an *attribute specification,* as follows:

```
[ SomeAttribute(arguments) ]
```

If the attribute doesn't take any arguments, you can omit the parentheses entirely.

Where the attribute is placed in the code often determines the target to which the attribute applies. When applied to an entity that takes modifiers, it precedes all modifiers.

```
[ MethodAttribute(arguments) ]
public static int SomeMethod([ParameterAttribute] param1);
```

Multiple attributes may be specified in a single pair of square brackets or may appear in sequential square brackets.

```
[ FirstAttribute(arguments), SecondAttribute(arguments) ]
```

or

```
[ FirstAttribute(arguments) ] [ SecondAttribute(arguments) ]
```

The attribute syntax also supports specifically stating what type of programmatic element the attribute is meant to apply to; this is useful in cases where the target may be ambiguous, for example, when applied to a return value.

```
[ returnvalue: ReturnValueAttribute(arguments) ]
ReturnType^ GetValue();
```

If unspecified, the preceding attribute would be applied to the method, not the return value.

The Attribute Class

All attributes inherit from the System::Attribute class, either directly or indirectly. By convention, attribute classes have Attribute as a suffix. The Attribute suffix may be omitted when referring to the name of the attribute in an attribute specification.

Attribute Parameters

Attribute constructors may take arguments. These arguments are passed in to the attribute's class constructor when it is applied to a program element. There are two ways to pass in the constructor arguments: the usual way involving the order of the parameters, and a second way in which the name of the parameter is given and the assignment operator is used to specify the value. The two methods are illustrated here:

```
[ SomeAttribute( "AttributeValue1", 200) ] // Positional parameters
[ SomeAttribute( Value = "AttributeValue1", IntegralValue = 200) ] // Named
parameters
```

Because attribute parameter evaluation occurs during startup, when the CLI programming environment is not yet fully initialized, the language design imposes restrictions on the types that may be used as attribute parameter types. Attribute parameter types are restricted to primitive types, string handles, object handles, handles to the Type class, enum classes that are publicly accessible (and, if nested, are nested in a publicly accessible type) as well as one-dimensional managed arrays of these types. These restrictions are in place in order to ensure that the runtime has access to the types when it needs them and that there are no dependencies on additional external assemblies.

Some Useful Attributes

The .NET Framework contains many attributes. Let's look at a few of them.

The Obsolete Attribute

The Obsolete attribute is one of the simplest of attributes. Try compiling the code in Listing 10-9.

Listing 10-9. *Using the Obsolete Attribute*

```
// obsolete.cpp
using namespace System;

ref class C
{
  public:
    void Method2() {}
    [Obsolete("This method is obsolete; use Method2 instead.")]
    void Method1() {}
};
```

```
int main()
{
    C^ c = gcnew C();
    c->Method1();
    c->Method2();
}
```

If you compile this, you should get output similar to the following:

```
obsolete.cpp(16) : warning C4947: 'C::Method1' : marked as obsolete
        Message: 'This method is obsolete; use Method2 instead.'
```

As you can see, attributes can be used to give a message to anyone who uses a class or method.

The Out Attribute

The Out attribute is useful when interoperating with other .NET languages, especially C#. It allows you to specify that a parameter is an out-only parameter, which to C# users means that its input value is not used (so it can be uninitialized). You must use a tracking reference as a parameter when using the OutAttribute (see Listing 10-10). Compiling with /clr:pure or /clr:safe makes interoperating with other .NET languages much easier, as you'll see in Chapter 12.

Listing 10-10. *Using the Out Attribute*

```
// outattribute.cpp
// compile with: /clr:safe or /clr:pure

using namespace System;
using namespace System::Runtime::InteropServices;

namespace OutAttrClass
{

    public ref class C1
    {
        public:

        void Func([Out] String^% text)
        {
            text = "testing";
        }
    };
}
```

```
// consume_outattr.cs
// compile with: csc /r:outattribute.dll consume_outattr.cs

using System;
using OutAttrClass;

public class C
{

    public static void Main()
    {
        C1 c1 = new C1();
        String str = "old value";
        c1.Func(out str);
        Console.WriteLine(str);
    }
};
```

The output of Listing 10-10 is as follows:

---

testing

Serialization Attributes

Some .NET Framework features rely heavily on attributes. For example, serialization of types
as XML is primarily supported through applying certain attributes to classes and fields. The
Serializable attribute, applied to a type, enables that type to be serialized as an XML stream.
It can then be stored and re-created later by reading the XML stream and reconstructing the
class. The NonSerialized attribute is used within a serializable class to identify a field that
doesn't participate in serialization. Both attributes are used in Listing 10-11.

Listing 10-11. *Using Serialization Attributes*

```
// serialization.cpp
#using "System.Xml.dll"

using namespace System;
using namespace System::IO;
using namespace System::Xml::Serialization;

// To participate in serialization, types must be public.
[Serializable]
public enum class SunEnum { FullSun, PartShade, Shade };
```

```cpp
[Serializable]
public enum class WaterEnum { Moist, Medium, Dry };

[ Serializable]
public ref class Plant
{
    // an internal counter to determine instance IDs
     static int counter;


    // The instance ID keeps track of the plant objects. It will be
    // a different ID when the object is deserialized, so this does not need
    // to be serialized. We use the NonSerialized attribute to indicate that.
    [NonSerialized]
     int InstanceID;

    public:
    property String^ Genus;
    property String^ Species;
    property String^ Cultivar;
    property String^ CommonName;
    property SunEnum Sun;
    property WaterEnum Water;
    property int Zone;


    Plant() {}

    Plant(String^ genus, String^ species, String^ commonName,
          String^ cultivar, SunEnum sun, WaterEnum water, int zone)
    {
        Genus = genus; Species = species; Cultivar = cultivar;
        Sun = sun; Water = water; Zone = zone;
        InstanceID = counter++;
    }

    static Plant() { counter = 0; }

};

void CreateAndSerialize(String^ genus, String^ species, String^ commonName,
        String^ cultivar, SunEnum sun, WaterEnum water, int zone)
{
    Plant^ p = gcnew Plant(genus, species, commonName, cultivar, sun,
                  water, zone);
```

```
    // The XmlSerializer takes the Type object as a parameter.
    XmlSerializer^ serializer = gcnew XmlSerializer(Plant::typeid);
    // Create a StreamWriter object to write to a file.
    StreamWriter^ sw = gcnew StreamWriter("plants.xml");

    // Serialize causes the XML to be generated.
    serializer->Serialize(sw, p);
    sw->Close();
}

Plant^ Deserialize()
{
    Plant^ p;
    XmlSerializer^ serializer = gcnew XmlSerializer(Plant::typeid);
    // To read the file, use a FileStream object.
    FileStream^ fs = gcnew FileStream("plants.xml", FileMode::Open);
    // Deserialize and cast to object type.
    p = safe_cast<Plant^>( serializer->Deserialize(fs) );
    return p;
}

int main()
{
    CreateAndSerialize("Ampelopsis", "brevipedunculata",
        "Porcelain Berry", nullptr, SunEnum::PartShade, WaterEnum::Medium,
        4);

    Deserialize();
}
```

Here is the plants.xml file Listing 10-11 produces:

```
<?xml version="1.0" encoding="utf-8"?>
<Plant xmlns:xsi="http://www.w3.org/2001/XMLSchema-instance" xmlns:xsd="http://w
ww.w3.org/2001/XMLSchema">
  <Zone>4</Zone>
  <Water>Medium</Water>
  <Sun>PartShade</Sun>
  <Species>brevipedunculata</Species>
  <Genus>Ampelopsis</Genus>
</Plant>
```

This example demonstrates serialization and deserialization of a simple class. The attributes are very simple, and because they take no arguments, the parentheses may be omitted. Only the presence or absence of the attribute makes a difference; there is no "internal structure" to these, the simplest of attributes.

Assembly and Module Attributes

Attributes may be applied at the assembly or the module level. You'll see this used in the default CLR project in the Visual C++ development environment. Look at the default file AssemblyInfo.cpp generated by Visual Studio, shown in Listing 10-12. The main purpose of AssemblyInfo.cpp is to contain assembly-level attributes.

Listing 10-12. *AssemblyInfo.cpp*

```
#include "stdafx.h"

using namespace System;
using namespace System::Reflection;
using namespace System::Runtime::CompilerServices;
using namespace System::Runtime::InteropServices;
using namespace System::Security::Permissions;

//
// General Information about an assembly is controlled through the following
// set of attributes. Change these attribute values to modify the information
// associated with an assembly.
//
[assembly:AssemblyTitleAttribute("green_dragon")];
[assembly:AssemblyDescriptionAttribute("Green Dragon")];
[assembly:AssemblyConfigurationAttribute("")];
[assembly:AssemblyCompanyAttribute("Creative Anarchy, Ltd.")];
[assembly:AssemblyProductAttribute("Wizard's Quest")];
[assembly:AssemblyCopyrightAttribute("Copyright (c)  2006")];
[assembly:AssemblyTrademarkAttribute(
    "Green Dragon is a Trademark of Creative Anarchy, Ltd.")];
[assembly:AssemblyCultureAttribute("")];

//
// Version information for an assembly consists of the following four values:
//
//      Major Version
//      Minor Version
//      Build Number
//      Revision
//
// You can specify all the values or you can default the Revision and Build Numbers
// by using the '*' as shown below:

[assembly:AssemblyVersionAttribute("1.0.*")];

// Is this assembly exposed to COM?
[assembly:ComVisible(false)];
```

```
// Indicate whether the program elements used comply with the Common Language
// Specification (CLS).
[assembly:CLSCompliantAttribute(true)];

// Control security settings.
[assembly:SecurityPermission(SecurityAction::RequestMinimum, UnmanagedCode = true)];
```

The attributes in this file are marked with assembly:, which means the attribute target is the assembly. As you can see, you can specify a variety of assembly metadata, such as its version, the associated product, the company that owns the assembly, and so on. To apply attributes to a .NET module, the syntax module: is used, as follows:

```
[module:ComVisible(false)];
```

Creating Your Own Attributes

To create a custom attribute, you create a class derived from System::Attribute. Consider the example in Listing 10-13.

Listing 10-13. *Creating a Custom Attribute*

```
// custom_attribute.cpp

using namespace System;

// This attribute is applied to custom attributes and indicates the targets for
// the attribute, among other things. In this case, we accept the defaults.
[AttributeUsageAttribute(AttributeTargets::All)]
public ref class OwnerAttribute : Attribute
{
  public:
      property String^ DevOwner;
      property String^ TestOwner;
      property String^ PMOwner;
      property String^ DocOwner;
      property DateTime^ CreationDate;

      OwnerAttribute()
      { }

      OwnerAttribute(String^ _DevOwner, String^ _TestOwner,
                     String^ _PMOwner, String^ _DocOwner)
      {
        DevOwner = _DevOwner;
        TestOwner = _TestOwner;
        PMOwner = _PMOwner;
        DocOwner = _DocOwner;
      }
};
```

```
// Parameter order
[ Owner("John Smith", "Jane Doe", "Hubert Eliason", "Edgar Odell")]
ref class C1
{
   // etc.
};

// Using named parameters
[ Owner(DevOwner="John Smith") ]
ref class C2
{
   // etc.
};
```

Now consider the code in Listing 10-14, in which we've made the fields into public properties and eliminated the constructor that takes arguments. Because the constructor is now gone, we must use the named parameters method of setting one or more values.

Listing 10-14. *Initializing an Attribute with Properties*

```
// custom_attribute2.cpp

using namespace System;

// Specify what targets this attribute may be applied to using the
// AttributeUsageAttribute.
[AttributeUsageAttribute(AttributeTargets::Assembly | AttributeTargets::Class)]
public ref class OwnerAttribute : Attribute
{
   public:
      // Public properties can be used as named parameters.
      property String^ DevOwner;
      property String^ TestOwner;

      OwnerAttribute() { }

};

// Using named parameters
[ Owner(DevOwner="John Smith") ]
ref class C2
{
   // etc.
};
```

Or, you could have both the constructor and the public properties and allow both methods. The named parameters don't have to be properties; public fields work just as well. The AttributeUsageAttribute is an attribute that you use when creating your own attribute types. This attribute is used to specify the targets your attribute may be applied to (the AttributeTargets property), whether or not multiple copies of the attribute may be applied to a single target (the Boolean AllowMultiple property), and whether or not the attribute is inherited by derived classes of a class that the attribute is applied to (the Boolean Inherited property).

To do more complex programming with your attributes, you'll need to get access to them at runtime. To do this, you'll use the static GetCustomAttribute method of the Attribute class, as demonstrated in Listing 10-15. GetCustomAttribute has many overloads, which are used to get attributes on various types of targets. The specific overload of GetCustomAttribute in Listing 10-15 takes two Type objects as parameters: the type of the target class and the type of the attribute you want.

Listing 10-15. *An Overload of GetCustomAttribute*

```
int main()
{
    Attribute^ attribute = Attribute::GetCustomAttribute( C1::typeid,
                            OwnerAttribute::typeid);
    if (attribute != nullptr)
    {
        Console::WriteLine("{0}", attribute);
    }
}
```

The Type class represents a CLI type and can be used to get all kinds of information about the type. You'll read a bit more about this in the next section.

Reflection

Now that you've defined all this metadata for a type, you'll want to access it programmatically. Getting attributes on an object is an example of the use of *reflection*, a .NET Framework feature that recalls the runtime type information (RTTI) feature in classic C++. Reflection enables you to query the attributes of an object at runtime, as well as other metadata associated with a type, such as the type name, inheritance relationships, properties, methods, and events of a type. Not only can you query for information, but you can also create new types, instantiate objects, and call methods on these objects from dynamically loaded assemblies, even if the type or method name is known only from reflection. Reflection does not work with mixed mode (compiled with /clr) executables; you must compile with /clr:pure or /clr:safe in order to use reflection on an assembly. This is because reflection only knows how to load MSIL; it has no knowledge of non-MSIL code that is present in mixed mode.

The Assembly::LoadFrom method we used in Chapter 9 is a good way to get started with reflection. Once we've loaded an assembly, we can get the types in the assembly as a collection of Type objects using the GetTypes method on the assembly class, as in Listing 10-16.

Listing 10-16. *Loading an Assembly and Reflecting on Types*

```
Assembly^ assembly = Assembly::LoadFrom("myassembly.dll");
array<Type^>^ types = assembly->GetTypes();
for each (Type^ t in types)
{
    Console::WriteLine(t->ToString());
}
```

The Type object is a gateway to all the information about the type, including the methods, method parameters, properties, constructors and so on. Throughout this book, you've seen multiple ways to get Type objects. If the type is accessible at compile time, you can get a type object by specifying ::typeid on a managed type. ::typeid is a compiler-defined way of getting the Type object.

```
Type^ t = String::typeid; // Get the static type.
```

For a type that is known only from an object, you can use the GetType method inherited from Object, so it's available on all managed types. The difference between GetType and typeid is that GetType returns the dynamic type, whereas typeid evaluates to the static type. The dynamic type may be different from the static type when, for example, a derived class object is represented by a base class pointer. In that case, the dynamic type is the real type of the object (e.g., Derived), but the static type is Base.

```
Type^ t = obj->GetType();  // Get the dynamic type.
```

You can also create a Type object using the text of a class name using a static method of the Type class.

```
Type^ t = Type::GetType("System::DateTime");
```

The Type class has methods like GetAttributes, GetMembers, and GetMethods to find out about the type, and, once the member names and parameter information is known, you can invoke methods with the InvokeMember method (see Listing 10-17). If you need an instance, you use the Activator::CreateInstance method (see Listing 10-18).

Listing 10-17. *Reflecting with Type Methods*

```
// reflection_general.cpp

using namespace System;
using namespace System::Reflection;

// a class to reflect upon

ref class Reflector
{
    public:
```

```cpp
    // Load an assembly, and print out the methods in the types in the
    // assembly, invoking the specified method on the specified type.
    void LoadAndReflect(String^ assemblyFileName)
    {
        Assembly^ assembly = Assembly::LoadFrom(assemblyFileName);
        array<Type^>^ types = assembly->GetTypes();
        for each (Type^ t in types)
        {
            Console::WriteLine(t->ToString());

            // Get the methods and loop over them.
            array<MethodInfo^>^ methods = t->GetMethods();
            for each (MethodInfo^ method in methods)
            {
                Console::Write("  {0} {1}(", method->ReturnType->ToString(),
                    method->Name);
                // Get the parameters and loop over them.
                array<ParameterInfo^>^ params = method->GetParameters();
                // We don't use for each here because we need to use the index
                // to determine whether a comma is needed.
                for (int i = 0; i < params->Length; i++)
                {
                    ParameterInfo^ param = params[i];
                    Console::Write("{0} {1}",
                        param->ParameterType->ToString(),
                        param->Name);
                    if (i < params->Length - 1)
                        Console::Write(", ");
                }
                Console::WriteLine(")");
            }
        }
    }
};

int main(array<String^>^ args)
{
    Reflector^ r = gcnew Reflector();
    // Pass the assembly file name and reflect over it.
    for each (String^ s in args)
    {
        Console::WriteLine("Reflection on {0}", s);
        r->LoadAndReflect(s);
    }
}
```

The output of Listing 10-17, when reflection_general.cpp is compiled with /clr:safe, is as follows:

```
C:\code\reflection>reflection_general reflection_general.exe
Reflection on reflection_general.exe
Reflector
   System.Void LoadAndReflect(System.String assemblyFileName)
   System.Type GetType()
   System.String ToString()
   System.Boolean Equals(System.Object obj)
   System.Int32 GetHashCode()
```

Reflection is certainly useful for writing tools that give you information about what's in an assembly. It's also useful for late binding, dealing with types about which nothing is known at compile time, perhaps downloaded from or uploaded to a web site. Listing 10-18 provides an example.

Listing 10-18. *Reflecting on Late Binding*

```cpp
// reflection2.cpp

using namespace System;
using namespace System::Reflection;

// A class to reflect upon

ref class Reflector
{
   public:

   void TestDynamicCall(String^ greeting)
   {
      Console::Beep();
      Console::WriteLine(greeting);
      Console::WriteLine("Dynamic Call succeeded!");
   }

   // Load an assembly and invoke the specified method on the specified type.
   void LoadAndReflect(String^ assemblyFileName, String^ typeName,
                       String^ methodName, array<Object^>^ parameterList)
   {
      // Load the assembly.
      Assembly^ assembly = Assembly::LoadFrom(assemblyFileName);
```

```
    // Get the type.
    Type^ t= assembly->GetType(typeName);

    // Get the method of interest.
    MethodInfo^ method = t->GetMethod(methodName);

    // Create an instance of the object.
    Object^ obj = Activator::CreateInstance(t);

    // Invoke the method.
    method->Invoke(obj, parameterList);

  }
};

int main()
{
  Reflector r ;
  // Pass the assembly file name, class name, and method name, and the
  // parameter list.
  array<Object^>^ params = gcnew array<Object^> { "Hello!" };
  r.LoadAndReflect("reflection2.exe", "Reflector", "TestDynamicCall", params);
}
```

The output of Listing 10-18 is shown here:

```
Hello!
Dynamic Call succeeded!
```

Application Domains

In any program, all the objects and other variables exist conceptually in a single application, but in classic C++, there is no named entity accessible to program code that represents this. Application domains, also called *app domains*, represent this abstraction and are named entities in CLI code. In the managed world, you can have multiple app domains in one application. This is like having more than one application to work with in the same program or process. All managed applications start off executing with a single default app domain. You can create additional app domains and run code in them. The code will run in the same process but as if it were a separate program entirely. This can be handy if you're calling into some code of unknown provenance that you fear might crash. Unless it's the initial app domain that the process started with, if something causes an app domain to crash, it will crash that app domain but not the overall process. Thus, app domains provide some measure of isolation and fault tolerance. This technique is used by database and web servers running user code for this reason.

In the example in the previous section, you could load an assembly and have it start in a new app domain instead of the default app domain. You can load many assemblies into these app domains. You can "run an assembly" and have its main method executed. To do all this, you use the AppDomain class. You can create an AppDomain object by calling the static CreateDomain method.

```
AppDomain^ newAppDomain = AppDomain::CreateDomain("My New App Domain");
```

You can then execute the Load method to load an assembly into the app domain.

```
Assembly^ assembly = newAppDomain->Load("myassembly.dll");
```

Loading an assembly doesn't execute anything in the assembly, but you can then use reflection to get information about the assembly, or use the methods of the Assembly class to create objects and use reflection to call methods. The AppDomain object itself has many overloads of the CreateInstance method that may be used to create objects. If you just want to run a program from within your program in its own app domain, you can call the ExecuteAssembly method.

```
appDomain->ExecuteAssembly("reflector2.exe");
```

Application domains are powerful and have low overhead, much lower than the alternative of creating a new process.

Summary

You first saw how exception handling is done in C++/CLI, along with the .NET Framework exceptions. Then you used the finally block, created your own exception class, and examined what happens when exceptions are thrown in constructors. You learned how to use exceptions not based on the Exception class and reviewed exception-handling best practices.

You then looked at the syntax for applying attributes to various targets, examined the Attribute class, and learned about some useful CLI attributes, including the Out parameter attribute, the Obsolete attribute, serialization attributes, and so on. You also saw how to define your own attributes.

Finally, you examined reflection, the .NET Framework feature that allows you to query for type information at runtime, and looked briefly at application domains.

In the next chapter, you'll study parameterized functions and types.

CHAPTER 11

■ ■ ■

Parameterized Functions and Types

A function or type is said to be *parameterized* when one or more types used in the declaration and definition are left unspecified, so that users of the type can substitute the types of their choice. Parameterized functions are functions that have a type parameter in their argument list (or at least the return type). There are two types of parameterized types in C++/CLI: templates, which are inherited from C++, and generics, which are the CLI parameterized type. This chapter will explore generics in detail, look at some useful collection classes and container types, and then look at managed templates and compare them with generics. It will also discuss when to use generics and when to use managed templates.

The syntax for generics is quite similar to that of templates. If you're familiar with the template syntax, some of the description of the syntax for generics in the first few sections of this chapter may be old hat.

Generics

The main question you may have is why generics were introduced to the C++/CLI language when templates already existed in C++. First, the CLI already supported generics, and it was necessary to be able to access these in C++/CLI. Second, generics are really different from templates in fundamental ways, and hence have different uses. Once compiled, templates cease to be parameterized types. From the point of view of the runtime, the type created from a template is just another type. You can't substitute a new type argument that wasn't already used as an argument for that template at compile time. Generics are fundamentally different because they remain generic at runtime, so you can use types that were not known at compile time as type arguments. However, generics, like templates, have limitations that make them unsuitable for certain uses, as you'll see later in this chapter. Let's look at how to use generics.

Type Parameters

Generic functions and types are declared with the contextual keyword `generic`, followed by angle brackets and a list of type parameters with the keyword `typename` or `class`. As with template declarations, both `typename` and `class` are equivalent, even if the type argument used is not a class. Type parameters are identifiers, and thus follow the same rules as other identifiers such as variable names. The type parameter identifier is used as a placeholder for the type in the function or type definition. Listing 11-1 shows a generic function declaration.

Listing 11-1. *Declaring a Generic Function*

```
generic <typename T>
void F(T t, int i, String^ s)
{
  // ...
}
```

This declaration creates a generic function, F, that takes three arguments, the first of which is an unspecified type. If more than one type parameter is to be used, they appear in a comma-separated list, as shown in Listing 11-2.

Listing 11-2. *Declaring Multiple Generic Parameters*

```
generic <typename T, typename U>
void F(T t, array<U>^ a, int i, String^ s)
{
  // ...
}
```

The type parameter in a generic class or function can be used anywhere a type is used, for example, directly as a parameter or in aggregate type such as an array. The type parameter is capable of standing in for both value types as well as reference types.

Generic Functions

Generic functions are declared, defined, and used as in Listing 11-3.

Listing 11-3. *Declaring, Defining, and Using a Generic Function*

```
// generic_functions1.cpp
using namespace System;

generic < typename T>
void GenericFunction(T t)
{
   Console::WriteLine(t);
}

int main()
{
   int i;
   // Specify the type parameter.
   GenericFunction<int>( 200 );
```

```
    // Allow the type parameter to be
    // deduced.
    GenericFunction( 400 );
}
```

As you can see in this example, the generic function is called by using the function name, possibly followed by angle brackets and the type arguments to be substituted for the type parameters. I say "possibly" because if type arguments are omitted, the compiler attempts to deduce them from the types supplied to the function as arguments. For example, if a generic function takes one parameter and the type of that parameter is a type parameter, and if the type of the object supplied is, say, String, the type argument is assumed to be String and may be omitted.

The type parameter need not be an actual argument type; however, it must appear in the argument list or as the return value. It may appear in a compound type, such as an array, as in Listing 11-4.

Listing 11-4. *Using a Generic Array As a Parameter*

```
// generic_functions2.cpp
using namespace System;

generic < typename T>
void GenericFunction(array<T>^ array_of_t)
{
    for each (T t in array_of_t)
    {
        Console::WriteLine(t);
    }
}

int main()
{
    array<String^>^ array_of_string;

    array_of_string = gcnew array<String^>
    { "abc", "def", "ghi" };

    // Allow the type parameter to be
    // deduced.
    GenericFunction( array_of_string );
}
```

While deduction works on compound types, it doesn't work if the type is used as a return value. The compiler won't try to deduce the generic type argument from the left side of an assignment, or any other use of a return value. When only the return value of a generic function is generic, or if the generic type parameter doesn't even appear in the function signature, the type argument must be explicitly specified, as in Listing 11-5.

Listing 11-5. *Explicitly Specifying a Type Argument*

```
// generic_return_value.cpp
using namespace System;

generic <typename T>
T f()
{
    return T();
}

int main()
{
    int i = f<int>();  // OK
    String^ s = f<String^>();  // OK
    double d = f(); // Error! Can't deduce type.
}
```

Generic Types

Like generic functions, the declaration of a generic type differs from a nongeneric declaration by the appearance of the contextual keyword generic followed by the type parameter list. The type parameter may then be used in the generic definition wherever a type is used, for example, as a field, in a method signature as an argument type or return value, or as the type of a property, as shown in Listing 11-6.

Listing 11-6. *Using a Generic Type*

```
// generic_class1.cpp
using namespace System;

generic <typename T>
ref class R
{
    T t;

    public:

        R() {}

        property T InnerValue
        {
            T get() { return t; }
            void set(T value) { t = value; }
        }
};
```

```
int main()
{
    double d = 0.01;
    int n = 12;

    // Create an object with T equal to double.
    R<double>^ r_double = gcnew R<double>();

    // Create an object with T equal to int.
    R<int>^ r_int = gcnew R<int>();

    r_double->InnerValue = d;

    r_int->InnerValue = n;

    Console::WriteLine( r_double->InnerValue );

    Console::WriteLine( r_int->InnerValue );
}
```

The types created from a generic type, such as R<double> and R<int> in Listing 11-6, are referred to as *constructed types*. Two or more types constructed from the same generic type are considered to be unique, unrelated types. Thus, you cannot convert from R<double> to R<int>.

When a generic class or function is compiled, a generic version of that function or class is inserted into the assembly or module created for that source code. At runtime, constructed types are created on demand. Thus, it is not necessary to know at compile time all the possible types that might be used as type parameters. However, this freedom also means that the compile-time restrictions must be greater; otherwise, you would risk adding an incompatible type in at runtime, which might not have all the features required. When the compiler interprets the code for a generic class, it only allows methods, properties and other constructs to be called on the unknown type that are certain to be available. This ensures the type safety of generic types, since otherwise it would be possible to create a generic type that compiled but failed at runtime when the method used was not available. This restriction imposes constraints on the code you can use in your generic functions and types.

For example, the code in Listing 11-7 won't compile.

Listing 11-7. *Compiler Restrictions on Generic Types*

```
// invalid_use_of_type_param.cpp

generic <typename T>
ref class G
{
    T t;

    public:
```

```
    G()
    {
        t = gcnew T("abc", 100); // Error: T may not have
                                 // a compatible constructor.
        t->F(); // Error: T may not have F.
    }

};
```

Listing 11-7 will produce the compiler error:

```
invalid_use_of_type_param.cpp(12) : error C3227: 'T' : cannot use 'gcnew' to
 allocate a generic type
invalid_use_of_type_param.cpp(14) : error C2039: 'F' : is not a member of
 'System::Object'
        c:\windows\microsoft.net\framework\v2.0.50727\mscorlib.dll : see
 declaration of 'System::Object'
```

As you can see, the first complaint is that gcnew is not available on a generic type parameter; the second error occurs because the compiler is only willing to allow methods that are available on System::Object.

There is a way to get around these restrictions. If you need to use specific features of a type, you must constrain the generic so that only types with those features are allowed to be used as type arguments. You'll see how to do that in the section "Using Constraints." But first, let's look at a typical generic class implementing a simple collection.

Generic Collections

Generics are most often used to implement collection classes. Generic collection classes are more type-safe and can be faster than the alternative—nongeneric collection classes relying on handles to Object to represent items in the collection. The main efficiency gain is that the retrieval of items from the collection can be done without the use of casts, which usually requires a dynamic type check when the type is retrieved from the collection, or maybe even when adding elements to the collection. Also, if you are using value types, you can often avoid boxing and unboxing entirely by using a generic collection class. In addition to efficiency gains, if you use a generic type, you automatically force the objects in the collection to be of the appropriate type. Since most collections hold objects of the same type (or perhaps types with a common base type), this helps avoid programmatic errors involving adding objects of the wrong type to the collection. In addition, having the strongly typed collection leaves no doubt as to type needed, which is a relief to anyone who has had to try to figure out what type(s) a poorly documented, weakly typed collection takes.

In order to use the for each statement on a generic collection, the collection must implement the IEnumerable interface, and you must implement an enumerator class to walk through each element of the collection. Listing 11-8 shows the use of generics to create a linked list class that supports the for each statement to iterate through the generic collection. The generic collection implements IEnumerable, and an enumerator class implementing the IEnumerator interface is created to allow the for each statement to work.

Listing 11-8. *Creating a Linked List That Can Be Traversed with for each*

```cpp
// generic_list.cpp
using namespace System;
using namespace System::Collections::Generic;

// ListNode represents a single element in a linked list.
generic <typename T> ref struct ListNode
{
    ListNode<T>(T t) : item(t) { }

    // The item field represents the data in the list.
    T item;
    // the next node in the list;
    ListNode<T>^ next;
};

// List represents a linked list.
generic <typename T> ref class MyList : IEnumerable<ListNode<T>^>
{
    ListNode<T>^ first;

public:

    property bool changed;

    // Add an item to the end of the list.
    void Add(T t)
    {
        changed = true;
        if (first == nullptr)
        {
            first = gcnew ListNode<T>(t);
        }
        else
        {
            // Find the end.
            ListNode<T>^ node = first;
            while (node->next != nullptr)
            {
                node = node->next;
            }
            node->next = gcnew ListNode<T>(t);
        }
    }
```

```cpp
    // Return true if the object was removed,
    // false if it was not found.
    bool Remove(T t)
    {
        changed = true;
        if (first == nullptr)
          return false;
        if (first->item->Equals(t))
        {
            // Remove first from list by
            // resetting first.
            first = first->next;
            return true;
        }
        ListNode<T>^ node = first;
        while(node->next != nullptr)
        {
            if (node->next->item->Equals(t))
            {
                // Remove next from list by
                // leapfrogging it.
                node->next = node->next->next;
                return true;
            }
            node = node->next;
        }
        return false;
    }

    property ListNode<T>^ First
    {
        ListNode<T>^ get()
        {
            return first;
        }
    }

private:
    virtual System::Collections::IEnumerator^ GetEnumerator_NG() sealed
            = System::Collections::IEnumerable::GetEnumerator
    {
        return GetEnumerator();
    }
```

```cpp
    virtual IEnumerator<ListNode<T>^>^ GetEnumerator_G() sealed
            = IEnumerable<ListNode<T>^>::GetEnumerator
    {
        return GetEnumerator();
    }

public:
    IEnumerator<ListNode<T>^>^ GetEnumerator()
    {
        ListEnumerator<T>^ enumerator = gcnew ListEnumerator<T>(this);
        return (IEnumerator<ListNode<T>^>^) enumerator;
    }

    // ListEnumerator is a struct that walks the list, pointing
    // to each element in turn.
    generic <typename T> ref struct ListEnumerator : IEnumerator<ListNode<T>^>
    {
        ListNode<T>^ current;
        MyList<T>^ theList;
        bool beginning;

        ListEnumerator<T>(MyList<T>^ list) : theList(list), beginning(true)
        {
            theList->changed = false;
        }

    private:
        virtual property Object^ Current_NG
        {
            Object^ get() sealed =
                System::Collections::IEnumerator::Current::get
            {
                return (Object^) Current;
            }
        }

        virtual property ListNode<T>^ Current_G
        {
            ListNode<T>^ get() sealed = IEnumerator<ListNode<T>^>::Current::get
            {
                return Current;
            }
        }

    public:
```

```
            property ListNode<T>^ Current
            {
                ListNode<T>^ get()
                {
                    if (theList->changed)
                        throw gcnew InvalidOperationException();
                    return current;
                }
            }

            virtual bool MoveNext()
            {
                if (theList->changed)
                    throw gcnew InvalidOperationException();
                beginning = false;
                if (current != nullptr)
                {
                    current = current->next;
                }
                else
                    current = theList->First;

                if (current != nullptr)
                    return true;
                else
                    return false;
            }

            virtual void Reset()
            {
                theList->changed = false;
                current = theList->First;
            }

            ~ListEnumerator() {}

        }; // end of ListEnumerator
    }; // end of MyList

int main()
{
    MyList<int>^ int_list = gcnew MyList<int>();

    int_list->Add(10);
    int_list->Add(100);
    int_list->Add(1000);
    int_list->Add(100000);
```

```
    int_list->Add(500);
    int_list->Remove(10);
    int_list->Remove(1000);
    int_list->Remove(500);
    int_list->Add(50);

    // Iterate through the list using the for each statement,
    // displaying each member of the list at the console.
    for each (ListNode<int>^ node in int_list)
    {
        Console::WriteLine(node->item);
        // int_list->Remove(50); // danger: modifying the collection
    }
}
```

The output of Listing 11-8 is as follows:

```
100
100000
50
```

There are a few points to notice about Listing 11-8. Recall the IEnumerable implementation on a deck of cards in Chapter 9 (Listing 9-15). In that example, we chose to implement the nongeneric IEnumerable. Implementing the generic IEnumerable<T> adds an additional layer of complexity because IEnumerable<T> also inherits from IEnumerable. That means MyList must implement two different versions of GetEnumerator: one for the generic IEnumerable and one for the nongeneric interface. This is done via explicit interface implementation. In fact, just as in Listing 9-15, we make the interface implementation methods private and define a public method that for each actually uses and that the private interface implementation functions call. This helps improve performance since the enumeration does not require a virtual function call.

Note also that we had to add a destructor to the ListEnumerator class. Without the destructor, the compiler complains that we did not implement IDisposable::Dispose. This is because IEnumerator<T> also inherits from IDisposable (the nongeneric IEnumerator does not). A C++/CLI destructor on a managed type is emitted as the Dispose method, as discussed in Chapter 6.

Finally, we have added a Boolean field in MyList that detects whether MyList is changed during the enumeration. As you may recall, in Listing 9-15, we made a copy of the card deck and used it in the enumerator class. With this version, you avoid the copy, which could be expensive for a large list, and instead generate an exception when the list is modified. To demonstrate the exception, try uncommenting the line calling the Remove method during the iteration. If we permitted the item to be successfully removed during the iteration, the collection would be considered corrupted, and the enumeration would produce undefined results. The behavior of for each would not be as expected and would be very confusing for consumers of the type. Unless you create a working copy of the collection, you should always implement some code that checks that the type has not been modified.

Using Constraints

The restriction noted previously on the use of methods, properties, and other constructs on a type parameter would severely limit the usefulness of generic types, were it not for the ability to get around the restriction by using constraints. Constraints are specific requirements put on a type parameter that limit, or constrain, the types that may be used as type arguments. Essentially, the constraints limit the possible type arguments to a subset of all possible types. By imposing constraints, you may write generic code that uses the methods, properties, and other constructs supported by the constrained subset of types. There are several types of constraints: interface constraints, class constraints, the gcnew constraint, and constraints that limit the type arguments to either reference types or value types.

Interface Constraints

Interface constraints indicate that the type parameter must implement the specified interface or interfaces. When an interface constraint is applied to the type parameter, you may use methods of that interface in your generic type definition (see Listing 11-9).

Listing 11-9. *Specifying Interface Constraints*

```
// interface_constraint.cpp

interface class I
{
    void f();
};

// The constraint is introduced with the where keyword
// and requires that T inherit from I.
generic <typename T> where T : I
ref class R
{
    T t;

    public:
        R(T t_in) : t(t_in)
        {
            // Call the method on I.
            // This code would not compile without
            // the constraint.
            t->f();
        }
};
```

```
ref class C : I
{
   public:
       virtual void f()
       {
           // ...
       }
};

int main()
{
    R<C^>^ r = gcnew R<C^>(gcnew C());
}
```

Class Constraints

A class constraint on a type parameter indicates that the type used must be derived from a specified type. When you specify a class constraint, you may then be sure that the members on that type are available, and you may use those members in the definition of the generic type (see Listing 11-10).

Listing 11-10. *Specifying Class Constraints*

```
// class_constraint.cpp
using namespace System;
ref class B
{
   public:
       virtual void f() {}
};

generic <typename T> where T : B
ref class G
{
    T t;

    public:
       G(T t_in) : t(t_in)
       {
           // For this example, C::f is
           // called.
           t->f();
       }
};
```

```
ref class C : B
{
   public:
      virtual void f() override
      {
          Console::WriteLine("C::f");
      }
};

int main()
{
    G<C^>^ r = gcnew G<C^>(gcnew C());
}
```

Here is the output of Listing 11-10:

```
C::f
```

Any class in the hierarchy under C can be used as the type argument for the generic type G in Listing 11-10.

There are other types of constraints, but before you proceed to them, let's look at reference types and value types in generic types and functions, which will give a better idea of why the other constraint types are needed.

Reference Types and Value Types As Type Parameters

Although the type parameter is written without a handle or any other adornment, when a type argument is supplied, it will either be a handle to a reference type or a value type. The same generic collection will work with both with the same syntax. The same constructs are interpreted differently depending on whether the type parameter is a value type or a reference type. Thus, the MyList class shown in Listing 11-8 works as well with a handle to a ref class, as demonstrated in Listing 11-11, as with the value type int used in Listing 11-8.

Listing 11-11. *Using a Generic List for Strings*

```
ref class R
{
   String^ name;

   public:

   R(String^ n) : name(n) {}
```

```
    virtual String^ ToString() override
    {
        return name;
    }
};

int main()
{
    MyList<R^>^ R_list = gcnew MyList<R^>();

    R_list->Add(gcnew R("test1"));
    R_list->Add(gcnew R("test2"));
    R_list->Add(gcnew R("test3"));

    for each (ListNode<R^>^ node in R_list)
    {
        Console::WriteLine(node->item);
    }
}
```

You cannot use a naked reference type (as opposed to a handle type) as a type parameter:

```
List<R>^ R_list = gcnew List<R>(); // illegal
```

You can make it work by either making R a value type or using a handle to R as the generic type argument.

When writing a generic class that can take either value types or handles, you need to understand something that may be surprising, especially if you're familiar with templates. And that is that regardless of the type argument, you code your generic class with the assumption that the unknown type is a handle. For example, you use the -> operator vs. the . operator for member access, as in Listing 11-12. You wouldn't expect to be able to do this with a pointer or a nonpointer type with the same template class, because different syntax would be required for each, but for generics, the unknown type is treated as if it were a handle, even if the type substituted is a nonhandle type. If the type argument is a value type, you could read the code as if the type parameter were a boxed value type. The actual implementation of the generic doesn't incur the overhead of boxing the value type unless a real boxing operation is needed, for example, if the type parameter is converted to Object^ or a method on Object is accessed.

Listing 11-12. *Assuming an Unknown Type Is a Handle*

```
// generic_reference_syntax.cpp

interface class I { void F(); };

value struct V : I { virtual void F() {} };

ref struct R : I { virtual void F() {} };
```

```
generic <typename T> where T : I
ref class G
{
    T t;

    public:
        G(T t)
        {
            // The handle syntax -> is used
            // even though T could be a value type.
            t->F();
        }
};

int main()
{
    V v;
    R^ r = gcnew R();
    G<V>^ gv = gcnew G<V>(v);
    G<R^>^ gr = gcnew G<R^>(r);
}
```

You might then wonder how you code for situations such as creating objects of the type parameter type inside the generic function or type. If you are to treat the unknown type as a handle, can you use gcnew to create the object, and if so, how? In fact, using gcnew is not allowed in a generic type without specifying a constraint on the type parameter that only allows types that support a default constructor to be used. These could be reference types or value types, even though normally you wouldn't use gcnew to create objects of value type.

The gcnew Constraint

The gcnew constraint indicates that the type parameter must have a default constructor that takes no arguments. The constraint is used if you need to use gcnew on the type parameter in the definition of the generic type. The use of gcnew on an unknown type is limited to the default constructor with no arguments. The gcnew constraint is used with an empty pair of parentheses as a reminder that only the default constructor is allowed (see Listing 11-13). Types that are used must have a public default constructor, either an implicit one (as for all value types) or an explicitly declared default constructor with public accessibility.

Listing 11-13. *Using the gcnew Constraint*

```
// generic_gcnew.cpp
using namespace System;

generic <typename T> where T: gcnew()
T CreateInstance()
{
```

```
    return gcnew T();
}

ref class R
{
    public:

    R() { }
};

int main()
{
    int i = CreateInstance<int>();
    R^ r = CreateInstance<R^>();
}
```

The gcnew constraint is useful, but you cannot specify a specific constructor other than the default constructor.

Value Type Constraints

Unconstrained type parameters can be either reference types or value types, and the same constructs will just work appropriately for either. When an assignment occurs in the generic type, if it's a value type, the value is copied, but if it's a reference type, the reference, not the value, is copied. In some cases, however, you will want to write an algorithm that assumes the semantics of one or the other. Perhaps your algorithm copies and then destroys or destructively modifies objects so it either wouldn't work or would corrupt any reference types that are used. It is possible to constrain a type parameter such that it may only be a value type, or only a reference type, if needed. The syntax is show in Listing 11-14.

Listing 11-14. *Using Value Type Constraints*

```
// valuetype_constraint.cpp

generic <typename T>
where T : value class
ref class G
{ /* ... */ };
```

As an example, suppose the List generic class removes nodes. The question you face when creating a collection class that deletes nodes is what to do with the objects when the node is deleted. If the collection uses a reference type as an argument, and it merely references the objects, but doesn't own them, it's fine to remove the references in the nodes. If the collection is considered to own the object, it might need to delete the object to make sure the destructor is called, perhaps to free up some scarce resource such as a database connection. But if you do that, you have to worry about whether any other references to that object are being held so that you don't destroy an object that's being used. If the objects in the nodes are value types, they are automatically owned by the collection, and they will get destroyed when the containing node is destroyed as part of the natural semantics of value types. Since they're value types, you never have to worry about another object holding a reference that is now invalid. The bottom line is that you can write your class to rely on the natural semantics of value types when you declare a value type constraint. If you don't, you have to write your class to handle both reference types and value types, and you have to deal with the question of object ownership.

As an example, take the MyList generic class used previously and change the Remove method to delete objects upon removal, as in Listing 11-15.

Listing 11-15. *A Collection That Owns the Objects and Deletes Them When Removed*

```
bool Remove(T t)
{
    changed = true;
    if (first == nullptr)
      return false;
    if (first->item->Equals(t))
    {
        // Remove first from list by
        // resetting first.
        first = first->next;
        return true;
    }
    ListNode<T>^ node = first;
    while(node->next != nullptr)
    {
        if (node->next->item->Equals(t))
        {
            delete node->next->item;
            // Remove next from list by
            // leapfrogging it.
            node->next = node->next->next;
            return true;
        }
        node = node->next;
    }
    return false;
}
```

You'd want to prevent the code in Listing 11-15 from being used with a reference type so that you aren't deleting objects for which references might be held in some other part of the program. You would add the constraint to the MyList class and the ListNode class as shown in Listing 11-16. Note that, as discussed previously, you still retain the handle syntax even though you are constraining the type argument to a value type. (It's not a problem using delete on a value type. From the perspective of the generic class, the value type is boxed as an object and can be deleted like any object.)

Listing 11-16. *Adding Constraints to MyList and ListNode*

```
// ListNode represents a single element in a linked list.
generic <typename T>
where T : value class
ref struct ListNode
{
    // same as before
};

generic <typename T>
where T : value class
ref class MyList : IEnumerable<ListNode<T>^>
{
    // same as before
};
```

Reference Type Constraints

Similarly, reference type constraints are specified using `ref class` in the constraint clause, as in Listing 11-17.

Listing 11-17. *Using ref class*

```
// refclass_constraint.cpp

generic <typename Z>
    where Z : ref class
ref class G
{ /* ... */ }
```

As an example of when this might be useful, consider a class that uses a lot of assignment expressions. You might want to create a version optimized for reference semantics and one that is optimized for value semantics. The two versions would be different types with unique names, for example Gref and Gvalue.

Multiple Constraints

You can use multiple constraints on a single type parameter or on different type parameters. Listing 11-18 shows some examples of the syntax.

Listing 11-18. *Using Multiple Constraints*

```
// generic_multiple_constraints.cpp
using namespace System;

interface class I;
ref class C;
```

```
// T must have a public default constructor and
// T must inherit from C and
// T must implement I.
generic <class T>
where T : gcnew(), C, I
void F(T t)
{
   // ...
}

interface class IKey;

// Use multiple where clauses to specify
// constraints for multiple type parameters.
generic <typename Key, typename Value>
where Key : IKey
where Value : value class
ref class Dictionary
{
   // ...
};
```

The Dictionary class requires keys to implement IKey and the values to be value types. The .NET Framework BCL Dictionary class doesn't have these restrictions. You'll learn more about the ArrayList and Dictionary collection classes in the next section.

.NET Framework Container Types

Containers, or collection classes, are types that hold objects, provide ways to access them, and may be used in a variety of algorithms. Lists, queues, stacks, trees, and so on are all examples of container classes. The .NET Framework container classes are in the namespaces System::Collections and System::Collections::Generic.

Generic vs. Nongeneric Container Classes

The .NET Framework provides two types of container classes: the nongeneric container classes that hold references to Object and the generic collection classes. The so-called weakly typed collections were made available in the 1.0 version of the .NET Framework, and are still available in later versions. The generic collections became available in .NET Framework 2.0 with Visual Studio 2005. The generic collections are strongly typed, meaning that the objects in the collection are restricted to a specific type, and compilers will detect any attempt to insert the incorrect type into the container.

In a weakly typed collection class, it is the responsibility of the user to ensure that objects inserted into the collection are of the appropriate type. Usually, objects are cast dynamically back to the appropriate type when they are retrieved from the collection. If objects of the wrong type are inserted, they will produce a runtime InvalidCastException when retrieved.

Using the Collection Class Interfaces

The .NET Framework collection classes have associated interfaces. It is a good idea to use the interfaces instead of the types directly. That way, code written for one collection type will work with other related collection types that implement the same interface. Collection types use different data structures and algorithms, but often share the basic interface. For example, an array-like class could be implemented as an array or as a linked list. Whether one or the other was more efficient would depend on how it is used. If you use the interface instead of the specific collection type, your algorithms and functions that take the interfaces will be independent of implementation, so you can easily switch to another implementation if you find that it is more efficient, and you can reuse code on a wider variety of collection types.

ArrayList

As you saw in Chapter 5, the ArrayList is a collection class that combines array-like access to objects with list-like functionality such as adding, removing, and inserting items. An array list is implemented like an array, so access to elements of the list is a O(1) process, just as is an array lookup.

There are two versions of the ArrayList class. One of them is a weakly typed collection (using handles to Object as the array element type), and the other is a generic, strongly typed collection. If all your elements are of the same type, the generic collection should be used since you will enjoy compile-time type enforcement and improved performance as described previously. If your objects are not of the same type, you could create a generic collection class in which the type parameter is constrained to an interface or common base type of the types you want to store. If there is no common interface or base, you could use the weakly typed, nongeneric ArrayList, as in Listing 11-19. Note the use of the object handle in the for each statement.

Listing 11-19. *Using a Weakly Typed, Nongeneric ArrayList*

```cpp
// arraylist.cpp
using namespace System;
using namespace System::Collections;

int main()
{
    ArrayList^ array_list = gcnew ArrayList();

    array_list->Add(1);

    array_list->Add("test");

    // Iterate using the for each operator.
    for each (Object^ o in array_list)
    {
        Console::WriteLine( o->ToString() );
    }
```

```
    // Iterate using indexing.

    for (int i = 0; i < array_list->Count; i++)
    {
        Console::WriteLine("{0} {1}", i, array_list[i]);
    }
}
```

Often, code that uses the generic collections, such as ArrayList, will use a cast when objects are retrieved from the collection. If the cast fails, InvalidCastException is thrown, and Listing 11-20 traps this.

Listing 11-20. *Trapping an Invalid Cast Exception*

```
// casting_from_object.cpp
using namespace System;
using namespace System::Collections;

ref class Book
{
    public:
        Book()
        { }
        Book(String^ _title) { Title = _title; }
        property String^ Title;
};

int main()
{
    ArrayList^ theList = gcnew ArrayList();

    theList->Add( gcnew Book("Of Mice and Men") );

    // Use a cast to retrive an object from the list
    // and convert to the appropriate type.
    Book^ book = safe_cast<Book^>( theList[0] );

    Console::WriteLine("OK. The object was retrieved and the title is "
                        + book->Title );

    // Now try putting an object of the wrong type
    // in the list and retrieving it using the same
    // method.
```

```
theList->Add( gcnew String("bad data"));
try
{
    book'= safe_cast<Book^>( theList[1] );
}
catch(InvalidCastException^ e)
{
    Console::WriteLine("An object of the wrong type was put on the list.");
}
}
```

Not only is the cast a performance hit, but also, as discussed in Chapter 10, it's inefficient to rely on a runtime exception to detect an incorrect use of the collection. To push this error to compile time, use the ArrayList: the List<T> generic type, or better yet, the IList<T> generic interface.

The generic List<T>, when used with a reference type, requires the type argument to be a handle type. In for each statements, the type argument is used directly, rather than a handle to Object, as is used when iterating the weakly typed collection (see Listing 11-21).

Listing 11-21. *Iterating with for each and with an Index*

```
// list_generic.cpp
using namespace System;
using namespace System::Collections::Generic;

int main()
{
    List<String^>^ list = gcnew List<String^>();
    // or IList<String^>^ list = gcnew List<String^>();

    list->Add("apple");
    list->Add("banana");

    // Iterate using the for each operator.
    for each (String^ s in list)
    {
        Console::WriteLine( s );
    }

    // Iterate using indexing.

    for (int i = 0; i < list->Count; i++)
    {
        Console::WriteLine("{0} {1}", i, list[i]);
    }
}
```

The output of Listing 11-21 is as follows:

```
apple
banana
0 apple
1 banana
```

In addition to the generic List, there is a generic IList interface that can be used, as mentioned in the comment.

Let's look at one more collection class before moving on to managed templates.

Dictionaries

Dictionaries provide associative array functionality based on key-value pairs. An *associative array* is an array in which one type, the key, is used to access a particular stored value, often of a different type. All the keys are usually the same type, and all the values are normally the same type as well. The name, Dictionary, suggests an analogy. Using a real dictionary, you look up a definition (value) using the word as the key. The generic Dictionary<TKey,TValue> class may be used directly and is probably the best bet for the associative array-like functionality. We'll also use the IDictionary interface in Listing 11-22.

Listing 11-22. *Using a Dictionary*

```cpp
// dictionary.cpp
using namespace System;
using namespace System::Collections::Generic;

int main()
{
   IDictionary<String^, String^>^ dict;
   dict = gcnew Dictionary<String^, String^>();

   // The add method takes the key and the value.
   dict->Add("hat", "head adornment");
   dict->Add("hot", "at a high temperature");
   dict->Add("hit", "to strike");

   // Use the KeyValuePair generic class when using the
   // for each statement.
   for each (KeyValuePair<String^, String^>^ pair in dict)
   {
       Console::WriteLine(" {0}: {1}", pair->Key, pair->Value);
   }
```

```
    // The remove method takes the key as an argument.
    dict->Remove("hat");

    // Use the KeyValuePair generic class when using the
    // for each statement.
    for each (KeyValuePair<String^, String^>^ pair in dict)
    {
        Console::WriteLine(" {0}: {1}", pair->Key, pair->Value);
    }
}
```

The output of Listing 11-22 is as follows:

```
hat: head adornment
hot: at a high temperature
hit: to strike
hot: at a high temperature
hit: to strike
```

When using the for each statement to iterate over a dictionary collection, use the KeyValuePair generic class as shown in the previous example.

If the key is not found, a KeyNotFoundException is thrown. If an attempt is made to add a duplicate key, an ArgumentException is thrown by the Add method.

Managed Templates

C++/CLI supports templates on managed types, generally known as *managed templates*. Managed templates differ from generics in several ways, although the syntax is very similar and both are parameterized types. The main difference is the templates are resolved at compile time, and so are considered to be fully specified types by the runtime, whereas generics remain "generic" at runtime as well. Another way of putting this is that for templates, the parameterization is handled by the compiler, whereas with generics, the parameterization is handled by the runtime. In this section, you'll see the implications of this difference in some detail, but before you get too far into the comparison of managed templates and generics, let's look at the basics of using templates on managed types.

The first example, Listing 11-23, shows a simple template class that is a ref class. Note the syntax that puts the template keyword first, followed by the template argument list, then any attributes, if any, and then the ref class keyword. Let's put the managed template declaration in a header file. The class template declares a member object and exposes it through a property, InnerObject, that in this simple example behaves just like a trivial property, but allows you to see how you use the type parameter in a managed type declaration.

Listing 11-23. *A Simple ref class Template*

```
// managed_template.h

template <typename T>
public ref class CTemplate
{
    T m_obj;

    public:

        CTemplate(T obj) { m_obj = obj; }

        property T InnerObject
        {
            T get() { return m_obj; }
            void set(T obj) { m_obj = obj; }
        }

};
```

The template is instantiated just as we would normally instantiate a native template class. In Listing 11-24, we instantiate the type with an int and, separately, a String handle.

Listing 11-24. *Using a Template with Different Types*

```
// managed_templates.cpp

#include "managed_template.h"

using namespace System;

int main()
{
    CTemplate<int>^ ct_int;
    CTemplate<String^>^ ct_string;

    ct_int = gcnew CTemplate<int>(55);
    ct_string = gcnew CTemplate<String^>("test");

    Console::WriteLine("{0} ", ct_int->InnerObject );
    Console::WriteLine("{0} ", ct_string->InnerObject );

}
```

In a similar manner, you can use all the other features of templates on your managed reference types, interfaces, and value types. Some managed types cannot be templates: you cannot declare template enum classes or delegate types. Otherwise, you can use nontype template parameters, you can use template functions, you can use template arguments, partial specialization, and so on. However, let's perform a little experiment with the template class in Listing 11-24 to illustrate an important limitation of managed templates: let's compile the template in two different assemblies. We'll also create some functions that take arguments of the specialized template types, so you can see what happens when we try to pass these template class types over an assembly boundary. We'll create two assemblies that include the managed template header file. One, compiled from assembly1.cpp (see Listing 11-25), will expose a class, CBridge, with a public static function that takes the template as a parameter. First, compile assembly1.cpp as an executable, then compile it as a library; and compile assembly2.cpp, which references assembly1.dll and tries to call the public static method CBridge::F, passing assembly2.cpp's instantiation of the managed template.

Listing 11-25. *An Assembly That Uses a Template Type in Its Public Interface*

```
// assembly1.cpp

#include "managed_template.h"

using namespace System;

public ref class CBridge
{
    public:

    static void F(CTemplate<int>^ ct_int)
    {
        Console::WriteLine("{0} ", ct_int->InnerObject );
    }
};

int main()
{
    CTemplate<int>^ ct_int;
    ct_int = gcnew CTemplate<int>(55);
    CBridge::F(ct_int);
}
```

Compile the code in Listing 11-25 as a DLL:

```
cl /clr /LD assembly2.cpp
```

Listing 11-26 is assembly2.cpp.

Listing 11-26. *Trying to Use the Template in Another Assembly*

```
// assembly2.cpp

#include "managed_template.h"

#using "assembly1.dll"

int main()
{
    CTemplate<int>^ ctemplate_int = gcnew CTemplate<int>(67);

    CBridge^ bridge = gcnew CBridge();
    bridge->F(ctemplate_int);
}
```

If we try to compile `assembly2.cpp` in Listing 11-26 as follows:

```
cl /clr assembly2.cpp
```

we'll get an error similar to the following:

```
assembly2.cpp
assembly2.cpp(12) : error C2664: 'CBridge::F' : cannot convert parameter 1 from
'CTemplate<T> ^' to 'CTemplate<int> ^'
        with
        [
            T=int
        ]
        No user-defined-conversion operator available, or
        Types pointed to are unrelated; conversion requires reinterpret_cast,
C-style cast or function-style cast
```

What's the problem? You can plainly see that `CTemplate<T>` with `T = int` is the same as `CTemplate<int>`, right? Well, no. The truth of the matter is that the `CTemplate<int>` compiled into the first assembly is not considered the same type as the `CTemplate<int>` compiled into the second assembly, because the runtime sees them as two different types. The compiler won't let you compile code that tries to do this.

The bottom line is that you should confine your template code to *intra-assembly* code. Don't expose your template classes as public classes. If you want a parameterized type to use in the public classes and methods of an assembly, use a generic type. You may often find yourself defining a generic interface to a template class. You can then use the generic interface over the assembly boundary, and use the template classes freely within each assembly. Listing 11-27 shows how you would declare such a thing.

Listing 11-27. *Declaring a Generic Interface*

```
// generic_interface.cpp
// Declare your generic interfaces and compile to a DLL.
// Reference the compiled assembly using #using.
// Do not reference the source as an included file.

generic <typename T>
public interface class IGInterface
{
    property T InnerObject;
};
```

Unlike the generic interface, the template is declared and defined in a header file, as shown in Listing 11-28.

Listing 11-28. *Declaring a Generic Interface for a Template*

```
// template_with_generic_interface.h

#using "generic_interface.dll"

template <typename T>
ref class CTemplate : IGInterface<T>
{
    T m_obj;

    public:

        CTemplate(T obj) { m_obj = obj; }

        virtual property T InnerObject
        {
            T get() { return m_obj; }
            void set(T obj) { m_obj = obj; }
        }

};
```

Now the `CBridge::F` function can be rewritten to use the generic interface handle instead of the template class directly (see Listing 11-29).

Listing 11-29. *Using a Generic Interface Instead of a Template*

```cpp
// template_with_generic_interface.cpp

#include "template_with_generic_interface.h"

using namespace System;

public ref class CBridge
{
   public:

   static void F(IGInterface<int>^ ct_int)
   {
      Console::WriteLine("{0} ", ct_int->InnerObject );
   }
};
```

And the second assembly can now call the CBridge::F function. It will include the template using #include and reference the generic interface (as well as the other assembly containing CBridge::F) with #using, as in Listing 11-30.

Listing 11-30. *Successfully Using a Template from Another Assembly*

```cpp
// assembly2_with_generic.cpp

#using "generic_interface.dll"
#using "template_with_generic_interface.dll"

#include "template_with_generic_interface.h"

int main()
{
   CTemplate<int>^ ctemplate_int = gcnew CTemplate<int>(67);

   CBridge^ bridge = gcnew CBridge();
   bridge->F(ctemplate_int);
}
```

The conversion from the template to the generic parameter of F is implicit, since it amounts to a simple derived class to base interface conversion.

The presence of both generics and templates in the language can be confusing. If you remember nothing else, remember that templates are good for use within assemblies, but that generics should be used for any interassembly functionality, and also for any cross-language functionality. The language you are interoperating with must also support consuming generics, which VB, C# and J# do.

You might also wonder, Why use managed templates at all? There are some limitations to the usefulness of generics, especially for those who are used to the full expressive power of templates in C++. Many features of templates are not available with generics, as described here:

- Templates support nontype template parameters; generics don't.

- Templates support specialization and partial specialization; generics don't.

- Templates work better with mathematical operations; unconstrained generics don't allow the use of mathematical operators on the unknown type parameter, and there are no viable constraints for families of primitive types (e.g., int, double, etc.).

- Generic types cannot inherit from the type parameter, as is possible with templates.

- Generics have no equivalent of template metaprogramming, that is, using template expansion by the compiler to perform operations.

- Templates are compiled at the time of instantiation; generics are compiled at the point of definition.

The last point bears some further explanation, since it has far-reaching implications in terms of what code is allowed in a generic class. The basic rule is that a generic class may not include any code that is not ensured to compile with any type argument. Think about the fact that the compiler will not even know what types might eventually be used as type arguments. You could compile G<T> today and deploy it somewhere, and years later someone could instantiate it with a type that never even existed when G<T> was compiled. This would not be possible if just any code were allowed to compile. That's the reason why constraints are so important in generic classes. In order to call a method on a type parameter, the compiler must be certain that that method is in fact available for every allowable type argument that may be used. The runtime must also be equally forceful in insisting that only types that meet the constraints are allowed to be used as type arguments. Contrast this with templates, in which you can make all kinds of unstated assumptions about the type (such as assuming the type has certain methods, operators, and so on) that might be used as a type parameter, without any worries because you know that when someone tries to instantiate your template, the compiler will check the template with the actual type that is being used. You don't have to constrain the template type parameter because the type never remains unknown at runtime.

To drive home the point, consider a template class that works with mathematical entities and assumes the existence of a + operator on the type, as in Listing 11-31.

Listing 11-31. *Assuming the Existence of an Operator*

```
template <class T>
ref class A
{
    // assumes T supports the + operator
    T add(T t1, T t2) { return t1 + t2; }
};
```

If you want a generic class that does this, you probably need to define an interface constraint and add that interface to any types that are to be used as a type argument, as in Listing 11-32.

Listing 11-32. *Using a Constraint to Guarantee the Existence of an Operator*

```
interface class IAddition
{
        static IAddition^ operator+(IAddition^, IAddition^);
};

generic <typename T> where T : IAddition
ref class G
{
   T add(T t1, T t2) { return t1 + t2; }
};
```

The problems arise when you try to use the primitive types, since, although they might have a + operator, they don't implement IAddition. Using templates, you can just use the + operator without the constraint, and if someone tries to instantiate the template with a type that is incompatible, it simply won't compile, but the template would work with int as well as with your types that define the + operator. There are certainly other examples of when you would want to use templates instead of generics. It is a trade-off, since the additional expressive power of templates does come at the cost of only having access to the templates with a single assembly, apart from generic interfaces you might set up for interassembly communication.

On the other hand, generics have many advantages when programming in the CLI environment. Advantages of generics are significantly greater runtime flexibility, since you can use types not envisioned at compile time; the ability to use generics across assembly boundaries; and the ability to interoperate with other CLI languages.

Summary

In this chapter, you looked at the two major language features supporting parameterized types: generics and templates. You saw how to declare, define, and use generic functions and types, and how to use constraints to allow generic code to use specific features of a specified subset of types. You also looked at a variety of .NET Framework collection classes, including ArrayList and Dictionary, and their associated helper classes. You learned the differences between the generic and nongeneric collection classes and when to use them, and you also learned another way to enumerate over collections using enumerators and the for each statement. Finally, you looked at managed templates and the differences between them and generics and you saw when to use one or the other.

In the next and final chapter, I'll cover how to use C++/CLI to interoperate with other technologies, including other .NET languages and native C++ code.

CHAPTER 12

■■■

Interoperability

Interoperability, or *interop* as it is usually called, refers to using or invoking program code from some other programming environment or language, for example, calling COM or native C++ code in a managed language. Interop is a complex but beautiful and extremely necessary thing. Many people think that the C++/CLI language for the .NET platform would be used primarily to extend existing code bases written in native C++. While there is no reason why you could not use C++/CLI as your .NET language of choice, the support that C++/CLI provides for native code interop on the .NET platform is indeed impressive. In many cases, you simply turn on the /clr compiler option and recompile your native code, producing managed code (or at least mixed code that's mostly MSIL but with a few native x86 or x64 instructions mixed in). This feature was called IJW or "it just works" when it was originally released along with Managed Extensions for C++. And for the most part, it was true. It's now called *mixed mode*. A huge amount of work went into making that type of interop possible. Also, even if you're writing an entirely new application that uses a native API, such as Win32, interop support in C++ makes it easier and much faster to call these APIs in C++ than it is in C#.

The Many Faces of Interop

There are several kinds of interop that you should be aware of. *Cross-language interop* is the one you'll see first, and that refers to the ability of C++/CLI to work closely with C# and Visual Basic, and other languages that target the CLR. Because of the common platform, common IL, and assembly and metadata formats, you can use a C# or Visual Basic assembly pretty much as you would another C++/CLI assembly. You can reference it with #using, you can create instances of the types declared in those assemblies, call methods, and so on. You can also go a step further and create inheritance hierarchies that cross language boundaries, such as a C# class that implements a C++/CLI interface, or a C++/CLI class that inherits from a class written in Visual Basic. Once these types are compiled to MSIL, there is little that indicates the original language in which they were authored.

In addition to cross-language interop, you may also need to interoperate with native C++ code. The way you choose to interoperate depends on whether you have source code available or only have a binary, whether the native API is exposed as a function or a class, whether the API is exposed via COM, and whether you can recompile the code.

Let's first consider the case where you don't have source access, and you simply have a library function in a native DLL that you'd like to call from a managed environment. The CLR provides a mechanism for doing this; it's usually referred to as *Platform Invoke*, or *P/Invoke*,

3

suggesting that you are invoking a platform-specific binary. Basically, P/Invoke lets you create a managed entry point to your native function. If the native code you want to call is not exposed as a native, exported function, you can't use P/Invoke. P/Invoke works well for calling Win32 APIs, and it is widely used in CLI languages for this purpose. There are some complexities in using P/Invoke, since you have to declare managed analogs for any native structs that are passed into the function, and this is sometimes tricky. Also, there is considerable overhead due to switching from managed to native code and back again, as you'll see.

In addition to P/Invoke, the CLR provides support for COM interop. You can create instances of proxy objects to COM objects in managed code. Usually this will involve creating a wrapper assembly that contains managed types that expose the COM interfaces to your managed code. Visual Studio contains several tools that simplify this process, such as tlbimp.exe, which creates a wrapper assembly from a typelib (TLB file) that is usually present with a COM library. You can also go the other way, exposing managed objects to COM. This process involves attributing the types with COM attributes, specifying, for example, the GUID for the type, and using tlbexp.exe to generate a type library that can be used to instantiate the managed objects from COM as COM objects.

All of the previously mentioned interop methods are available to all CLR languages, but in C++/CLI, you have the option of an additional type of interop if you have the C++ source code and can recompile it with the /clr option. Most C++ code will compile with the /clr compiler option with minimal changes, if any. If you do this, you can re-create your native DLL as an assembly. The types are still native, but the instructions are compiled into IL. This code can be used from C++/CLI code (at least in mixed mode) in the same way as you would normally use native C++ code: include the header file and link to the DLL's import library. In pure mode and safe mode, you cannot link in native object files and have the resulting file remain pure or safe. If you can link together object files of different modes, the resulting assembly is "downgraded" to the lowest common denominator; for example, if you link pure and mixed mode object files, the result is a mixed mode assembly.

You can put both native classes and types and managed classes and types in the same assembly in pure and mixed mode. This is useful if you want to expose native classes and types to other .NET languages such as C# or Visual Basic. A typical scenario might be that you would take a native class library's source code, recompile it with the /clr option, and, in the same assembly, add managed classes that wrap the native classes that you want to export to other managed languages. These managed wrappers would be marked public and would be visible to the other language. However, the native classes in the DLL would not be accessible to the clients who use the assembly.

To support all this, there are various language features and CLR features. Cross-language interop, P/Invoke, and COM interop are CLR features. I'll discuss cross-language interop, P/Invoke, and COM interop in brief. Using native types and managed types together in the same assembly, for example, in order to create a managed wrapper for a native class library, is the main focus of this chapter. You'll learn how to reference a native type in a managed type, and how to reference a managed type in a native type. You'll see pointer types that help in working with interoperability scenarios, such as interior pointers and pinning pointers. You'll also look into converting types between native and managed equivalents. This type of conversion is usually called *marshaling*.

Interop is an intriguing, complex subject. A full discussion of all the subtle aspects of interop would be impossible in an introductory text, so this chapter will focus on some basic scenarios to give you an idea of what is possible. You could write an entire book on C++ interop.

For more information, you may want to consult *Expert Visual C++/CLI* by Marcus Heege (Apress, forthcoming).

Interoperating with Other .NET Languages

It is straightforward to use types created in another .NET Language in C++/CLI. In fact, you do this all the time, since much of the .NET Framework is written in C#. When interoperating with C# or VB or any of a number of non-Microsoft languages, you need to be aware of what features of C++/CLI are available in other languages, and what are not. For example, C# does not support global functions. If you define a global function and make it public, you cannot call it from C#. You could call such a function through a public static method of a public class. If you want a managed language that lets you do everything, IL is the answer—see *Expert .NET 2.0 IL Assembler* by Serge Lidin (Apress, 2006) for more details. It is fair to say that IL is the language below C++/CLI on the CLR, just as assembler is the one language lower than C++ on many platforms.

Using pure or safe mode makes sense for cross-language interop, since it's easy to reference MSIL assemblies from VB or C#. If you were to compile in mixed mode, you'd need to create a managed wrapper to ensure that the code can be accessed from the other languages, as shown in Listings 12-1 and 12-2.

Listing 12-1. *Wrapping a Global Function*

```cpp
// global_function.cpp
// Compile with cl /clr:safe /LD global_function.cpp.

using namespace System;

namespace G
{

    void FGlobal()
    {
        Console::WriteLine("Global C++/CLI Function.");
    }

    public ref class R
    {
        public:
        static void FMember()
        {
            Console::WriteLine("C++/CLI Static Member Function.");
            FGlobal();
        }
    };
};
```

Listing 12-2. *Consuming a Wrapped Global Function in C#*

```
// consume_cpp.cs
// Compile with csc /r:global_function.dll consume_cpp.cs.

using G;

class C
{
    public static void Main()
    {
        // FGlobal();    // Error: global functions not available in C#.
        R.FMember();      // OK
    }
};
```

The output of Listing 12-2 is as follows:

```
C++/CLI Static Member Function.
Global C++/CLI Function.
```

Listing 12-3 shows a C++/CLI interface that is then implemented in a VB class in Listing 12-4.

Listing 12-3. *Creating an Interface in C++*

```
// interface_example.cpp
// Compile with cl /clr:pure /LD interface_example.cpp.

public interface class ITest
{
    void F();
    void G();
};
```

Listing 12-4. *Using an Interface in Visual Basic*

```
' implement_example.vb
' Compile with vbc /r:interface_example.dll implement_example.vb.

Public Class VBClass
    Implements ITest

    Public Sub F Implements ITest.F
        Console.WriteLine("F in VB")
    End Sub
```

```
Public Sub G Implements ITest.G
      Console.WriteLine("G in VB")
End Sub

Public Shared Sub Main
    Dim Test As ITest = New VBClass
    With Test
    .F()
    .G()
    End With
  End Sub 'Main
End Class 'VBClass
```

Here is the output of Listing 12-4:

```
F in VB
G in VB
```

To minimize problems with cross-language interop, a Common Language Specification (CLS) was created that specifies common constructs across .NET languages that are usable across language boundaries. If you are careful to utilize only those features that are CLS compliant in the publicly visible portions of public types, you can be sure that your code is accessible to C# and VB and any other CLR language that recognizes CLS-compliant types. You can safely use noncompliant features inside the methods of a public type, or in private types, but the public signatures of public types must be CLS compliant for the type to be considered CLS compliant. There are many C++/CLI features that are not CLS compliant. Table 12-1 lists C++/CLI features that are not CLS compliant and suggests alternatives that are.

Table 12-1. *Major Features of C++/CLI That Are Not CLS Compliant, and Some Possible Alternatives to Them*

Feature	Possible CLS-Compliant Alternatives
Boxed value types	Use System::Object, System::ValueType, or System::Enum.
Global functions	Use static methods instead.
Native code	Create CLS-compliant wrappers.
Templates	Use generics or create generic interfaces.
Pointer types	Use IntPtr.
Exceptions that don't inherit from System::Exception	Use only exceptions that inherit from System::Exception.
Interfaces with static members	Use only nonstatic methods, properties, and events.
Properties with accessors that have different modifiers, for example, one virtual accessor and one nonvirtual)	Use only properties with consistent modifiers on their accessors.

Table 12-1. *Major Features of C++/CLI That Are Not CLS Compliant, and Some Possible Alternatives to Them (Continued)*

Feature	Possible CLS-Compliant Alternatives
Overriding virtual methods that change accessibility	Use only types that don't do this.
Operator overloading	Provide methods with similar functionality, for example, int Add(int a) for int operator+(int).
Traditional varargs, for example, printf("%d%s", ...)	Use the new parameter array syntax: for example, f(String^ s, ... array<R^>^ params).

Using Native Libraries with Platform Invoke

Remember that I said in Chapter 3 that there are several compilation modes supported in C++/CLI: mixed mode (the /clr option), pure mode (/clr:pure), and safe mode (/clr:safe). (There's also /clr:oldSyntax, which enables the syntax for Managed Extensions for C++ that was used in Visual Studio .NET 2002 and 2003.) In previous chapters, most of the code compiles just as well in mixed, pure, or safe mode, except in a few cases where explicitly noted otherwise. When dealing with interop, the choice of compilation mode matters, because native code is potentially unsafe. P/Invoke is used when you need to invoke a function in a native DLL in safe mode. Even though native code cannot be verified to be safe, it is the safest way to invoke native code from managed code. P/Invoke is used widely in C#, but there are other alternatives in C++/CLI that may often be used instead in pure and mixed modes. The other methods will be described later in the chapter. If you are using safe mode, P/Invoke is your only option for invoking native functions.

The basic idea of P/Invoke is that you create a new function declaration and use attributes to associate it with an existing native function, naming the DLL that exports the function. That is the straightforward part. The complexity arises with the types that will be used as parameters to the function. These types must be created in C++/CLI code and must be exactly the same as the native types the function expects.

Let's say you want to call the MessageBox function. The Windows SDK documentation tells us that MessageBox is stored in user32.dll, and its header file is WinUser.h. Looking up its declaration, we find it as shown in Listing 12-5.

Listing 12-5. *MessageBox Declaration*

```
int MessageBox( HWND hWnd, // handle to owner window
                LPCTSTR lpText, // text in message box
                LPCTSTR lpCaption, // message box caption
                UINT uType // message box type );
```

This function call can be exposed for use in managed code using the DllImport attribute. Listing 12-6 shows how the Win32 MessageBox function is declared and used in C++/CLI code.

Listing 12-6. *Calling a Win32 Function in C++/CLI*

```cpp
// pinvoke.cpp
using namespace System;
using namespace System::Runtime::InteropServices;

// Note the use of managed equivalents of native types.
[DllImport("user32.dll", CharSet=CharSet::Auto)]
int MessageBox(IntPtr, String^ text, String^ caption,
    unsigned int type);

int main()
{
    MessageBox(IntPtr::Zero, "Hello, World!", "Win32 Message Box", 0);
}
```

You can easily verify that this code works just fine in mixed mode (with the /clr option), pure mode (with the /clr:pure option), and safe mode (with the /clr:safe option).

The DllImport attribute takes the DLL name as an argument, as well as an argument that specifies how string arguments are to be treated. As you know, in native code strings may be ANSI or MBCS (type char) or Unicode (type wchar_t). The managed string type is always Unicode, but a lot of APIs take ANSI strings. The CharSet parameter allows you to tell the system to convert the managed string to the desired native string type. Also, it actually controls whether the Unicode or the ANSI version of a Win32 function is called. The CharSet parameter has three possible values: CharSet::Ansi, CharSet::Auto, and CharSet::Unicode. CharSet::Auto lets the system choose the right marshaling on its own. You may know that there is no actual function MessageBox. In WinUser.h, you can see that MessageBox is a macro that resolves to one of the real function names: MessageBoxA for the ANSI version and MessageBoxW for the Unicode version. If you specify CharSet::Unicode, the function called will actually be MessageBoxW. If you specify CharSet::Ansi, it will be MessageBoxA. This mechanism is independent of whether or not UNICODE is defined. This is one of the ways that P/Invoke is fine-tuned for use with the Win32 APIs, although it may be used for any native DLL. If you are using P/Invoke with your own DLL and you want to disable CharSet's automatic mapping to ANSI or Unicode versions of function names, you can set the Boolean property ExactSpelling to true, like this:

```cpp
[DllImport ("mydll.dll", CharSet = CharSet::Ansi, ExactSpelling = true)]
```

Another thing you might be wondering about in Listing 12-6 is the use of IntPtr for the HWND parameter and the use of IntPtr::Zero as the parameter. IntPtr is a useful struct in interop programming since it can be used for a pointer type in native code, but it doesn't appear to be a pointer in managed code. It is CLS compliant, unlike native pointers, so is usable in other languages. The size of IntPtr is dependent on the pointer size for the platform, so it can represent a 32-bit pointer or a 64-bit pointer. It can be converted easily to a 32-bit or 64-bit integer or to an untyped pointer (void *). The IntPtr type may be used to hold values of native OS handles (such as an HWND) and pointers obtained from other P/Invoke calls.

If the function you want to import has a name conflict with one you're already using, you can use the EntryPoint property on DllImport to specify the desired native function, and then name the function something else that won't conflict, as in Listing 12-7.

Listing 12-7. *Using DllImport's EntryPoint Property*

```cpp
// pinvoke_rename_entry_point.cpp

#using "System.Windows.Forms.dll"

using namespace System;
using namespace System::Runtime::InteropServices;
using namespace System::Windows::Forms;

[DllImport("user32.dll", CharSet=CharSet::Auto, EntryPoint="MessageBox")]
int NativeMessageBox(IntPtr, String^ text, String^ caption,
   unsigned int type);

int main()
{
   NativeMessageBox(IntPtr::Zero, "Hello, World!", "Win32 Message Box", 0);
   MessageBox::Show("Hello, Universe!", "Managed Message Box");
}
```

In general, with P/Invoke, you should be sure that you know the calling convention of the target function. As long as you are calling Win32 functions, you don't need to worry about the calling convention used, because all Win32 functions use the __stdcall calling convention (WINAPI in the Windows headers evaluates to this), and that is the default for DllImport. However, if you are using your own native DLL compiled with Visual C++, for which the default calling convention is __cdecl, you may need to set the CallingConvention property on the DllImport attribute. For example, you need to set the CallingConvention to CallingConvention::Cdecl if you are calling any CRT function via P/Invoke. For example, the Bessel functions are not available in the .NET Framework API, so you could expose them from the CRT via the following declaration:

```cpp
[DllImport("msvcr80.dll", CallingConvention=CallingConvention.Cdecl)]
extern double _jn(int n, double x); // Bessel function of the first kind
```

This code would be useful in safe mode only, since in pure mode you can call CRT functions directly using the managed CRT.

The CallingConvention property can be used to call a method on a class that is exported from a DLL. Let's look at this possibility in Listings 12-8 and 12-9.

Listing 12-8. *Compiling a Native Class into a DLL*

```cpp
// nativeclasslib.cpp
// Compile with cl /LD nativeclasslib.cpp.

#include <stdio.h>
```

```cpp
class __declspec(dllexport) NativeClass
{
    private:
        int m_member;
    public:
        NativeClass() : m_member(1) { }

        int F( int i )
        {
            // __FUNCSIG__ is a compiler-defined macro evaluating
            // to the current function signature.
            printf("%s\n", __FUNCSIG__);
            return m_member + i;
        }

        static NativeClass* CreateObject()
        {
            printf("%s\n", __FUNCSIG__);
            return new NativeClass();
        }

        static void DeleteObject(NativeClass* p)
        {
            printf("%s\n", __FUNCSIG__);
            delete p;
        }
};

// If you do not want to use the obfuscated names, you can use these exports:

extern "C" __declspec(dllexport) NativeClass* CreateObject()
{
    return NativeClass::CreateObject();
}

extern "C" __declspec(dllexport) void DeleteObject(NativeClass* p)
{
    NativeClass::DeleteObject(p);
}

/* The mangled names were obtained by running the command.
    link /DUMP /EXPORTS nativeclasslib.dll
   which outputs:

    ordinal hint RVA       name
```

```
    1    0 00001000 ??0NativeClass@@QAE@XZ
    2    1 000010D0 ??4NativeClass@@QAEAAV0@ABV0@@Z
    3    2 00001050 ?CreateObject@NativeClass@@SAPAV1@XZ
    4    3 000010A0 ?DeleteObject@NativeClass@@SAXPAV1@@Z
    5    4 00001020 ?F@NativeClass@@QAEHH@Z
    6    5 000010F0 CreateObject
    7    6 00001100 DeleteObject
*/
```

Listing 12-9. *Using the CallingConvention Property*

```cpp
// pinvoke_thiscall.cpp
// Compile with cl /clr:safe pinvoke_thiscall.cpp.

using namespace System;
using namespace System::Text;
using namespace System::Runtime::InteropServices;

namespace NativeLib
{
    [ DllImport( "nativeclasslib.dll",
    EntryPoint="?F@NativeClass@@QAEHH@Z",
    CallingConvention=CallingConvention::ThisCall )]
    extern int F( IntPtr ths, int i );

    // static NativeClass* NativeClass::CreateObject();
    [DllImport( "nativeclasslib.dll", EntryPoint=
                "?CreateObject@NativeClass@@SAPAV1@XZ" )]
    extern IntPtr CreateObject();

    // static void NativeClass::DeleteClass( NativeClass* p )
    [ DllImport( "nativeclasslib.dll", EntryPoint=
                "?DeleteObject@NativeClass@@SAXPAV1@@Z" )]
    extern void DeleteObject( IntPtr p );
}


int main()
{
    IntPtr ptr = NativeLib::CreateObject();
    int result = NativeLib::F( ptr, 50 );
    Console::WriteLine( "Return value: {0} ", result );
    NativeLib::DeleteObject( ptr );
}
```

The output of Listing 12-9 is shown here:

```
class NativeClass *__cdecl NativeClass::CreateObject(void)
int __thiscall NativeClass::F(int)
Return value: 51
void __cdecl NativeClass::DeleteObject(class NativeClass *)
```

As you can see, in order to use P/Invoke with class functions, whether static or nonstatic, you need the obfuscated names, which we obtain by running dumpbin.exe or link.exe /DUMP /EXPORTS as explained in the code comments. The static functions do not require a special calling convention, since they use the __cdecl calling convention. The member function F required the __thiscall calling convention, because the implicit parameter for any member function is a pointer to the object.

The declaration of the P/Invoke function creates a managed name for the native function, as well as a small piece of code that in turn calls the native function. This piece of code is called a *managed entry point* to a native function, and it involves what is called a *context switch* between managed and native code. This is also called a *managed to native transition* or vice versa. Context switches add overhead to the function call. During a context switch, parameters are marshaled between native and managed types. The penalty is incurred again when the context switches back to managed code. You might say that execution is detained at the border for a time when crossing between managed and native code.

Data Marshaling

A lot of what is happening during the context switches is marshaling of parameters between native types and managed types. Marshaling for primitive types is straightforward and actually doesn't involve any work at runtime. Marshaling character, string, and structure types is not as straightforward. Table 12-2 shows the default mappings used. So, if the type used in the native function you're calling is as shown in one of the first two columns, the type in the P/Invoke signature should be one of the types in the last two columns.

Table 12-2. *Default Mappings Used When Marshaling Types Between Native and Managed Code*

Windows Type	Native Code	C++/CLI	CLR
HANDLE, DWORD_PTR	void *	void *	IntPtr, UIntPtr
BYTE	unsigned char	unsigned char	Byte
SHORT	short	short	Int16
WORD	unsigned short	unsigned short	UInt16
INT	int	int	Int32
UINT	unsigned int	unsigned int	UInt32
LONG	long	long	Int32
BOOL	long	bool	Boolean
DWORD	unsigned long	unsigned long	UInt32

Table 12-2. *Default Mappings Used When Marshaling Types Between Native and Managed Code (Continued)*

Windows Type	Native Code	C++/CLI	CLR
ULONG	unsigned long	unsigned long	UInt32
CHAR	char	char	Char
LPCSTR	char *	String ^ [in], StringBuilder ^ [in, out]	String ^ [in], StringBuilder ^ [in, out]
LPCSTR	const char *	String ^	String
LPWSTR	wchar_t *	String ^ [in], StringBuilder ^ [in, out]	String ^ [in], StringBuilder ^ [in, out]
LPCWSTR	const wchar_t *	String ^	String
FLOAT	float	float	Single
DOUBLE	double	double	Double

You can change the default marshaling by using the MarshalAs attribute. Marshaling for more complex types is not as simple. The Marshal class in the namespace System::Runtime::InteropServices provides many useful methods for interoperability. This book will cover only a few of the most useful. Future versions of Visual C++ may include a marshaling template library, which should make marshaling much more convenient. A full discussion would be outside the scope of this book.

If you instead use other interop methods described later, you can include the relevant header files that define all the types used in the parameter list, and not only avoid the trouble of re-creating them in managed code, but in many cases avoid the context switch to native code and vice versa. Still, if you do need to use P/Invoke, you should avail yourself of Internet resources for P/Invoke programming, such as www.pinvoke.net, which includes prepared code for many Win32 calls.

Interop with COM

COM interop can occur in two ways (three, if you count recompiling a COM object with the /clr option). You can access a COM object from managed code, or you can expose your managed object as a COM object.

Using a COM object from managed code involves creating a wrapper assembly that exposes the COM object via a set of managed wrapper classes and interfaces. The wrapper assembly can be created automatically from a type library or COM DLL or executable using tlbimp.exe. Using tlbimp.exe creates a set of wrapper classes with default marshaling of managed and native types. If you need more custom marshaling, you can also create these wrappers manually.

The wrapper assembly may be referenced with #using, and you can then call into the COM objects, assuming they are properly registered. If you use #import (the usual way to import COM types from a DLL or type library) with managed code, this will cause code to be generated that is not compilable with /clr:pure or /clr:safe.

COM interop is a CLR feature, not specifically a C++/CLI language feature, so it is not described here in depth. There are excellent books available on COM interop, such as *COM and .NET Interoperability* by Andrew Troelsen (Apress, 2002) and *.NET and COM: The Complete Interoperability Guide* by Adam Nathan (Sams, 2002).

Using Native Libraries Without P/Invoke

Native libraries may be used in C++/CLI code without using P/Invoke. As native object files, they can be linked in. If source is available, you can recompile the source as managed code, often without changing it. If you only have a binary and a header file, you can include the header and link with the native object file, static library, or import library for a DLL. The Visual Studio 2005 linker can also handle linking native and managed files into a single assembly.

You won't be able to use these techniques in safe mode; in safe mode, P/Invoke is the only way to go. You can use native libraries in pure mode and mixed mode.

The C Runtime (CRT) Library and the Standard C++ Library are available as pure MSIL. The DLL names are a bit different: msvcm80.dll as opposed to msvcr80.dll. The m indicates managed code. If you compile code that uses the CRT with either the /clr option or the /clr:pure option, you'll get the appropriate pure MSIL CRT linked in instead of the native CRT. When using interop, you should know and care about whether you are calling into a native function or calling into native code that was recompiled to MSIL (such as a function in the pure mode CRT) because it is a lot faster to avoid a context switch from managed code (MSIL) to native code whenever possible. In general, from managed code, it is faster to call other managed code, and from native code, it is faster to call other native code. Did I mention how slow the context switch is? Because of the slowness of the context switch, it's usually better to recompile your native code as managed code if you want to use it frequently from managed code, as we do by providing the managed CRT.

Consider some simple code that uses the Win32 API, as in Listing 12-10.

Listing 12-10. *Using the Win32 API*

```
// message_box.cpp

#include <windows.h>

int main()
{
    MessageBox( 0, "Hello, World!", "Win32 Message Box", 0);
}
```

The MessageBox function code lives in user32.dll and is an exported function there. To produce a native executable, we would to link to the import library user32.lib.

```
cl message_box.cpp user32.lib
```

However, we could also do the following:

```
cl /clr message_box.cpp user32.lib
cl /clr:pure message_box.cpp user32.lib
```

The only change is to compile with the /clr or /clr:pure option enabled. That is a big difference, because it means that the object file contains managed code, not native code. The linker is able to link the managed code with a native import library without any problem. What this means to you is that you can call a function in a native DLL from managed code simply by including the header file and invoking the function as usual. This works just as well in both mixed and pure modes. In the Visual Studio IDE, you would have to make a few changes in the project properties to recompile your code that uses Win32 with the CLR option. You already know (because we discussed it in Chapter 3) about the Common Language Runtime property. What might not be obvious is that to refer to a library like user32.lib you might need to change the Linker property for Additional Dependencies. If you created a CLR project, it is set to $(NOINHERIT). You'll have to remove that to enable CLR projects to link with Win32 DLLs.

The drawback to this method is context switching from native to managed code and vice versa. Although it may be easy to invoke the MessageBox method from managed code, a context switch takes place at each transition point—and that is every time a native function is called from managed code. As long as you can live with this performance penalty, this interop method is useful. It's also the recommended method when you don't have access to the source code for your native functions. If you do have source to your native DLL, recompiling it as managed code might be better and might help avoid expensive context switches between managed and native code.

Incidentally, if you try /clr:safe, good luck wading through the thousands of lines of compiler errors as the C++/CLI compiler tries to interpret the Windows headers in safe mode. Here's a small excerpt of the output:

```
C:\Program Files\Microsoft Visual Studio 8\VC\PlatformSDK\include\imm.h(151) : e
rror C4959: cannot define unmanaged struct 'tagIMECHARPOSITION' in /clr:safe bec
ause accessing its members yields unverifiable code
C:\Program Files\Microsoft Visual Studio 8\VC\PlatformSDK\include\imm.h(157) : e
rror C4956: 'tagIMECHARPOSITION *' : this type is not verifiable
C:\Program Files\Microsoft Visual Studio 8\VC\PlatformSDK\include\imm.h(157) : e
rror C4956: 'tagIMECHARPOSITION *' : this type is not verifiable
C:\Program Files\Microsoft Visual Studio 8\VC\PlatformSDK\include\imm.h(157) : e
rror C4956: 'tagIMECHARPOSITION *' : this type is not verifiable
C:\Program Files\Microsoft Visual Studio 8\VC\PlatformSDK\include\imm.h(159) : e
rror C4956: 'BOOL (__stdcall *)(HIMC,LPARAM)' : this type is not verifiable
C:\Program Files\Microsoft Visual Studio 8\VC\PlatformSDK\include\imm.h(315) : e
rror C4956: 'int (__stdcall *)(LPCSTR,DWORD,LPCSTR,LPVOID)' : this type is not v
erifiable
C:\Program Files\Microsoft Visual Studio 8\VC\PlatformSDK\include\imm.h(316) : e
rror C4956: 'int (__stdcall *)(LPCWSTR,DWORD,LPCWSTR,LPVOID)' : this type is not
 verifiable
```

Because pointers and unmanaged structs are not allowed in safe mode, you can't use the Windows headers.

But we haven't done any real interop yet, we've just done the first step. In any interop scenario, you're going to have managed types in the picture, so let's expand the simple call to MessageBox with some managed code. Listing 12-11 shows a case where you are writing a managed class that calls some Win32 functions in its implementation.

Listing 12-11. *Using Win32 Functions in a Managed Class*

```cpp
// interop_messagebox.cpp

#include <windows.h>
#include <vcclr.h> // for PtrToStringChars

using namespace System;

public ref class MessageBoxClass
{
    public:

    property String^ Message;
    property String^ Caption;

    int DisplayBox()
    {
        // Use pinning pointers to lock down the data while it's being
        // used in native code.
        pin_ptr<const wchar_t> message = PtrToStringChars(Message);
        pin_ptr<const wchar_t> caption = PtrToStringChars(Caption);
        return MessageBoxW( 0, message,  caption, MB_OK);
    }
};

int main()
{
    MessageBoxClass m;
    m.Message = "Managed string used in native function";
    m.Caption = "Managed Code using Win32 Message Box";
    m.DisplayBox();
}
```

In Listing 12-11, we use the Unicode form of the MessageBox function, MessageBoxW, since we're starting with a Unicode string. We start to see some more complex operations as we marshal the managed String type to a native LPCWSTR parameter. LPCWSTR is a typedef for const wchar_t*. The PtrToStringChars function is a convenience provided in vcclr.h that gives you a pointer to the underlying character array. The data is of type Char, which is the same as wchar_t. Because the array is in an object on the managed heap, you need to use pinning pointers (pin_ptr) to make sure that the data isn't moved by the garbage collector during these operations. We'll discuss pinning pointers in more detail later in this chapter, but for now, suffice it to say that the way pinning pointers work is that whatever they point to is marked as fixed in memory as long as the pinning pointer exists. If the pinning pointer points to the internals of an object, the containing object is pinned. Once the pinning pointer goes out of scope, the object is free to move again. The pinning pointer has a defined conversion to its underlying pointer type, so it doesn't require a cast when passed to MessageBoxW. You must be careful to use pinning pointers for any pointers you pass to native code. You can also use pinning pointers when you need to use pointer arithmetic on data that's on the managed heap, as you saw in Chapter 5 when you looked at how to iterate over the elements of a managed array using pointer arithmetic.

The call to MessageBoxW is a transition to native code, just as in the case where P/Invoke was used to call MessageBox. As long as the native functions are called infrequently and the main action is in the managed code, this form of interop makes sense. If all you have is a binary, you don't have any other options available to you. In the next section, you'll see how if you have access to the source for the native library and can recompile it, you can avoid the context switch between native and managed code.

Recompiling a Native Library As Managed Code

At this point, you've seen how to call native functions in two ways from managed code—using P/Invoke and by linking with the appropriate binary and including the appropriate header. You've gotten a taste of the conversions that are used and some of the concerns when calling native code, such as pinning movable data.

Now let's look at another alternative, and that is recompiling native code as managed code. This could be an attractive option if you own the source code for the native library and plan to extensively call your native code from managed code. This is the option of choice for a frequently used library that is to be used primarily from managed code, maybe even from another language, such as C# or VB. It's an attractive option because you can avoid the context switches between managed and native code. Compiling your native code as managed code doesn't mean it will run slower. Remember that all managed code is compiled on demand at runtime to native code before it gets executed by the CLR. That's what the JIT (Just In Time) compiler does, and is a reason that managed code and native code can have comparable execution performance. Of course, there is always the overhead of the JIT compilation itself and runtime services such as garbage collection.

Consider a native class library, as in Listing 12-12. It uses the Windows headers and the CRT.

Listing 12-12. *Creating a Native Message Box Class*

```
// native_message_box_class.h

#include <wchar.h>
#include <windows.h>

enum MessageBoxType
{
    OK, OKCANCEL, ABORTRETRYIGNORE,
    YESNOCANCEL, YESNO,
    RETRYCANCEL, CANCELTRYCONTINUE,
    ICONHAND = 0x10,
    ICONQUESTION = 0x20,
    ICONEXCLAMATION = 0x30,
    ICONASTERISK = 0x40,
    TYPEMASK = 0xF,
    ICONMASK = 0xF0
};
```

```cpp
class MessageBoxClass
{

    wchar_t* m_message;
    wchar_t* m_caption;
    MessageBoxType m_type;
    static const size_t sz = 1024;

    public:

    MessageBoxClass(const wchar_t* message, const wchar_t* caption,
                    MessageBoxType type)
        : m_type(type)
    {
        m_message = new wchar_t[sz];
        m_caption = new wchar_t[sz];
        wcscpy_s(m_message, sz, message); // using the "safe" CRT
        wcscpy_s(m_caption, sz, caption);
    }

    void SetMessage(const wchar_t* message)
    {
        if (message != NULL)
        {
            wcscpy_s(m_message, sz, message);
        }
    }
    const wchar_t* GetMessage() const { return m_message; }

    void SetCaption(const wchar_t* caption)
    {
        if (caption != NULL)
        {
            wcscpy_s(m_caption, sz, caption);
        }
    }
    const wchar_t* GetCaption() const { return m_caption; }

    MessageBoxType GetType() const { return m_type; }
    void SetType(MessageBoxType type){ m_type = type; }



    int Display()
    {
        return MessageBoxW(0, m_message, m_caption, m_type);
    }
}
```

```
~MessageBoxClass()
{
    delete m_message;
    delete m_caption;
}

};
```

Listing 12-13 shows the corresponding source file containing the main method.

Listing 12-13. *Using Your Message Box Class*

```
// native_message_box.cpp
#include "native_message_box_class.h"

int main()
{
    MessageBoxClass* messageBox = new MessageBoxClass(
        L"Do you like this example?", L"Native message box",
        static_cast<MessageBoxType>(YESNOCANCEL | ICONASTERISK));

    int result = messageBox->Display();

    wchar_t wstr[1024];
    swprintf_s( wstr, L"The dialog result was %d", result);
    messageBox->SetMessage(wstr);
    messageBox->SetType(OK);
    messageBox->Display();

}
```

Try recompiling the code in Listing 12-13 with the /clr option. It works fine. You can also use the /clr:pure option in this case. As you've seen before, the Windows headers and the CRT are both supported in pure mode. Whether you compile with /clr or not, the link command line is the same, and the executable looks similar, but they are in fact very different.

Once you've recompiled, if you want to expose the native libraries to other managed assemblies, you need to write a wrapper layer. The wrapper layer is compiled into the same assembly as the recompiled native code. Listing 12-14 shows a wrapper layer for the message box example. Here, we use several techniques to optimize performance. We use PtrToStringChars to get a direct pointer to the character data in the String class. This is a pinned pointer, of course, since it is to be passed to native code. Alternative methods, such as using ToCharArray and then working with the array to get something suitable to pass as a const wchar_t *, would involve copying the string characters.

Listing 12-14. *Wrapping Your Message Box Class*

```cpp
// message_box_wrapper.cpp

#include "native_message_box_class.h"
#include <vcclr.h>

using namespace System;

enum class MessageBoxTypeEnum
{
  OK, OKCANCEL, ABORTRETRYIGNORE,
  YESNOCANCEL, YESNO,
  RETRYCANCEL, CANCELTRYCONTINUE,
  ICONHAND = 0x10,
  ICONQUESTION = 0x20,
  ICONEXCLAMATION = 0x30,
  ICONASTERISK = 0x40,
  TYPEMASK = 0xF,
  ICONMASK = 0xF0
};

wchar_t* MarshalString(String^ s, size_t sizeInCharacters)
{
  pin_ptr<const wchar_t> pinnedChars = PtrToStringChars(s);
  wchar_t* wcs = new wchar_t[sizeInCharacters];
  wcscpy_s(wcs, sizeInCharacters, pinnedChars);
  return wcs;
}

public ref class MessageBoxWrapper
{

  MessageBoxClass* nativeMessageBox;
  literal unsigned int maxSize = 1024;

  public:

  MessageBoxWrapper(String^ message, String^ caption, MessageBoxTypeEnum type)
  {
    pin_ptr<const wchar_t> pinnedMessage = PtrToStringChars(message);
    pin_ptr<const wchar_t> pinnedCaption = PtrToStringChars(caption);

    nativeMessageBox = new MessageBoxClass(
      pinnedMessage, pinnedCaption,
      static_cast<MessageBoxType>(type));
  }
```

```cpp
property String^ Caption
{
    String^ get()
    {
        return gcnew String(nativeMessageBox->GetCaption());
    }
    void set(String^ s)
    {
        nativeMessageBox->SetCaption( MarshalString(s, maxSize) );
    }
}
property String^ Message
{
    String^ get()
    {
        return gcnew String(nativeMessageBox->GetCaption());
    }
    void set(String^ s)
    {
        nativeMessageBox->SetMessage( MarshalString(s, maxSize) );
    }
}
property MessageBoxTypeEnum Type
{
    MessageBoxTypeEnum get()
    {
        return static_cast<MessageBoxTypeEnum>(nativeMessageBox->GetType());
    }
    void set(MessageBoxTypeEnum t)
    {
        nativeMessageBox->SetType( static_cast<MessageBoxType>( t ));
    }
}
int Display()
{
    if (nativeMessageBox != NULL)
      return nativeMessageBox->Display();
    else return -1;
}

~MessageBoxWrapper()
{
    this->!MessageBoxWrapper();
}
```

```
    !MessageBoxWrapper()
    {
        delete nativeMessageBox;
    }

};

int main()
{
    MessageBoxWrapper^ wrapper = gcnew MessageBoxWrapper(
        "Do you like this message box?",
        "Managed wrapper message box.",
        MessageBoxTypeEnum::YESNO);
    Console::WriteLine("Message is: {0}", wrapper->Message);
    int result = wrapper->Display();
    Console::WriteLine("Result was {0}", result);
}
```

The next step (see Listing 12-15) is to use the wrapper from another assembly, or even from another .NET language such as C#, effectively exposing a native class library to C#. Cross-language work is best done in the IDE, since the development environment does a lot of complicated things for you, such as embedding the native manifests in your C++ code with mt.exe, which is a required step in Visual C++ 2005. (For information on Visual C++ native manifests, see the product documentation.) Be sure to compile the C++/CLI code to a DLL rather than an executable, then add a project reference from the C# project to the C++/CLI code.

Listing 12-15. *Using a Wrapper from a C# Assembly*

```
// Program.cs
using System;
using System.Collections.Generic;
using System.Text;

class Program
{
    static void Main(string[] args)
    {
        MessageBoxWrapper wrapper =
            new MessageBoxWrapper("I hope you love this message box!",
                "C# using Native Message Box", MessageBoxTypeEnum.OKCANCEL);
        wrapper.Display();
    }
}
```

A successful wrapper layer will likely involve a lot of conversions between native and managed types. How you handle these conversions can involve a surprising amount of code and have a big impact on the performance of the wrapper class system. When writing managed code that calls into native code frequently in a tight loop, you need to be particularly careful to minimize transitions. Consider the code in Listing 12-16, which demonstrates the performance effect of native to managed transitions. It also demonstrates the use of #pragma to include both native and managed code in the same file. In this case, everything after #pragma unmanaged and before #pragma managed is interpreted as native code. No managed constructs are allowed there. By moving these pragmas around in code, you can see what the effects are of having various portions of the code native or managed.

Listing 12-16. *Using #pragma managed and #pragma unmanaged*

```
// context_switch.cpp
#include <stdio.h>
#include <time.h>
#include <stdlib.h>
#include <math.h>
#include <string.h>

#pragma unmanaged
int native_function(wchar_t* str1, wchar_t* str2 )
{
    int i = 0;
    while (*str1++ = *str2++) i++;
    return i;
}

#pragma managed

wchar_t* random_string(wchar_t* wcs, int n)
{
    for (int i = 0; i < n - 1; i++)
    {
        wcs[i] = (wchar_t) floor(((double) rand() / (double) RAND_MAX * 26)) + L'A';
    }
    return wcs;
}
// Try commenting out the pragma above random_string and uncomment this:
// #pragma managed.

int main()
{
    wchar_t wcs1[100];
    wchar_t* wcs2 = new wchar_t[100];
    memset(wcs1, 0, 100 * sizeof(wchar_t));
    clock_t t = clock();
    const int num_iter = 100000;
```

```
    for (int i = 0; i < num_iter; i++)
    {
      random_string(wcs1, 100);
      native_function(wcs2, wcs1);
    }
    double time_elapsed = (clock()-t)/(double)CLOCKS_PER_SEC;
    printf("total time elapsed: %2.2f seconds\n", time_elapsed);
}
```

On my system, when I execute the code in Listing 12-16 with native_function as native code and random_string as managed code, the execution time is 1.3 seconds. On the other hand, if both native_code and random_string are made native by moving the comment as suggested, we can avoid the transition on each loop and the execution time gets down to .73 seconds, which is just as fast (at least to two decimal places) as fully native code compiled with /O2, also .73 seconds.

Next, we turn to a discussion of the interior pointer and pinning pointer types, which we've used here and there throughout the text. These constructs are particularly useful when dealing with mixing native and managed types.

Interior Pointers

Sometimes a real pointer is needed to do some fast pointer arithmetic on a collection type in a performance-critical algorithm. It would have to be a pointer into a managed type that is itself on the managed heap. The *interior pointer*, interior_ptr<*type*>, provides this functionality. It is called an interior pointer because it points to an address *inside* a managed object. An interior pointer supports pointer arithmetic just like an ordinary pointer, but it is updated by the garbage collector if the object is moved in memory, just like the underlying address in a handle. Interior pointers may not be used to point to anything that isn't part of a managed object.

To assign a value to an interior pointer, use the address-of operator (&) on a managed object (see Listing 12-17).

Listing 12-17. *Using an Interior Pointer*

```
// interior_ptr.cpp
using namespace System;

ref struct S
{
  array<int>^ array1;

  S()
  {
    array1 = gcnew array<int>(10)
       { 0, 10, 20, 30, 40, 50, 60, 70, 80, 90 };
  }
```

```
void f()
{
    interior_ptr<int> p = &array1[0];
    for (int i = 0; i < 10; i++)
    {
        Console::WriteLine(*p++);
    }
}
};
```

Note that when you dereference an interior pointer, you get the object, just like a regular pointer. If you take the address of an interior pointer, you get a native pointer that is the address that the interior pointer designates. However, it's not a good idea to do that since the native pointer won't necessarily continue to point to the object. Once the garbage collector moves that object around in memory, the address of the object will no longer match the native pointer.

Pinning Pointers

As you have already seen, it is possible to prevent the garbage collector from moving an object around in memory by creating what is called a *pinning pointer* and setting it to point to a member of the object. Any object that has an element pointed to by a pinning pointer will not be moved by the garbage collector as long as that pinning pointer is in scope and is tied to the object. The object is said to be *pinned*. The syntax pin_ptr<*type*> is used.

Pinning pointers cannot be used as return values, parameters, or members of a type. You also cannot cast to a pinning pointer. They can only be used as automatic variables on the stack. This is because pinning pointers make use of a runtime feature that is only available on automatic stack-based variables, due to the nature of the pinning mechanism.

Pinning pointers are necessary when you need to use a native API call that takes a native pointer as a parameter. You'll need to create a pinning pointer to mark that object as fixed in memory for the duration of the native function call. You've seen this use of pinning pointers elsewhere in this chapter. Interior pointers won't work for this purpose because they (like handles) are subject to being updated when the containing object is moved.

Because a pinning pointer pins an entire managed object when it is pointed at one part of the object, you can take advantage of this in order to write some efficient algorithms. For example, you can pin a managed array by pinning one of its elements. Then you can use native pointers to work on the array without concern that the managed array might be moved in memory. You should not overuse pinning pointers because pinning objects on the managed heap reduces the efficiency of the garbage collector. For this reason, be careful of the scope of a pinning pointer. You want to make sure it either goes out of scope as soon as possible after it is no longer needed, or it is assigned to nullptr, which has the same effect.

You must take particular care when assigning values to pinning pointers to ensure that the resulting pointers are not allowed to persist beyond the limited scope in which the pinning pointer is declared. Therefore, do not return a pinning pointer as a return value, and do not return a pointer that has been assigned to a pinned pointer as a return value. If you do, then you will have a pointer that points to somewhere in the managed heap, not necessarily to an object at all (once the garbage collector moves the original pinned object). This type of programming error is known as a *GC hole*. Listing 12-18 shows an example of a GC hole.

Listing 12-18. *Demonstrating a GC Hole*

```cpp
// gc_hole.cpp
using namespace System;

ref struct R
{
    array<int>^ a;

    R()
    {
        a = gcnew array<int> { 1, 2, 3, 4, 5 };
    }
};

void F(int* ptr)
{
    if (ptr)
        Console::WriteLine(*ptr);   // possible crash
}

int* GcHole(R^ r)  // gc hole
{
    pin_ptr<int> pinp = &r->a[0];
    int *ptr;
    ptr = pinp;  // pointer assigned to pinning pointer
    // ...
    return ptr;  // pointer into gc heap returned (!)
}

int main() {
    R^ r = gcnew R;
    F(GcHole(r));
}
```

Native Objects and Managed Objects

You may sometimes need to mix objects of managed and native types. You'll next learn what you need to do if you need to have a managed object encapsulated in a native type, as well as how to include native objects in managed types.

But first, a little background and context. When would you need to write code like this? If you are extending a native application with managed types, you'll probably need to use the native types in your managed types. If in addition the native types need to refer to managed types, then you need to use the gcroot template to refer to them, as you will see in the next section.

Using a Managed Object in a Native Class

In a native class, you cannot simply declare a handle. Native types do not know what a handle is and what to do with one as a member. The code in Listing 12-19 is illegal.

Listing 12-19. *Misusing a Handle*

```
// native_in_managed_bad.cpp

using namespace System;

ref class R {};

class N
{
   R^ r;  // illegal

   public:
      N()
      {
         r = gcnew R();
      }

};
```

There is a way to properly contain a handle in a native type, and that is to use the gcroot template, with the handle to the reference type as an argument. In Chapter 6, you saw how this was done with the gcroot and the auto_gcroot templates. Listing 12-20 illustrates the difference between the gcroot template and the auto_gcroot template.

Listing 12-20. *gcroot vs. auto_gcroot*

```
// auto_gcroot.cpp

#include <msclr/gcroot.h>
#include <msclr/auto_gcroot.h>
using namespace System;
using namespace msclr;

ref class R
{
   public:
     void f()
     {
        Console::WriteLine("managed member function");
     }
```

```
    ~R()
    {
        Console::WriteLine("destructor");
    }

};

class N
{
    gcroot<R^> r_gcroot;
    auto_gcroot<R^> r_auto_gcroot;

    public:
        N()
        {
            r_gcroot = gcnew R();
            r_gcroot->f();
            r_auto_gcroot = gcnew R();
            r_auto_gcroot->f();
        }

};

int main()
{
    N n;
    // When n gets destroyed, the destructor for the auto_gcroot object
    // will be executed, but not the gcroot object.
}
```

The output of Listing 12-20 is as follows:

```
managed member function
managed member function
destructor
```

As you can see, the destructor was called only once, for the auto_gcroot object. Now, if we have a function that takes a handle to a managed object, we can pass in the gcroot or auto_gcroot handle instead. Both gcroot and auto_gcroot have implicit conversions to the underlying handles. They also both work with boxed value types.

Using a Native Object in a Managed Type

Also in Chapter 6, you saw one way to include a native object in a managed type. A somewhat cleaner way to include this is to use a template class that takes care of making sure that the native class gets cleaned up properly automatically when the enclosing class exits. Listing 12-21 defines a template reference type native_root that encapsulates the native pointer and can be used somewhat like auto_gcroot. We use the native class to open a file, and we see that it is closed when delete is called on the enclosing reference type or the enclosing object goes out of scope.

Listing 12-21. *Encapsulating a Native Pointer*

```cpp
// native_in_managed.cpp

#include <stdlib.h>
#include <stdio.h>
#include <time.h>

using namespace System;
using namespace System::Runtime::InteropServices;

// template for embedding a native class
// in a reference type
template<typename T>
ref class native_root
{
  T* t;

  !native_root()
  {
    if (t)
    {
      delete t;
      t = NULL;
    }
  }

  ~native_root()
  {
    this->!native_root();
  }

public:

  native_root() : t(new T) {}

  // These must be static to prevent them from being used
  // within the class (e.g. when we use this-> in ~native_root).
```

```
      // allows access to the underlying pointer
      static T* operator&(native_root% n) { return n.t; }
      // allows -> to be used to access members
      static T* operator->(native_root% n) { return n.t; }
};

class native_exception {};

// typical native class
class NativeClass
{
   FILE* fp;
   static const int TIME_BUFFER_SIZE = 32;

   public:
     NativeClass()
     {
        printf("Opening the file.\n");
        // Open a file for Unicode writing.
        int errcode = fopen_s(&fp, "myfile.txt", "a+, ccs=UNICODE");
        if (errcode != 0)
        {
           throw new native_exception;
        }
     }

     void OutputText(const wchar_t* text)
     {
        if (fp)
        {
           wprintf(text);
           fwprintf(fp, text);
        }
        else
        {
           throw new native_exception;
        }
     }

     void TimeStamp()
     {
        tm newtime;
        __time32_t time;
        wchar_t time_text[TIME_BUFFER_SIZE];
        _time32( &time );
        _localtime32_s( &newtime, &time );
        _wasctime_s(time_text, TIME_BUFFER_SIZE, &newtime);
```

```
            if (fp)
            {
                wprintf(time_text);
                fwprintf(fp, time_text);
            }
            else
            {
                throw new native_exception;
            }
        }

        ~NativeClass()
        {
            printf("Closing the file.\n");
            if (fp)
            {
                fclose(fp);
            }
        }
};

// A reference type enclosing a Native Class
ref class R
{
    native_root<NativeClass> n;

    public:

        R() { }

        // Marshal the String to a Unicode string
        // and pass the pointer to the native class method
        void OutputToFile(String^ s)
        {
            IntPtr ptr = Marshal::StringToHGlobalUni(s);
            n->OutputText(static_cast<wchar_t*>( ptr.ToPointer()));
            n->TimeStamp();
            Marshal::FreeHGlobal(ptr);
        }
};

int main()
{
    R^ r1 = gcnew R();
    r1->OutputToFile("Output through native class!\n");
    delete r1; // the file is closed
```

```
R r2;
r2.OutputToFile("More output\n");
// File is closed again when r2 is cleaned up.
}
```

The output of Listing 12-21 is something like the following:

```
Opening the file.
Output through native class!
Tue Sep 05 23:39:57 2006
Closing the file.
Opening the file.
More output
Tue Sep 05 23:39:57 2006
Closing the file.
```

Notice that a static member, StringToHGlobalUni of the Marshal class, is used to convert from String to wchar_t*. This creates a new wide character array and returns a pointer to it in the form of an IntPtr, which must be freed. We can free the memory with Marshal::FreeHGlobal to say in managed code rather than calling the native API GlobalFree to free the memory. IntPtr has the ToPointer method, which returns a void pointer that we then cast to the desired type for the managed function call.

Native and Managed Entry Points

A native function is said to have a *native entry point*, which is its address. Similarly, a managed function has a *managed entry point*. A function that may be called by both native and managed code has two separate entry points, one that is the actual function, and another that is a small compiler-generated function known as a *thunk*, which handles the context switch between native and managed code, and then calls the real function.

You know that functions in Visual C++ have calling conventions specifying how parameters are handled by a function—you looked at some earlier. The native calling conventions, such as __cdecl, __stdcall, and __thiscall, specify certain ways of passing parameters. Managed functions similarly have a calling convention, __clrcall, that characterizes the particulars about how managed functions are called. A function with the __clrcall calling convention only has a managed entry point. There is no native entry point generated for it.

The calling convention for managed functions, and hence the set of entry points that get generated for a function, depends on the compilation mode. In pure mode and safe mode, __clrcall is the default for all managed functions. If you compile in safe mode or pure mode, a managed function will be generated with a managed entry point only, because in those modes, there is no native code that would require a native entry point. However, when you compile in mixed mode (/clr), as is likely in an interop scenario, both native and managed entry points are generated. This is because the calling convention is a native calling convention (__thiscall for methods and likely __cdecl for global functions, but this may be changed by a compiler option).

If you use __declspec(dllexport) on a managed function, which causes it to be made available to callers outside the DLL, you create a native entry point that can be used by native callers that can then use __declspec(dllimport) to reference the function.

How to Avoid Double Thunking

You should be cognizant of the subtleties involved in native and managed entry points, because of the concern that you could make unnecessary context switches between native and managed code, if you aren't careful to avoid it. The scenario of concern is calling a managed function via a native entry point from managed code, rather than the far more efficient route of calling the managed entry point directly. The existence of the native entry point makes it a possible route that your managed code can use to access the function. If you call a function in this way, you have to first switch to native code to access the native entry point, which is a small piece of code called a thunk, and then you have to switch to managed code to call the managed function, another thunk. All this unnecessary switching between contexts is known as *double thunking* and can really slow down an application.

The compiler will try to get the right entry point; however, it sometimes needs some help. Using the __clrcall calling convention is one way to avoid the problem. You can use the __clrcall calling convention on a managed function as long as you don't need to call your function from native code. If there's no native entry point, then there's no way it can be used improperly. The __clrcall calling convention is only needed when compiling in mixed mode (with /clr), because in pure mode and safe mode, the default is __clrcall and no native entry point is generated anyway.

In the other situation where double thunking can occur (exporting a managed function from a DLL), you should avoid using __declspec(dllexport) and __declspec(dllimport) to invoke managed functions from managed code. Instead, you should use #using to reference the managed assembly.

Managed and Native Exceptions

You might be wondering, if you have managed code calling into native code, how do errors and exceptions get propagated from native code to managed code? In this section you explore this.

Interop with Structured Exceptions (__try/__except)

Structured Exception Handling (SEH) is used on the Windows platform in C and C++ for many hardware and software error conditions. Possible error codes are listed in the Windows headers. If an SEH exception is allowed to propagate into managed code, it is wrapped as a .NET exception of some type. Many structured exceptions are mapped to specific .NET exception types. For example, EXCEPTION_INT_DIVIDE_BY_ZERO is mapped to DivideByZeroException. If there is no specific mapping, a System::Runtime::InteropServices::SEHException is generated.

In Listing 12-22, two ways of handling structured exceptions are demonstrated. The exception in native code is an integer division by zero. In the first branch, the exception is allowed to propagate to managed code and is caught as an SEHException. In the second branch, it is caught as a native SEH exception in a __try/__catch statement.

Listing 12-22. *Handling Structured Exceptions*

```cpp
// try_except.cpp
#include <stdio.h>
#include <windows.h> // for EXCEPTION_INT_DIVIDE_BY_ZERO
#include <excpt.h>

using namespace System;
using namespace System::Runtime::InteropServices;

#pragma unmanaged
void generate_SEH_exception()
{
   int i = 0;
   // Divide by zero generates an SEH exception.
   int x = 2 / i;
}

void generate_AV()
{
   int *pn = 0;
   int n = *pn; // generates an access violation
}

int filter_div0(unsigned int code, struct _EXCEPTION_POINTERS *ep)
{

   if (code == EXCEPTION_INT_DIVIDE_BY_ZERO)
   {
      return EXCEPTION_EXECUTE_HANDLER;
   }
   else
   {
      return EXCEPTION_CONTINUE_SEARCH;
   };
}

// This must be a native function because __try/__except is not
// allowed in the same function as code that uses try/catch.
void try_except(bool bThrowUnhandledAV)
{
   __try
   {
      if (bThrowUnhandledAV)
         generate_AV();
      else
         generate_SEH_exception();
   }
```

```cpp
    __except( filter_div0(GetExceptionCode(), GetExceptionInformation()))
    {
        printf_s("Divide by zero exception caught via SEH __except block.");
    }
}

#pragma managed

int main(array<String^>^ args)
{
    if (args->Length < 1)
    {
        Console::WriteLine("Usage: try_except [NET|SEH|AV]");
        return -1;
    }
    if (args[0] == "NET") // Demonstrate catching SEH as a .NET Exception
    {
        try
        {
            generate_SEH_exception();
        }
        catch(DivideByZeroException^ e)
        {
            Console::WriteLine(e->ToString());
        }
    }
    else if (args[0] == "SEH")  // Demonstrate handling SEH exception natively.
    {
        // Call native function with try/except block
        // and filter out division by zero exceptions.
        try_except(false);
    }
    else if (args[0] == "AV")  // Demonstrate filtering of what exceptions to handle
                               // natively and what to allow through.
    {
        try
        {
            // AVs, however, are not filtered and are allowed
            // to propagate to managed code.
            try_except(true);
        }
        catch(AccessViolationException^ e)
        {
            Console::WriteLine(e->ToString());
        }
    }
}
```

The output of Listing 12-22 with the command line try_except NET is

```
System.DivideByZeroException: Attempted to divide by zero.
   at generate_SEH_exception()
   at main(String[] args
```

the output with the command line try_except SEH is

```
Divide by zero exception caught via SEH __except block.
```

and the output with the command line try_except AV is

```
System.AccessViolationException: Attempted to read or write protected memory.
This is often an indication that other memory is corrupt.
   at try_except(Boolean )
   at main(String[] args)
```

Note that you cannot include CLR exception handling in the same function as structured exception handling, since the two mechanisms are not compatible and, if used together, would corrupt the stack. However, as the version with the access violation demonstrates, you can filter on what exceptions you want SEH to handle and handle others in managed code.

Interop with Win32 Error Codes

You cannot simply call GetLastError via P/Invoke after a Windows API call and expect to get the error code corresponding to the Win32 function invoked on the last P/Invoke call, because there is no guarantee that between the function call of interest and the call to GetLastError any error value is preserved. The proper way to get at the error code is to call Marshal::GetLastWin32Error, as shown in Listing 12-23.

Listing 12-23. *Handling Win32 Error Codes*

```cpp
// getlasterror.cpp

#using "System.dll"

using namespace System;
using namespace System::ComponentModel; // for Win32Exception
using namespace System::Runtime::InteropServices;

[DllImport("kernel32.dll", SetLastError=true)]
extern bool SetVolumeLabel(String^ lpRootPathName, String^ lpVolumeName);
```

```
bool TestGetLastWin32Error()
{
    if (SetVolumeLabel("BAD:\\", "VolumeName"))
    {
        System::Console::WriteLine("Success!");
        return true;
    }
    else
    {
        throw gcnew Win32Exception(Marshal::GetLastWin32Error());
    }
    return false;
}

int main()
{
    try
    {
        TestGetLastWin32Error();
    }
    catch(Win32Exception^ e)
    {
        Console::WriteLine(e->ToString());
    }
}
```

The output of Listing 12-23 is as follows:

```
System.ComponentModel.Win32Exception: The filename, directory name, or volume
label syntax is incorrect
    at TestGetLastWin32Error()
    at main()
```

Interop with C++ Exceptions

C++ exception handling can exist alongside CLR exception handling. You can use subsequent catch blocks, with C++ exceptions in some catch filters and CLR exceptions in other catch filters. Remember that in Chapter 10 you saw what happens when throwing a type that does not derive from System::Exception to code in another .NET language. In that case, the nonexception type was wrapped as a RuntimeWrappedException. Wrapping also occurs when a native type is thrown from native code—it is wrapped as SEHException in C++/CLI managed code and, if not caught by a matching catch block, will be caught by catch filters that match SEHException, ExternalException (the base class of SEHException), or Exception. Listing 12-24 shows the behavior with both a throw by value and via a native pointer.

Listing 12-24. *Coexistent C++ and CLR Exception Handling*

```cpp
// native_exception.cpp
#include <wchar.h>

using namespace System;
using namespace System::Runtime::InteropServices;

#pragma unmanaged

class NativeException
{
    wchar_t m_str[1024];

    public:

        NativeException(wchar_t* s)
        {
            wcscpy_s(m_str, s);
        }

        const wchar_t* GetMessage() { return m_str; }
};

void throw_native_exception(bool byval)
{
    if (byval)
        throw NativeException(L"Native Exception By Value");
    else
        throw new NativeException(L"Native Exception on Native Heap");
}

#pragma managed

int main()
{
    bool byval = true;

    try
    {
        throw_native_exception(byval);
    }
    catch(NativeException& native_exception)
    {
        wprintf(L"Caught NativeException: %s\n", native_exception.GetMessage());
    }
```

```
catch(SEHException^ e)
{
    Console::WriteLine("{0}\nErrorCode: 0x{1:x}",
            e->ToString(), e->ErrorCode);
}

byval = false;

try
{
    throw_native_exception(byval);
}
catch(NativeException* native_exception)
{
    wprintf(L"Caught NativeException: %s\n", native_exception->GetMessage());
}
catch(SEHException^ e)
{
    Console::WriteLine("{0}\nErrorCode: 0x{1:x}",
            e->ToString(), e->ErrorCode);
}
}
```

The output Listing 12-24 is shown here:

```
Caught NativeException: Native Exception By Value
Caught NativeException: Native Exception on Native Heap
```

Interop with COM HRESULTs

A COM HRESULT is wrapped as an exception. It may appear as a specific exception type, such as OutOfMemoryException for the HRESULT E_OUTOFMEMORY, or, if there is no specific mapping provided, as a COMException, which has an ErrorCode property that has the original HRESULT value.

Summary

This chapter covered various aspects of interoperability—interop with other .NET languages, interop with native code including P/Invoke, the various compilation modes available, and how to expose native code to other .NET languages. The text touched briefly on COM interop. You also saw pointer types useful in interop, such as interior_ptr and pin_ptr, native and managed entry points, the __clrcall calling convention, double thunking and how to avoid it, how to include a native class in a managed class, how to include a managed class in a native class with gcroot and auto_gcroot, and finally, how exceptions and errors in native code surface in managed code.

Quick Reference

This appendix covers the new keywords introduced in C++/CLI, specifies which are also reserved words, and defines and lists contextual keywords and whitespaced keywords. This appendix includes a reference table for features available in native, mixed, pure, and safe modes. You'll also find a summary of the syntax introduced in C++/CLI.

Keywords and Contextual Keywords

Some new keywords were introduced in the C++/CLI bindings. Many new keywords introduced in C++/CLI are sensitive to the context in which they are used, so as to avoid creating new reserved words in order not to interfere with existing identifiers. When used in the proper syntactic position, contextual keywords are interpreted with the keyword meaning. When used in any other position, they may be used as identifiers. This enables your code to continue to use a variable that happens to collide with a C++/CLI contextual keyword without any special marking or modification. This also enables C++/CLI to use keywords that otherwise would be common variable names. There are several new keywords that are not contextual, as described in Table A-1: gcnew, generic, and nullptr. Table A-2 shows the new contextual keywords.

Table A-1. *C++/CLI Keywords*

Keyword	Description	Usage
gcnew	Allocates instances of reference types on the garbage-collected (managed) heap	R^ r = gcnew R();
generic	Declares a parameterized type (generic) that is recognized by the runtime	generic <typename T> ref class G { /* ... */ };
nullptr	Evaluates to the null value for a pointer, indicating an unassigned pointer	R^ r = nullptr;

Table A-2. *C++/CLI Contextual Keywords*

Contextual Keyword	Description	Usage
abstract	Declares a class that has some unimplemented methods, used as a base class. Objects cannot be instantiated from this class. When used on a method, declares that the method will not be implemented.	`ref class Base abstract { /* ... */ };`
delegate	Declares an object that represents a type-safe function pointer.	`delegate void MyDelegate(int);`
event	Declares an event, an occurrence that triggers method calls.	`event EventHandler ClickEvent;`
finally	Captures program flow after a try/catch block.	`finally { /* ... */ }`
in	Used in the for each statement.	`for each (R^ r in collection) { /* ... */ }`
initonly	Specifies a field that can only be modified in a constructor.	`initonly int i;`
internal	Specifies that access to a member is restricted to within an assembly.	`public ref class R { internal: void f(); }`
literal	Specifies a value that is a literal constant.	`literal int SIZE = 150;`
override	Indicates that a function is intended to be a virtual override of the base class function of the same name.	`virtual int f(int a, int b) override;`
property	Declares a field-like member on a type.	`property int P;`
sealed	Indicates a type that cannot be used as a base class or a method cannot be overridden.	`virtual int f(int a, int b) sealed;`
where	Used in the declaration of generics to specify constraints on the types that may be used as type arguments for a generic type or function.	`generic <typename T> where T : R ref class G { /* ... */};`

Whitespaced Keywords

Some of the keywords in C++/CLI are two words containing whitespace, which are referred to as whitespaced keywords. For example, ref class is a whitespaced keyword. Spaces and tabs may be used between the two words, but comments (despite technically being whitespace after preprocessing) may not be used. Table A-3 lists the whitespaced keywords of C++/CLI.

Table A-3. *Whitespaced Keywords*

Whitespaced Keyword	Description	Usage
enum class	Declares an enumeration with all members public	enum class Color { Red, Green, Blue};
enum struct	Declares an enumeration with all members public	enum struct Color { Red, Green, Blue };
for each	Used to iterate over collection classes	for each (R^ r in collection) { /* ... */ }
interface class	Declares an interface with all members public	interface class I { /* ... */ };
interface struct	Declares an interface with all members public	interface struct I { /* ... */ };
ref class	Declares a managed type with private default accessibility	ref class R { /* ... */ };
ref struct	Declares a managed struct with public default accessibility	ref struct S { /* ... */ };
value class	Declares a value type with private default accessibility	value class V { /* ... */ };
value struct	Declares a value type with public default accessibility	value struct S { /* ... */ };

Keywords As Identifiers

You can specify __identifier to use a keyword as an identifier. Use it when you migrate existing code to C++/CLI that uses one of the new keywords: gcnew, generic, or nullptr, or if you are dealing with another code from another language that has an identifier that matches a C++/CLI keyword, as in Listing A-1.

Listing A-1. *Using __identifier*

```
// identifier.cpp
using namespace System;

int main()
{
    int __identifier(switch) = 10;

    __identifier(switch)++;
```

```
switch( __identifier(switch) )
{
    case 10:
        break;
    case 11:
        Console::WriteLine("Switch is {0}", __identifier(switch));
        break;
    default:
        break;
}

}
```

The output of Listing A-1 is as follows:

```
Switch is 11
```

The following sections describe features not otherwise covered in this book: how to detect CLR compilation, and XML documentation comments.

Detecting CLR Compilation

Listing A-2 demonstrates how to detect CLR compilation.

Listing A-2. *Detecting CLR Compilation*

```
// detecting_clr.cpp
#include <stdio.h>
int main()
{
#ifdef _MANAGED
    System::Console::WriteLine("Must be compiling with /clr...");
#else
    printf("Not compiling with /clr.");
#endif
}
```

The output of Listing A-2 is as expected with or without the /clr option:

```
C:\code\appendix>cl /clr detecting_clr.cpp
Microsoft (R) C/C++ Optimizing Compiler Version 14.00.50727.42
for Microsoft (R) .NET Framework version 2.00.50727.42
Copyright (C) Microsoft Corporation.  All rights reserved.
```

```
detecting_clr.cpp
Microsoft (R) Incremental Linker Version 8.00.50727.42
Copyright (C) Microsoft Corporation.  All rights reserved.

/out:detecting_clr.exe
detecting_clr.obj

C:\code\appendix>detecting_clr
Must be compiling with /clr...

C:\ code\appendix>cl detecting_clr.cpp
Microsoft (R) 32-bit C/C++ Optimizing Compiler Version 14.00.50727.42 for 80x86
Copyright (C) Microsoft Corporation.  All rights reserved.

detecting_clr.cpp
Microsoft (R) Incremental Linker Version 8.00.50727.42
Copyright (C) Microsoft Corporation.  All rights reserved.

/out:detecting_clr.exe
detecting_clr.obj

C:\ code\appendix>detecting_clr
Not compiling with /clr.
```

XML Documentation

XML files may be generated from code comments written in the CLR XML doc format by writing comments in the format in code and compiling with the /doc compiler option. You can use these XML files to generate formatted documentation. The tool xdcmake.exe is used to generate the XML files from doc comments. Table A-4 lists the XML tags available.

Table A-4. *XML Doc Comment Reference*

XML Tag	Description
`<c>inline code</c>`	Inline code
`<code>code block</c>`	Lines of code
`<example>example section</example>`	Defines a section containing text description and an optional code example
`<exception cref="member">description</exception>`	Specifies exceptions that may be generated
`<include file="filename" path="tagpath">`	Includes XML comments from a file
`<list>`	Defines a bulleted or numbered list or table

Table A-4. *XML Doc Comment Reference (Continued)*

XML Tag	Description
`<para>text</para>`	Defines a paragraph
`<param>description</param>`	Describes a function parameter
`<paramref name="name">`	Specifies a hyperlink to the parameter
`<permission cref="member">`	Specifies access (e.g., public)
`<remarks>description</remarks>`	Specifies the detailed description
`<returns>description</returns>`	Specifies the return value information
`<see cref="member">`	Specifies a cross-reference
`<seealso cref="member">`	Lists additional references
`<summary>text</summary>`	Specifies text that gives a brief synopsis
`<value>description</value>`	Specifies a property description

Listing A-3 illustrates the use of the XML comment format and the generation of XML documentation from the comments.

Listing A-3. *Using XML Documentation*

```
// xml_comments.cpp
// compile with: /LD /clr /doc
// then run: xdcmake xml_comments.xdc

using namespace System;

/// Ref class R demonstrates XML Documentation Comments.
/// <summary> A class demonstrating documentation comments </summary>
/// <remarks> A detailed description of R goes into the remarks block
/// </remarks>
public ref class R
{
public:
    /// <summary>F is a method in the R class.
    /// <para>You can break the comments into paragraphs.
    /// <see cref="R::G"/> for related information.</para>
    /// <seealso cref="R::G"/>
    /// </summary>
    void F(int i) {}
```

```
/// The method G is a method in the R class.
/// <summary>Counts the number of characters in two strings.</summary>
/// <param name="s1"> Description for s1</param>
/// <param name="s2"> Description for s2</param>
/// <returns>The sum of the length of two strings.</returns>
int G(String^ s1, String^ s2){ return s1->Length + s2->Length; }
};
```

Listing A-3 is compiled with

```
cl /clr /doc /LD xml_comments.cpp
```

The documentation comments are generated with

```
xdcmake xml_comments.xdc
```

The resulting xml_comments.xml file, with some minor whitespace alterations, is as follows:

```
<?xml version="1.0"?>
<doc>
    <assembly>
        xml_comments
    </assembly>
    <members>
        <member name="M:R.G(System.String,System.String)">
            The method G is a method in the R class.
            <summary>Counts the number of characters in two strings.
            </summary>
            <param name="s1"> Description for s1</param>
            <param name="s2"> Description for s2</param>
            <returns>The sum of the length of two strings.</returns>
        </member>
        <member name="M:R.F(System.Int32)">
            <summary>F is a method in the R class.
                <para>You can break the comments into paragraphs.
                <see cref="M:R.G(System.String,System.String)" />
                    for related information.
                </para>
                <seealso cref="M:R.G(System.String,System.String)" />
            </summary>
        </member>
        <member name="T:R">
            Ref class R demonstrates XML Documentation Comments.
            <summary> A class demonstrating documentation comments </summary>
            <remarks> A detailed description of R goes into the remarks block
            </remarks>
        </member>
    </members>
</doc>
```

It is up to you to then render this in the desired user-friendly documentation format. For example, you could generate documentation in various formats using a tool such as Sandcastle, available from the Microsoft download center (http://www.microsoft.com/downloads).

Summary of Compilation Modes

This book has covered many aspects of the various modes, but not all. Table A-5 summarizes the features available in each compilation mode.

Table A-5. *Features Available in Various Compilation Modes*

Feature	Native	Mixed	Pure	Safe
Define and use native types	Yes	Yes	Yes	No
Define and use managed types	No	Yes	Yes	Yes
Define native functions	Yes	Yes	No	No
Define managed functions	No	Yes	Yes	Yes
Native instructions*	Yes	Yes	No	No
Managed instructions (IL)	No	Yes	Yes	Yes
Build 32-/64-bit agnostic assemblies	No	No	No	Yes
Use the NET Framework	No	Yes	Yes	Yes
Use the CRT	Yes	Yes	MSIL CRT	No
Use the Standard C++ Library	Yes	Yes	MSIL version	No
Use ATL	Yes	Yes	No	No
Use MFC	Yes	Yes	No	No
App domain aware	No	No	Yes	Yes
Reflection on built assembly	No	DLLs only	Yes	Yes
Call functions via P/Invoke	N/A	Yes	Yes	Yes
Use unsafe casts**	Yes	Yes	Yes	No
Include native header	Yes	Yes	Depends on header	No
Include managed header	No	Yes	Yes	Yes
#using managed assembly	No	Yes	Yes	Yes
#import COM typelib/DLL	Yes	Yes	No	No
Compile C code	Yes	No	No	No
Floating-point control (__controlfp, etc)	Yes	No	No	No
std::set_terminate and SIGTERM	Yes	No	No	No

Table A-5. *Features Available in Various Compilation Modes*

Feature	Native	Mixed	Pure	Safe
Nonvirtual calls to virtual functions	Yes	Yes	Yes	No†
Command-line arguments in main	Yes	Yes	Yes	No
Throw exceptions by value	Yes	Yes	Yes	No
Pointer arithmetic on interior pointers	No	Yes	Yes	No
Explicit keyword	For constructors	For conversions	For conversions	No
Export native functions (__declspec(dllexport))	Yes	Yes	No	No
Import native functions (__declspec(dllimport))	Yes	Yes	Yes	No
Custom alignment (__declspec(align))	Yes	No	No	No
__declspec(naked)	Yes	Yes	Yes	No
#pragma unmanaged	No	Yes	No	No
#pragma pack	Yes	Yes	Yes	No
__based	Yes	Yes	Yes	No
Structured Exception Handling	Yes††	Yes††	Yes††	No

* *Inline asm, most compiler intrinsics*
** *Including downcasts with* static_cast *and all uses of* reinterpret cast
† *Not detected by Visual C++ 2005 compiler*
†† *Not in the same function as managed or C++ exception handling*

Syntax Summary

In these examples, assume R is a reference type (ref class) and V is a value type (value class), I is an interface (interface class), and P is a property (property int P). Also assume r is a handle to R and v is an instance of V. Assume i, j, and k are integer fields or local variables, s is a handle to String, and ai is a one-dimensional managed array of integers. Assume Base and Derived are reference classes in an inheritance relationship. Assume d is typed as a handle to Derived and b has type handle to Base, but could be an actual instance of a Base or Derived object, or nullptr.

The order of the examples is the order in which they are covered in the text.

Handle

```
R^ r;        // Declare a handle.
R r1 = *r;   // Dereference a handle.
i = r1->P;   // Access a member using the -> operator.
```

Tracking Reference

```
// Declare a tracking reference and initialize to dereferenced handle.
R% rref = *r;
i = rref.P;    // Access a member using the . operator.
```

The gcnew Keyword

```
R^ r = gcnew R;            // gcnew using default constructor
r = gcnew R();             // gcnew using default constructor
r = gcnew R(100, "xyz");   // gcnew with args
```

The nullptr Keyword

```
r = nullptr;   // Set handle to null.
```

The main Method

```
int main(array<String^>^ args)
{
    /* body of main method */
    return i;  // optional return statement
}
```

Managed Arrays

```
// Declare an array of reference types but don't create it.
array<R^>^ refArray;
// Declare array of value types but don't create it.
array<V>^ valueArray;
// Declare and create 1D array of integers with size
// determined by given initial values.
array<int>^ ai = gcnew array<int> { 0, 1, 2, 3 };
// Declare and create 1D array of integers with given size.
array<int>^ ai = gcnew array<int>(4);
// array with two dimensions, four by two
array<int, 2>^ ai2d = gcnew array<int, 2>(4, 2)
        { { 0, 1 }, { 2, 3 }, { 4, 5 }, { 6, 7} };
```

The for each Statement

```
// for each statement for array of integers
for each (int i in ai) { /* body */ }
// for each statement for collection of ref objects
for each (R^ r in rCollection) { /* body */ }
```

Reference Classes

```
ref class R { /* body */ };
// public abstract ref class inheriting from Base
[ SomeAttribute ]
public ref class R abstract : Base { /* class body */ };
```

Value Classes

```
value class V { /* class body */ };
// value class inheriting from interface I
[ SomeAttribute ]
public value class V : I { /* class body */ };
```

Enum Classes

```
// enum with some values
enum class MyEnum { Zero, One, Two, Three = 3, Ten = 10 };
// enum with char as underlying type
enum class MyEnum : char { Zero, One, Two };
```

Interface Classes

```
interface class I { /* class body */ };
public interface class I : IBase { /* class body */ };
```

Safe Cast

```
try
{
    d = safe_cast<Derived^>(b);
}
catch(InvalidCastException^ e)
{
    // Handle the exception.
}
```

Dynamic Cast

```
d = dynamic_cast<Derived^>(b);
if (d == nullptr) { /* cast failed*/ }
```

Static Cast

```
unsigned int u;
i = static_cast<int>(u); // no overflow check
int* pi;
void* pv;
pi = static_cast<int*>(pv);
```

Const Cast

```
const wchar_t* cwcs = L"xyz";
wchar_t* wcs = const_cast<wchar_t*>(cwcs);
```

C-Style Cast

```
Base^ b = gcnew Derived();
try
{
    d = (Derived^) b; // evaluates to safe_cast<Derived^> ( b );
}
catch(InvalidCastException^ e)
{
    // Handle the exception.
}
```

Access Modifiers

```
public ref class R { };

private ref class R { };

ref class R
{
    public:
      void F() {}

    private:
      void G() {}

    protected:
      void H() {}

    internal:
      void I() {}

    protected private:
      void K() {}

    protected public:
      void L() {}
};
```

Stack Semantics Declaration

```
void f()
{
   R r;
   r.P = 100;   // Use the . operator to access a member.
}
```

Initonly Fields

```
ref class R
{
   initonly int i;
   public:
      R() i(5) { }
};
```

Literal Fields

```
ref class R
{
   literal int SIZE = 100;
   literal String^ NAME = "Test";
};
```

Static Constructor

```
ref struct R
{
   private:
      static R() { /* body */ }
};
```

Finalizer

```
ref struct R
{
   ~R() { this->!R(); }  // implements IDispose::Dispose
   !R() { /* finalizer body */ }
};
```

Properties .

```
ref struct R
{
    property int P1;  // trivial property
    // nontrivial property with int backing store
    int value;
    property int P2
    {
        int get() { return value; }
        void set(int i) { value = i; }
    }
    // indexed property
    array<String^>^ names;  // backing store
    property String^ P[ int ]
    {
        String^ get(int index) { return names[index]; }
        void set(int index, String^ s) { names[index] = s; }
    }
    // default indexed property
    property String^ default[ int ]
    {
        String^ get(int index) { return names[index]; }
        void set(int index, String^ s) { names[index] = s; }
    }
};
```

Delegates

```
// Declare delegate type.
delegate void MyDelegate(int, String^);

void f()
{
    // Create delegate to method F on object r.
    MyDelegate^ del = gcnew MyDelegate( r, &R::F);
    del += gcnew MyDelegate(r, &R::G); // Add target function.
    del -= gcnew MyDelegate(r, &R::G); // Remove target function.
    del += gcnew MyDelegate(&R::StaticMethod); // Add static method.
    del(100, "xyz");  // Invoke delegate.
    del->Invoke(200, "abc");  // Invoke delegate.
}
```

Events

```
ref class R
{
   public:
    event EventHandler^ E1;   // trivial event
    EventHandler^ evt;
    event EventHandler^ E2
    {
          void add(EventHandler^ e)
          {
               evt += e;
          }
          void remove(EventHandler^ e)
          {
              evt -= e;
          }
          void raise(Object^ o, EventArgs^ args)
          {
               evt(o, args);
          }
     }

   void F(Object^ o, EventArgs^ args) { /* event handler body */ }

   void f()
   {
       E1 += gcnew EventHandler(r, &R::F);
   }
};
```

Static Operators

```
ref class R
{
    // member operator:
    R^ operator+(int i) { /* body */ }

    // static operator:
    static R^ operator+(int i, R^ r)
    {
          return r + i;  // Call member operator + (above).
    }
};
```

Virtual Functions

```
ref struct Base
{
        virtual int f(int i) { /* ... */ }
        virtual void g(String^ s) { /* ... */ }
};
ref struct Derived : Base
{
        virtual int f(int i) override { /* body */ } // Override Base::f.
        virtual void g(String^ s) new { /* body */ }    // no override
};
```

Abstract Classes

```
ref struct R abstract
{
        virtual void F(int, String^) abstract;
};
```

Abstract Methods

```
ref struct R
{
        virtual void F(int, String^) abstract;
};
```

Sealed Classes

```
ref struct Base
{ virtual void F(int i) { /* method body */} };

ref class Derived sealed : Base
{
   public:
      virtual void F(int i) override { /* method body */ }
};
```

Sealed Methods

```
ref struct Base { virtual void F(int i) { /* body */ } };
ref struct Derived : Base {  virtual void F() sealed { /* body */ } };
```

Interface Implementation

```
interface class I
{
    int F(int i, String^ s);
    void g();
};
ref class R : I
{
    public:
        virtual int F(int i, String^ s) { /* implement I::F */ }
        virtual void g() { /* implement I::g */ }
};
```

Explicit Interface Implementation

```
interface class I
{
    int F(int i, String^ s);
    void g();
};
ref class R : I
{
    public:
      virtual int F(int i, String^ s)  =  I::F
      { /* implement I::F */ }
      virtual void x() = I::g { /* implement I::g */ } // possibly different name
};
```

Exceptions

```
R^ r = gcnew R();
try
{
    if ( /* ... */ )
        throw gcnew SomeException();
}
catch(SomeException^ e)
{
    // Handle SomeException;.
}
catch(SomeOtherException^ e)
{
    // Handle SomeOtherException.
}
```

```
finally
{
    // Clean up code.
    if (r != nullptr)
      delete r;
}
```

Attributes

```
// attribute intialized with constructor applied to method f
[ SomeAttribute("Arg1", "Arg2") ] void f();
// attribute initialized with public properties P and Q
[ SomeAttribute( P = "Arg1", Q = "Arg2") ] void f();
// attribute applied to return value (target syntax)
[ returnvalue : SomeAttribute() ] R^ f(int i);
```

Type Identification

```
Type^ type = R::typeid;     // Get static type from class.
Type^ type = r->GetType();  // Get dynamic type from object.
```

Managed Template Classes

```
template <typename T>  // or template < class T>
public ref class R
{
    T t; // type parameter as a member
    public:
        // method using type parameter in parameter list
        void f(T t, array<T>^ a)
        { /* method body */ }
    /* class body */
};
```

Managed Template Functions

```
template < typename T >
int TemplateFunction(T t) { /* body */ };
```

Generic Classes

```
generic <typename T>  // or generic < class T>
where T : I
ref class G
{
    /* body of generic class */
};
```

```
generic < typename T, typename U >
where T : R, gcnew()   // multiple constraints on one type parameter
where U : value class   // constraints on multiple type parameters
public ref class G abstract
{
    /* body of generic abstract class */
        T t;   // reference type handle
        U u;   // value type object
    public:
        G() { t = gcnew T(); }
};
```

Generic Functions

```
generic <typename T>
[ SomeAttribute ]  // Attributes go after the generic preamble.
T f(array<T>^ at)
{  /* method body */ }

int g()
{
    array<int>^ a;
    // call generic function
    return f<int>(a);
}
```

Interior Pointers and Pinning Pointers

```
ref struct R
{
    array<int>^ a;
    public:
        int f()
        {
            int sum = 0;
            // interior pointer
            interior_ptr<int> pi = &a[0];
            for (int i = 0; i < a->Length; i++)
            {
                // using pointer arithmetic
                sum += *pi++;
            }
            return sum;
        }
```

```
      int g()
      {
            // pinning pointer
            pin_ptr<int> pinp = &a[0];
            return native_function(pinp);
      }
};
```

The auto_handle Template

```
#include <msclr\auto_handle.h>
using namespace msclr;
auto_handle<R> auto_r = R::ReturnHandleToNewR();
```

The lock Class

```
#include <msclr\lock.h>
using namespace msclr;
void f(R^ r)
{
   lock lockr(r);
   /* sensitive code using r */
} // stack semantics, lock released
```

The gcroot Template

```
#include <msclr\gcroot.h>
using namespace msclr;
class N
{
   gcroot<R^> r;
   void f()
   {
      r = gcnew R();
      r->F();   // Call method F on r.
   }
};
```

The auto_gcroot Template

```
#include <msclr\auto_gcroot.h>
using namespace msclr;
class N
{
    auto_gcroot<R^> r;
    void f()
    {
        r = gcnew R();
        r->F();    // Call method F on r.
    }
};  // r's destructor is called when containing object is deleted.
```

Index

You Need the Companion eBook

Printed in the United States
By Bookmasters